D1250021

Africapitalism

Africa is on the rise. Enabled by natural resources, commodity trading and the recent discovery by the global market that Africa is the last frontier of capitalism, African entrepreneurs are now being empowered as economic change agents. How can this new economic elite engage in the sustainable development of the continent? 'Africapitalism', the term coined by Nigerian entrepreneur Tony O. Elumelu, describes an economic philosophy embodying the private sector's commitment to the economic transformation of Africa through investments generating economic prosperity and social wealth. The concept has attracted significant attention in both business and policy circles. Promoting a positive change in approach and outlook towards development in Africa, this book consolidates research and insights into the Africapitalism movement, and will appeal to scholars, researchers and graduate students of African studies, international business, business and society, corporate social responsibility, strategic management, economic thought, international political economy, leadership, and development studies.

PROFESSOR KENNETH AMAESHI is chair in Business and Sustainable Development and director of the Sustainable Business Initiative at the University of Edinburgh Business School. Amaeshi's research focuses on sector-level policies for sustainability and sustainability strategy in organisations. He has an expert-level knowledge of developing and emerging economies.

DR ADUN OKUPE is the Africapitalism Research Fellow (post-docto-rate) at the Sustainable Business Initiative of the University of Edinburgh. Her research interests are in the role of leadership as an instrument for societal change.

DR UWAFIOKUN IDEMUDIA is an associate professor in the Department of Social Science at York University, Toronto. Idemudia's research interests are in the area of critical development studies, business and development, and natural resource extraction and conflict in Africa.

Africapitalism

Rethinking the Role of Business in Africa

Edited by

KENNETH AMAESHI
University of Edinburgh

ADUN OKUPE
University of Edinburgh

UWAFIOKUN IDEMUDIA
York University, Toronto

CAMBRIDGE
UNIVERSITY PRESS

CAMBRIDGE
UNIVERSITY PRESS

University Printing House, Cambridge CB2 8BS, United Kingdom

One Liberty Plaza, 20th Floor, New York, NY 10006, USA

477 Williamstown Road, Port Melbourne, VIC 3207, Australia

314–321, 3rd Floor, Plot 3, Splendor Forum, Jasola District Centre, New Delhi – 110025, India

79 Anson Road, #06–04/06, Singapore 079906

Cambridge University Press is part of the University of Cambridge.

It furthers the University's mission by disseminating knowledge in the pursuit of education, learning, and research at the highest international levels of excellence.

www.cambridge.org
Information on this title: www.cambridge.org/9781107160705
DOI: 10.1017/9781316675922

© Cambridge University Press 2018

This publication is in copyright. Subject to statutory exception and to the provisions of relevant collective licensing agreements, no reproduction of any part may take place without the written permission of Cambridge University Press.

First published 2018

Printed in the United States of America by Sheridan Books, Inc.

A catalogue record for this publication is available from the British Library.

Library of Congress Cataloging-in-Publication Data
Names: Amaeshi, Kenneth, editor. | Okupe, Adun, editor. | Idemudia, Uwafiokun, editor.
Title: Africapitalism: rethinking the role of business in Africa / edited by Kenneth Amaeshi, Adun Okupe, Uwafiokun Idemudia.
Description: New York : Cambridge University Press, 2018.
Identifiers: LCCN 2017052803 | ISBN 9781107160705
Subjects: LCSH: Capitalism – Africa. | Capitalists and financiers – Africa. | Africa – Economic conditions – 21st century. | Africa – Economic policy. | Social responsibility of business – Africa.
Classification: LCC HC800.Z9 C323 2018 | DDC 338.96–dc23
LC record available at https://lccn.loc.gov/2017052803

ISBN 978-1-107-16070-5 Hardback
ISBN 978-1-316-61370-2 Paperback

Cambridge University Press has no responsibility for the persistence or accuracy of URLs for external or third-party internet websites referred to in this publication and does not guarantee that any content on such websites is, or will remain, accurate or appropriate.

Contents

Figures

Tables

Contributors

Emmanuel Adegbite is Professor of Accounting, Governance and Responsibility at De Montfort University, UK. He previously held senior academic positions at the University of Birmingham and at Durham University. His widely cited research has been published in leading academic outlets and has attracted generous funding as well as prestigious awards.

Kenneth Amaeshi is Professor of Business & Sustainable Development, and Director of the Sustainable Business Initiative, at the University of Edinburgh Business School, UK. His research focuses on entrepreneurship and business model innovation for sustainable development. His other interests include sustainability, corporate responsibility, ethics and governance. He is widely published.

Amon Chizema is Professor of Corporate Governance and Strategy at the University of Birmingham, UK. His research focuses on the intersection of corporate governance and leadership issues. He is an associate editor of *Africa Journal of Management* and an editorial member of *Journal of Management Studies and Corporate Governance: An International Review.*

George Ferns is Lecturer in Management, Employment and Organisation at Edinburgh University. His research broadly concerns how organisations engage with social and environmental issues; focusing on topics such as corporate social responsibility, corporate responses to climate change, and environmental activism.

Diane Holt is Professor of Management at Essex Business School, University of Essex. She has extensive research experience in Africa including running the Trickle Out Africa Project that looks at the role of social and environmental enterprises in poverty alleviation and sustainable development across 19 African nations.

Uwafiokun Idemudia is Associate Professor of Development Studies and African Studies at York University, Toronto, Canada. His research focuses on business, natural resources, conflict, and development. He has published widely in international journals including but not limited to, *Organization and Environment, Business Strategy and the Environment,* and *Accounting, Auditing and Accountability.*

Ken Kamoche is Professor of Human Resource Management and Organisation Studies at the University of Nottingham where he also serves as Director of the Africa Research Group. He has written extensively on human resources, jazz improvisation, knowledge management and African management issues. His current focus is Africa–China relations.

Konan Anderson Seny Kan is a Senior Lecturer at Otago Business School (New Zealand). He is interested in the configural analysis of management practices. He has published in journals such as *African Management Studies, Journal of Business Ethics, Journal of Business Research, Society and Business Review* and *Harvard Business Review* (professional). He serves as an Editorial Review Board member of the *Journal of Business Research* and is a co-guest editor for special issues in *European Management Journal* and *Management International.* He also serves as a Vice-chair of COMPASSS.

Adrian Kitimbo is a research associate at the Gordon Institute of Business Science (GIBS), University of Pretoria. Previously, he was the Machel Mandela Fellow at the Brenthurst Foundation. His research interests cut across a number of areas, including international business, African politics and international migration.

David Littlewood is Lecturer in Strategic Management at University of Sheffield Management School, UK. His research interests lie in the business and society domain, and relate more specifically to corporate social responsibility (CSR); sustainability, green business and environmental entrepreneurship; organisation stakeholder relationships; social entrepreneurship and innovation; and the informal economy.

Aminu Mamman is a reader at the Global Development Institute, University of Manchester, United Kingdom. His research interests focus on human capital development in Africa and the management of organisations in development contexts. His recent books include *Development Management: Theory and Practice* (co-edited 2017); *SMEs* and *Poverty Reduction: Strategic Management Perspective.*

Franklin Nakpodia is Lecturer in Accounting at Newcastle Business School, Northumbria University, UK. He has PhD in Accounting from Northumbria University. He has published articles in *Journal of Business Ethics, Accounting Forum, Business & Society,* among others. He has research interests in corporate governance and corporate social responsibility.

Stella M. Nkomo is a professor in the Department of Human Resource Management at the University of Pretoria, South Africa. Her research focuses on race, gender, diversity, leadership and management in Africa. She is an associate editor of the *British Journal of Management* and is currently the president of the *Africa Academy of Management.*

Nceku Nyathi is a senior lecturer at the Graduate School of Business, University of Cape Town, South Africa. He is an associate editor of *Equality, Diversity and Inclusion: An International Journal.* His research explores the development of individuals, groups, organisations, and nations and the modernising of Africa through management and leadership.

Adun Okupe is an independent researcher and practitioner with interests in leadership and tourism development for societal change. Her research focuses on leaders as instruments of societal change. Adun was the Africapitalism Research Fellow at the University of Edinburgh, a project that explored the role of business leaders in Africa's development.

Olorunfemi A. Onakoya is currently a doctoral candidate at Covenant University, Nigeria. He previously practised and held different management positions in the industry spanning risk management, business advisory consulting and banking. He also holds directorship positions in consulting and education firms. His research interests are in the fields of corporate governance and business ethics.

Olutayo Otubanjo is Senior Lecturer at Lagos Business School. He holds a PhD in Marketing with emphasis on corporate identity. He attended the University of Hull, UK and Brunel University, London. He has published in *Academy of Marketing Science Review, Management Decisions, Marketing Review, Journal of Product and Brand Management, Corporate Reputation Review*, etc.

Lyal White is the founding senior director of the Johannesburg Business School at the University of Johannesburg, South Africa. He is an associate professor in International Business, previously at the Gordon Institute of Business Science, University of Pretoria. White's work focuses on comparative political economy and international business, specifically in Africa and Latin America.

Hamza Bukari Zakaria is a PFM Specialist at the Swiss State Secretariat for Economic Affairs in Ghana. He taught at the Ghana Institute of Management and Public Administration, and has published in peer-reviewed journals. His research focuses on public management, performance management, local governance and capacity development in Africa.

Foreword

For decades, Africans and non-Africans alike have hypothesised about Africa's potential, designing a variety of routes and road maps to reach the desired destination of opportunity and prosperity for *all* Africans fostered by inclusive and sustainable systems. My response to this evergreen subject of realising Africa's rise is the economic philosophy of Africapitalism, which outlines a new approach to capitalism and private-sector responsibility on the continent.

The concept of Africapitalism is defined as the private sector's commitment to African development through long-term investments in strategic sectors of the economy that create both economic prosperity and social wealth. Africapitalism focuses on private-sector growth as the primary driver of Africa's development, and at its heart calls for a new kind of capitalism: one that focuses on long-term investment in key sectors to spark the growth of African-owned businesses, stimulate the creation of jobs and create, in a sustainable form, both economic and social good. Essentially, Africapitalism embodies a private-sector-led approach to solving some of Africa's most intractable development problems.

How practical is Africapitalism? Africa offers compelling economic and business opportunities that can, at the same time, meet a range of social objectives. In fact, Africa's burgeoning private sector and its growing domestic industries have already delivered significant returns to investors and entrepreneurs, while also addressing many of Africa's persistent structural challenges. Consider for example my own experience building what is now one of the largest banks in Africa – United Bank for Africa (UBA) with more than 14 million customers, nearly 25,000 employees and operations in nineteen African countries, the United States, the United Kingdom and France.

The story of today's UBA is one I often share. In 1997, a group of investors and I took over a shuttered bank, and rapidly built the bank into one of Nigeria's largest by reaching out to the over 90 per cent of the Nigerian population (at the time 110 million people) who did not have bank accounts and were excluded from the financial services sector. In the process of democratising Nigerian – and later African – banking, we built Standard Trust Bank, and subsequently, the United Bank for Africa, into a pan-African financial services institution that not only created substantial value for the shareholders, but also created social wealth for a broader set of previously unbanked and under-banked stakeholders. Not only were we doing well and earning substantial returns for our investors, we were also doing good by enabling broader inclusivity in the financial services sector, solving people's problems, easing access to finance for small businesses and improving their productivity and eliminating persistent inefficiencies in what had been a very undemocratic banking sector.
We accomplished all this in addition to effectively meeting the increasing demand for trade finance and cross-border finance as intraregional investment and commerce strengthened.

Upon retiring from the bank in 2010, I sought to do the same thing for other sectors in Africa. I established Heirs Holdings as a proprietary investment company that would invest in sectors and businesses that created both economic prosperity and social wealth in line with Africapitalism. Today, we invest in strategic sectors of the African economy – agriculture, financial services, real estate, energy, oil and gas, health care and hospitality – creating the jobs, opportunity and wealth necessary to transform Africa for good.

Africapitalism is coming to life all over Africa and beyond as business leaders, government leaders and entrepreneurs respond to its call to action. Africans must take primary responsibility for Africa's development, and non-Africans must now evolve their thinking about the best ways to channel their investments on the continent and shake up the old aid-based approach. The case study of Andrew Rugasira, a young Ugandan entrepreneur who defied all odds to build

Good African Coffee, which has now become the first company to sell an African-owned coffee brand directly to the United Kingdom retailers, is inspiring and demonstrates Africapitalism in action.

Good African Coffee has enjoyed significant profits, all the while placing community development at the centre of its strategy – proof that economic and social wealth need not compete but can coexist. The story affirms Africapitalism's trust in the power of private capital to transform society and strengthens my own resolve to support as many entrepreneurs as I can across the continent. My foundation, the Tony Elumelu Foundation, continues to empower thousands of African entrepreneurs whose business ideas – from all fifty-four countries on the continent – have the potential to transform Africa.

Overall, I commend all those who contributed to the production of this book, which I am confident will go a long way in provoking critical thought and changing mindsets as far as Africa's development is concerned. *Africapitalism: Rethinking the Role of Business in Africa* and the contributions of soon-to-come publications on Africapitalism will ensure that Africa will continue progressing towards the prosperity and stability that it yearns for, and so richly deserves.

Tony O. Elumelu CON

I Introduction

Uwafiokun Idemudia, Kenneth Amaeshi and Adun Okupe

Capitalism as 'a mode of economic coordination ... fundamentally anchored on the principles of freedom (liberty), individuality (self-interest), diligence (thrift and self-discipline), rights (private property) and equity (fairness)' (Amaeshi and Idemudia, 2015: 213) is not new in Africa. However, Chitonge (2016) has recently suggested that since not all people have the same understanding of what a capitalist society is, scholarly debates on capitalism in Africa continue to be highly contested. This contestation means that a significant amount of work has been done on the nature, dynamics and consequences of capitalism in Africa. For instance, the nature of capitalism, as well as the presence or absence of an effective capitalist class, has often been at the centre of the debates on capitalism in Africa since the 1980s (see Lubeck, 1987; Callaghy, 1988). Indeed, a key aspect of this debate focused on whether African societies can be described as capitalist or pre-capitalist (see Guy, 1987; Jerven, 2016), and what this might mean for the nature and the pattern of the evolution of capitalism in the continent (see Saul and Leys, 1999; Hyden, 1983).

Chitonge (2016) attributed this capitalist versus pre-capitalist debate to the fact that capitalist formations in Africa were often analysed based on some idealised model of the capitalist path. Since this idealised path often did not materialise in Africa as expected, there has often been a strong temptation among analysts to see African societies as non-capitalist. This conclusion tends to imply that African societies and economies are pre-capitalist. For instance, Iliffe (1983) suggested that the nature of capitalism in Africa is partly a function of its pre-capitalist cultural context and the 'very late stage in the global history of capitalism' reached when capitalism penetrated Africa (cited Leys, 1994: 22). Hence, based on local political

1

climates, Iliffe (1983) identified three variants of local capitalism that seem to have taken form since independence. The first was the 'anti-capitalist' regime, which was avowedly committed to socialist development and thus systematically sought to suppress the development of indigenous capital (e.g., Ethiopia, Tanzania and Ghana).The second category was 'parasitic capitalism', as in the case of Liberia and Zaire at the time, where state officials and politicians often used their hold on state power and access to resources, via neo-patrimonial networks, to promote their own private accumulation and that of their supporters with little regard for individualism or free market principles. The third category took form in countries like Nigeria and Kenya, where the governments were committed to 'nurture capitalism' via some genuine attempt to promote the development of an indigenous business class in some segment of the economy while recognising the advantages of competition and free market. However, Heilman and Lucas (1997) have suggested that 'nurtured capitalism' as in the case of Nigeria might be better characterised as pro-business and not necessarily pro-capitalist. This is because governmental policies allowed for the accumulation of private wealth via rent-seeking. However, it did not facilitate the productive investment of capital.

Similarly, after suggesting that African capitalist classes were at a stage of development that is comparable to where their European precursors were 200 years ago (Kennedy and Kennedy, 1988), Kennedy (1994) argued that the question of whether or not traditional cultures and social institutions are sufficiently 'appropriate' and capable of supporting a viable local capitalist ethos, is largely irrelevant – especially, if the states have failed to create the institutional basis for a fully commoditised and competitive market economy. This is because 'the barriers to African capitalism are only likely to be overcome, if governments are willing and able to make certain crucial decisions and actions that they and they alone have the power to undertake' (Kennedy, 1994:192) (see also Carmody, 2016). For Kennedy, traditional cultures are likely to disappear or become irrelevant once the commanding logic of capitalism takes hold, and cultural factors may even become potential resources to be used by indigenous entrepreneurs to build new business structures (Kennedy, 1994).

In contrast, Cox and Negi (2010, 77) argued that capitalism in Africa has assumed a *stunted form* because for the most part the necessary cultural conditions for its development have been missing. They pointed out that indirect rule during colonialisation froze property rights in their pre-capitalist form and that the extensiveness of these pre-capitalist property relations blocks the development of capitalism in the continent. One implication of this contrasting perspective is that 'African culture' is blamed for the failure of capitalism not taking the form of the idealised path. Paradoxically, at the same time that it is being described as irrelevant, African culture is also seen as a potential resource that can be used to strengthen the development of capitalism in the continent. This is not surprising given that most of the analyses of the advance and/or stagnation of capitalism in Africa tend to adopt a structural or systemic framework that emphasises factors such as class relations, role in world economy, degree of proletarianisation/peasantisation and emergence of the capitalist state (Heilman and Lucas, 1997). In other instances, scholars have tended to focus on African entrepreneurs so as to examine where they come from and whether they can overcome the limitations of their origins and be competitive (Leys and Berman, 1994).

In response, drawing on social movement theory so as to highlight the role of ideas and human agency, Heilman and Lucas (1997) have suggested an analytical frame for examining capitalism in Africa. According to them, 'business communities' can be useful units of analysis and viewed as coalitions of sectoral interest groups with a shared common goal of facilitating the development of the capitalist system in Africa. They conclude that where the power of capital is not yet fully institutionalised, the fate of capitalism may well depend on the ability of capitalist social movements to promote the policies, institutions and reforms necessary for the development of capitalism in Africa. Indeed, McDade and Spring (2005) recently identified a new generation of African entrepreneurs and their business networks that seek both to expand intra-African business activities and investments, and to create a favourable climate for private-sector investments. They concluded that this new growing segment of the African entrepreneurial landscape can serve as a catalyst for the improvement of economic conditions and the stimulation of development led by the private sector in the continent.

These debates about capitalism in Africa have been insightful. Indeed, the extant literature has demonstrated at least two key dynamics with regard to capitalism in Africa. The first is that some form of capitalism has emerged there. This is because from the time that Africa came into contact with the 'foreign' capitalist system, it became part of this system, largely as a 'periphery of the periphery' (Chintonge, 2016). This point is informed by the fact that African entrepreneurs have a long history of developing linkages and adapting methods of economic interactions based on the situations at hand (Cooper, 2014: 34). Second, this capitalism is flawed in ways that have rendered its ability to promote economic development problematic (Heilman and Lucas, 1997). However, a great deal is left unexamined if Africa is understood simply in terms of everything Europe pretends not to be (Cooper, 2014). This is particularly the case given that the history of capitalism in Africa can be characterised as one of domination, adaption and resistance. Hence, the tendency to simply posit Africa as the problem in the analysis of the nature and consequences of capitalism in the continent via either culturalist explanations or institutional failure arguments amounts to looking both too broadly and too narrowly. According to Cooper (2014, 36; emphasis added), '"too narrowly" because the analyst fails to see the long history that linked the peoples inhabiting the African continent to the expansion of capitalism, and "too broadly" because of the failure to see the different ways in which production and commerce across that space have actually worked'.

Although the practice and diffusion of capitalism tend to evoke a homogenous understanding of capital accumulation and profit-seeking behaviours, capitalism as a set of practices and institutions differs from context to context. The continental European form of capitalism is different from the North American version. The Nordic form of capitalism is equally different from the Asian type of capitalism. These varieties of capitalism often point to differences in cultures and institutions. In other words, capitalism is a practice mediated by such cultures and institutions, and it works well where there is a good alignment between it and these national cultures and institutions. This understanding is at the heart of the literature on comparative capitalism (Hall and Soskice, 2001). Comparative capitalism refers 'to a diverse set of approaches and analytical frameworks with common concerns in understanding the institutional foundations of diverse national "varieties" of business organization' (Deeg and Jackson, 2007:149–150). The varieties of capitalism model (Hall and Soskice, 2001), as one of the variants of the comparative capitalism tradition, offers a comparative framework to understand the political economy of firm behaviour and performance. As an offshoot of institutional theory, it seeks to explain variations and change within the capitalist system, since the late 1980s, following the demise of the competing threat of communism as a viable alternative (Kang, 2006).

The central theme of the varieties of capitalism model is the macro-economic dichotomisation of institutional contexts in which firms operate, based on such indices as legal and governance systems, sources of finance and skills, and other socio-legal indices like degree of labour unionisation and incursions of regulatory authorities. It is not uncommon in comparative capitalism literature to stylise Coordinated Market Economies (CME) as stakeholder-oriented and Liberal Market Economies (LME) as shareholder-oriented (Dore, 2000). The CME is society oriented, and firms within it thus focus on meeting broad range of stakeholders' needs (e.g., employees, suppliers, shareholder, etc.), whereas the LME is market-oriented and focuses more on meeting shareholders' needs than those of any other stakeholder groups (Dore, 2000; Amable, 2003; Hall and Soskice, 2001; Fiss and Zajac, 2004; Jackson, 2005; Hancke et al., 2007). Japan and Germany are prime examples of CME whereas the UK and the USA are prime examples of LME. In this regard, it is argued that different national and institutional contexts provide some sort of comparative advantages to firms within them. The varieties of capitalism theoretical framework has been applied to the study of the role of business in the society (Amaeshi and Amao, 2009; Matten and Moon, 2007). For instance, Amaeshi and Amao (2009) suggest that the behaviour of MNEs in the Nigerian oil and gas sector is to a large extent influenced by their varieties of capitalism. This has been one of the challenges of capitalism in Africa as it is largely shaped by MNEs and other external actors: e.g., multilateral institutions and governments.

Africans have always engaged in capitalist economic transactions. For example, Leys (1995: 22) noted that the indigenous African capitalism that existed here and there before colonialism was overwhelmed by competition from advanced capital in the metropoles backed by the colonial government. Consequently, the dominant and formal capitalism in Africa today, arguably, tends to reflect foreign cultures entrenched in colonial histories and attributes. The formal mode of economic coordination still mirrors colonial establishments and influences. As such, contemporary capitalism and democracy suffer the same fate in Africa, as borrowed cultures in search of stability and domestication in the continent.[1] Hence, when one talks about capitalism in Africa, it could be different from capitalism in other parts of the world due to different practices of capitalism anchored in different cultures and institutions (Hall and Soskice, 2001; Witt et al., 2017).

Although Philips (1977) dismissed talks of 'African capitalism' as meaningless, Carmody (2016) has suggested that there is a need to move beyond talking about a monolithic capitalism in Africa, while recognising its global nature. Consequently, Macamo (2016) argues that the analysis of 'capitalism in Africa' cannot just be about how

---

[1]   Indeed, much of the analysis of capitalism in Africa tends to also suffer from what Oyovbaire(1983) described as the 'tyranny of borrowed paradigm', in which African realities are made to fit into western social science construct and as such distort the academic representation of the reality of social existence in Africa.

economic circumstances of the continent are consistent with the semantic and the analytical field implied by capitalism, as a concept in political economy. She notes that 'it is also about how to make social science concepts work well when they cross borders' (p. 16). There is therefore a need to find new tools and ways to re-examine capitalism in Africa in a way that yields new insights into its intricate operations and how these shape society in its peculiar context (Chitonge, 2016). As such, we take seriously the structural disconnect between modern capitalism and African socio-cultural realities, especially as capitalism in Africa tends to be overly informed and driven by agendas set by outsiders who primarily see Africa merely as a 'market'.

The conception of Africa as a market occludes the fact that Africans are peoples with real human needs and challenges. Indeed, by framing Africa as merely a market, Africa becomes a 'non-place' that signals the loss of politics. The rise of transaction over interaction, as the forces of global capital, see in Africa only an amiable space to both invest and reduce human life, in their quest to maximise and optimise their power (Sharma, 2009). This is because all 'non-places' ask of you is to plug in and pass through as if they were spaces where people cohabitate without living together (Augé, 1995). The consequence of this discourse is that capitalism in Africa is based on a business-society relationship model framed in terms of *business and society*. This framing or logic allows for *a loss of connectivity* (Kunstler, 1993) and a change in the meaning of the *social obligations* of business (Augé, 1995). Hence there is a need to rethink the nature of the business-society relationship in Africa from *business and society* to *business in society*, partly as a way to restore the connectivity between business and society, and to reaffirm business's social obligations to societies in view of both the particularities of the African context and the unique competences businesses bring to Africa in pursuit of their private interests. It is these notions of connectivity, social obligations and business competences that can be leveraged to serve societal good that informs the concept of 'Africapitalism'.

However, 'is Africapitalism good old capitalism in new clothes, or an endogenous "African" version?' (see Macamo, 2016). What is unique about Africapitalism? How is it different from the capitalism we already know? Capitalism is capitalism, so where is the novelty in Africapitalism? Despite the relevance of these questions, they tend to conflate two things: 1) capitalism as a set of practices supported by institutions and 2) capitalism as a discourse or an idea, which is capable of informing and shaping practices and institutions. Capitalism as a set of practices is about a reality (present or past), while capitalism as a discourse could be about an idea of a future – i.e., a possible re-imagination of capitalism and what it could be. If the latter is successful, it becomes the former (i.e., a successful idea is realised in practice).

It is often claimed that it takes about 3,000 raw ideas for one commercial success (Stevens and Burley, 1997). Capitalism as a discourse of ideas also has the potential not to be realised, as not all ideas often materialise in practice. In that regard, the distinction between capitalism as a practice and capitalism as a discourse is equally useful and critical. However, the practice and discourse of capitalism often manifest and reinforce each other contemporaneously. The current critique of the excesses of modern capitalism is a classic example of the fusion between practice and discourse, and this fusion embodies the creative destruction upon which capitalism has continued to sustain and extend its reach. In other words, the critique of capitalism enables it to adapt to situations, adjust to criticisms and re-emerge in new forms. It is through these acts of adaptation, adjustment and renewal that the legitimacy of capitalism, as an economic system, is enhanced, sustained and diffused.

However, Africapitalism is a nascent idea based on an ideal economic philosophy that is meant to provide both the principles and the discourse that can inform business practices and stimulate a 'social movement' of businesses for a form of capitalism (see McDade and Spring, 2005) that can serve the needs of African societies. Indeed, one of the problems of capitalism in Africa is that it is not always aligned to the societal needs of the continent. It tends to be overly informed and driven by agendas set by outsiders who primarily see Africa as a market for exploitation and are obsessed by the consequent profits of such exploitations. This is reflected in some of the excesses of the MNEs operating in Africa, which have become the only role models for many African entrepreneurs. In the process, they foster a measure of corporate success and performance predicated upon individualism – not on collective interests. This is antithetical to the value of collectivism prevalent in most African societies (Lutz, 2009), which Africapitalism tends to capture.

Whilst it is possible to hold an abstracted notion of global capitalism, as an economic coordination mechanism and ideology, enacted in practice, this global capitalism (what could be also called 'capitalism in the world') and capitalism in Africa are different but interrelated practices. Hence, one can talk about 'capitalism in Africa', which is different from capitalism in other parts of the world (Witt et al., 2017); and both are, in turn, different from 'Africapitalism', as illustrated in Figure 1.1.

Africapitalism is underpinned by the notions of hybridity that seek to marry modern management practices with African values in a manner that is responsive to the particularities of the African context. It is therefore more of a pragmatic than an ideological response to the failure of capitalism in the region. The principles of Africapitalism are already captured in some of the behaviour and attitudes McDade and Spring (2005) found among a network of a new generation of African entrepreneurs. According to them, these new generations of African entrepreneurs not only incorporate modern management practices in their business operations, they also appear not to have a 'holier than thou' attitude towards conventional business practices. Importantly, 'they are concerned with result and not just ideology and they truly believe that transparency and honesty promote efficiency and strengthen the business community'. In addition, '[t]heir aim is to conduct business and advocate for policies that can contribute to *economic equity'* (McDade and Spring, 2005: 38, 36).

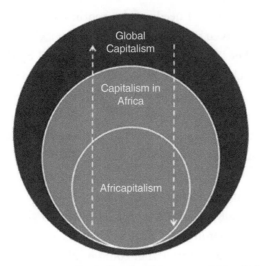

FIGURE I.I: Capitalism in Africa versus Africapitalism

Furthermore, since Africapitalism takes *the sense of place* (see Chapter 2) seriously. The role of place and how it shapes the behaviour of the new generation of African entrepreneurs identified by McDade and Spring (2005) constitutes an Africapitalism approach to business and society relations. McDade and Spring (2005) described these Africapitalist entrepreneurs as 'upwardly mobile entrepreneurs who are interested in economic and political reform'; embrace 'profits but not profiteering'; and can be distinguished from dominant political, military and trading elites by their ethics and commitments to working hard, being self-starters, business savvy, collaborative, transparent and refusing political patronage'. Similarly, rather than expressing anguish over business constraints such as poor infrastructure, poverty, spread of HIV/AIDS and corruption, network members expressed attitudes of confidence and empowerment in their ability to improve these conditions. 'They do not discount these problems they face. Rather, they have challenged and changed these conditions' (26). Put differently, network members view the role of business in society on a broad scale and interpret Africa's economic crises not as hopeless, but as fertile ground for corporate innovation that can create social and economic value for its stakeholders (see Muthuri et al., 2012).

AFRICAPITALISM FOR AFRICA'S DEVELOPMENT: INSIGHTS AND POSSIBILITIES

Given that there is no satisfactory definition of 'development' that does not already imply 'capitalism' (Philips, 1977), it is not surprising that recent debates on capitalism in Africa now also focus on the role of business in the drive for sustainable development in the region. While some of the challenges to Africa's development can be attributed to a wide range of internal and external factors such as a long and chequered history of colonialism, bad governance, poverty, weak institutions and a feeble civil society, the question of what to do about these challenges remains largely unresolved. This is because there is now some agreement that the traditional 'state versus market' debate, which has largely informed much of the discussion on how to resolve the problem of underdevelopment, while insightful, has failed to spur the kind of developmental progress expected for the continent. Addressing this impasse in development theory in the era of globalisation has led to a renewed emphasis on collaborative governance as a mechanism for harmonising the roles and responsibilities of the different key societal institutions (i.e., the state, private sector and civil society), in the pursuit of development objectives in Africa. Central to this shift is an understanding of business as not just part of the problem but also as part of the solution to the problem of underdevelopment (Idemudia, 2014).

Hence, questions about how business can contribute to development are only just emerging (Idemudia, 2008). Unfortunately, concepts such as corporate social responsibility, shared value and bottom of the pyramid, while useful, continue to seek to make African realities fit into boxes prescribed by Western management theories, as opposed to seeking to provide African management theories that are conversant with African realities, or perhaps adapt Western management theories to be more directly applicable to African realities.

Consequently, Bagire and Namada (2015), for instance, have argued that the question of how the local workforce in Africa can acquire management knowledge, which is in tandem with African values, but with a global outlook for industrial competitiveness in modern times, remains unanswered.

Hence, Africapitalism is about the role of 'business' as an agent of capitalism in African societies and the ways in which internal principles, management practices and modes of business decision-making can positively contribute to development in Africa. Our aim in putting together the collection of chapters of this book is to move beyond the traditional debate on 'capitalism in Africa' and instead focus on the potentials and the ways in which an alternative business management model rooted in Africapitalism can facilitate the contribution of the private sector to development in Africa.

Hence, in Chapter 2 Amaeshi and Idemudia suggest that while the idea of Africapitalism enables a creative space for rethinking the business-society relationship from a development perspective, the failure to clarify what underpins the idea and how it differs from similar western constructs potentially limits both its analytical and practical usefulness. This chapter attempts to address this gap by seeking to initiate a conversation around the set of values that might underpin the concept. It also explores the implications of Africapitalism for management in Africa.

Building on Chapter 2, Ferns, Okupe and Amaeshi in Chapter 3 situate the emergence of Africapitalism within the larger effort geared towards alternative forms of capitalism meant to challenge the dominant forms of market-based capitalism. The chapter seeks to understand what underlies the heterogeneity amongst these 'new capitalisms'. Drawing on both social movement theory and identity theory, the chapter explores how the proposed philosophies of the different new capitalisms are framed and how social position shapes such framing activities. As such, this chapter identifies how such underlying differences help either constrain or enable the continuity of each new capitalism. The chapter suggests lessons for the

Africapitalism philosophy, as it seeks to influence business leaders' role in the society in Africa.

While the foregoing chapters seek to clarify the links between the principles that underpin Africapitalism and the African context as well as highlight its unique contribution to an evolving business-society relation in Africa, in Chapter 4, Adegbite, Nakpodia, Seny Kan and Onakoya explore how the cardinal values of Africapitalism (see Chapter 2) can inspire discerning corporate governance practices and address corporate governance challenges in Africa. The chapter explores how an Africapitalist corporate governance framework will promote economic prosperity while addressing social problems. Similarly, Mamman, Kamoche and Zakaria in Chapter 5 adopt the four cardinal values of Africapitalism (see Chapter 2) to articulate a foundation for the new approach to human capital development. The chapter advocates a reconceptualisation of human capital in Africa so that knowledge and skills will be viewed as communal endowments rather than personal property for the pursuit of self-interest. Using the philosophies of Africapitalism and Ubuntu the chapter also advocates the co-production and co-sponsorship of human capital development by the state, international companies, international development agencies and non-state actors such as NGOs and civil societies. To operationalise Africapitalism in human capital development, the chapter argues for the inclusion of cultural, emotional and spiritual dimensions in the African educational and vocational systems (see Chapter 9).

In Chapter 6, Otubanjo explores the implications of the pillars of Africapitalism (Chapter 2), as a management paradigm, for corporate branding, as another management practice. Drawing from an analysis of the four pillars of Africapitalism within the context of four corporate branding concepts, namely 'corporate advocacy advertising', 'corporate co-branding', 'corporate green brand' and 'corporate brand loyalty, the chapter proposes an Africapitalism brand framework which takes the sense of place seriously. Essentially, this framework serves as a channel for corporate differentiation, recognition and positive corporate image and reputation. It offers a practical approach to the actualisation of the tenets of Africapitalism through corporate branding.

In Chapter 7, Okupe and Amaeshi posit that Africapitalism calls for private-sector leaders in Africa to be Africapitalists. They then go on to address the role of private sector leaders in the sustainable development of Africa. The chapter attempts to answer the question by exploring what being an Africapitalist can mean and interrogating leadership for sustainable development alongside the cardinal values of Africapitalism (see Chapter 2). With emphasis on transformational and responsible leadership theories, they propose an expansion of the leadership objective to include sustainable development as one way to understand what it means to be an Africapitalist. The chapter concludes by asserting that the Africapitalism philosophy can be a useful management philosophy to shape the future of the private sector in Africa by encouraging leaders to be instruments for sustainable development in Africa.

In Chapter 8, Holt and Littlewood explore the connections between social entrepreneurship in Africa and Africapitalism, drawing on both qualitative and quantitative data. It begins with a review of extant literature identifying key themes and critical issues. It then draws upon quantitative research undertaken with social enterprises across 19 countries in Eastern and Southern Africa to reflect on how social entrepreneurship in Africa differs from (and is similar to) entrepreneurship in other regions globally. The chapter concludes by considering conceptual and practical connections between social entrepreneurship in Africa and Africapitalism.

In Chapter 9, Chizema and Nyathi explore the connection between Foreign Direct Investment (FDI) – as a management practice – and Africapitalism by focusing on the case of Chinese FDI in Africa. The central concern for this chapter lies in the question of the extent to which Chinese investments respond to sustainable development consistent with Africapitalism, i.e., to the form of sustainable development identifiable within the context of African values. With China increasingly becoming a significant trading partner for almost all African countries, engaging in various industrial activities, it is important that this relationship be understood within a framework of sustainable development that is consistent with Africapitalism. While African countries do have heterogeneous institutions among them, certain aspects of economic and social life are common, and what is espoused in the definition of Africapitalism is what will guide this chapter.

In Chapter 10, White and Kitimbo present a practical example of Africapitalism in action. They demonstrate how the case of Good African Coffee, a Small-to-Medium Size Enterprise (SME), embodies the idea of Africapitalism. They argue that by placing community development at the centre of its business strategy, Good African Coffee's business model shows how the idea of Africapitalism can be put into practice and presents strategies for agri-businesses with a vested interest in social responsibility and economic empowerment.

Finally, in Chapter 11, which serves as a conclusion of this book, Nkomo reflects upon the implications of Africapitalism for the education of current and future generations of managers in and for Africa. In the first part of the chapter, she explores the relation between the African context and the basic tenets of Africapitalism (see Chapter 2). She then proposes how management education should be approached to support Africapitalism. She offers ten propositions that are broad but applicable for undergraduate, postgraduate and executive management education.

REFERENCES

Amable, B. 2003. *The Diversity of Modern Capitalism*. Oxford: Oxford University Press.

Amaeshi, K. and Amao, O. 2009. Corporate Social Responsibility in Transnational Spaces: Exploring the Influences of Varieties of Capitalism on Expressions of Corporate Codes of Conduct in Nigeria. *Journal of Business Ethics*, 86(2): 225–239.

Amaeshi, K. and Idemudia, U. 2015. Africapitalism: A Management Idea for Business in Africa?. *Africa Journal of Management*, 1(2): 210–223.

Augé, M. 1995. *Non-places: An Introduction to Anthropology of Supermodernity*. New York: Verso.

Callaghy, Thomas M. 1988. The State and the Development of Capitalism in Africa: Theoretical, Historical and Comparative Reflections. In *The Precarious Balance: State and Society in Africa*. Edited by D. Rothschild and N. Chazan, 67–99.Boulder, CO: Westview Press.

Carmody, P. 2016. Variegated Capitalism in Africa: The Role of Industrial Policy. Available at http://roape.net/2017/01/04/variegated-capitalism-africa-role -industrial-policy/. Accessed 25 January 2018.

Chitonge, H. 2016. Capitalism in Africa: The Old and the New lyrics. Available at http://roape.net/2017/01/12/capitalism-africa-old-new-lyrics/. Accessed 25 January 2018.

Cooper, F. 2014. *Africa in the World: Capitalism, Empire, Nation State*. Cambridge, MA: Harvard University Press.

Cox, K. R. and Negi, R. 2010. The State and the Question of Development in Sub-Saharan Africa. *Review of African Political Economy*, 37(123): 71–85.

Deeg, R. and Jackson, G. 2007. The State of the Art: Towards a More Dynamic Theory of Capitalist Variety. *Socio-Economic Review*, 5: 149–179.

Dore, R. 2000. *Stock Market Capitalism: Welfare Capitalism, Japan and Germany Versus the Anglo-Saxons*. Oxford: Oxford University Press.

Fiss, P. C. and Zajac. E. J. 2004. The Diffusion of Ideas over Contested Terrain: The (Non)adoption of a Shareholder Value Orientation among German Firms. *Administrative Science Quarterly*, 49: 501–534.

Guy, J. 1987. Analysing Pre-Capitalist Societies in Southern Africa. *Journal of Southern African Studies*, 14(1): 18–37.

Hall, P. A. and Soskice, D. (eds.). 2001. *Varieties of Capitalism – The Institutional Foundations of Comparative Advantage*. Oxford: Oxford University Press.

Hancke, B., Rhodes, M. and Thatcher, M. 2007. Introduction: Beyond Varieties of Capitalism. In *Beyond Varieties of Capitalism: Conflict, Contradictions, and Complementarities in the European Economy*. Edited by B. Hancke, M. Rhodes and M. Thatcher, 2–42. Oxford: Oxford University Press.

Heilman, B. and Lucas, J. 1997. A Social Movement for African Capitalism? A Comparison of Business Associations in Two African Cities. *African Studies Review*, 40(2): 141–171.

Hyden, G. 1983. *No Shortcut to Progress: African Development in Perspective*. London: University of California Press.

Idemudia, U. 2008. Conceptualising the CSR and Development Debate: Bridging Existing Analytical Gaps. *Journal of Corporate Citizenship*, 29: 1–20.

Idemudia, U. 2014. Corporate Social Responsibility and Development in Africa: Issues and Possibilities. *Geography Compass*, 8(7): 421–435.

Iliffe, J. 1983. *Emergence of African Capitalism*. London: Macmillan.

Jerven, M. 2016. Capitalism in Pre-Colonial Africa: A Review. African Economic History Working Paper Series, Number 27. Available at www.aehnetwork.org/wp-content/uploads/2016/06/AEHN-WP-27.pdf. Accessed 27 November 2017.

Kang, N. 2006. A Critique of the 'Varieties of Capitalism' Approach. ICCSR Working Paper Series, Number 46. Nottingham University Business School. Available at www.nottingham.ac.uk/business/ICCSR/pdf/ResearchPdfs/45-2006.pdf. Accessed 25 January 2018.

Kennedy, P. T. and Kennedy, P. M. 1988. *African Capitalism: The Struggle for Ascendency*. Cambridge: Cambridge University Press.

Kennedy, P. 1994. Political Barriers to African Capitalism. *Journal of Modern African Studies*, 32(02): 191–213.

Kennedy, P. T. and Kennedy, P. M. 1988. *African Capitalism: The Struggle for Ascendency*. Cambridge: Cambridge University Press.

Kunstler, J. H. 1996. Home from Nowhere. *Atlantic Monthly*, 2783: 43–66.

Kuper, A. 1988. *The Invention of Primitive Society: Transformations of an Illusion*. London: Routledge.

Leys, C. 1994. African Capitalists and Development: Theoretical Questions. In *African Capitalists in African Development*. Edited by B. J. Berman and C. Leys, 11–38. Boulder, CO: Lynne Rienner Pub.

Leys, C. and Berman, B. J. 1994. Introduction. In *African Capitalists in African Development*. Edited by B. J. Berman and C. Leys, 1–10. Boulder, CO: Lynne Rienner Pub.

Lubeck, P. M. (ed.). 1987. *The African Bourgeoisie: Capitalist Development in Nigeria, Kenya, and the Ivory Coast*. Boulder, CO: Lynne Rienner Publishers.

Lutz, D. W. 2009. African Ubuntu Philosophy and Global Management. *Journal of Business Ethics*, 84(3): 313–328.

Macamo, E. 2016. Blinded by Capitalism: Words That Think (for Us). Available at http://roape.net/2016/12/07/blinded-capitalism-words-think-us/.

Matten, D. and Moon, J. 2007. 'Implicit' and 'Explicit' CSR: A Conceptual Framework for a Comparative Understanding of Corporate Social Responsibility. *Academy of Management Review*, 33(2): 404–424.

McDade, B. E. and Spring, A. 2005. The 'New Generation of African Entrepreneurs': Networking to Change the Climate for Business and Private Sector–Led Development. *Entrepreneurship & Regional Development*, 17(1): 17–42.

Muthuri, J. N., Moon, J. and Idemudia, U. 2012. Corporate Innovation and Sustainable Community Development in Developing Countries. *Business & Society*, 51(3): 355–381.

Phillips, A. 1977. The Concept of 'Development'. *Review of African Political Economy*, 4(8): 7–20.

Saul, J. S. and Leys, C. 1999. 'Sub-Saharan Africa in Global Capitalism'. *Monthly Review*, 51(3): 13.

Sharma, S. 2009. Baring Life and Lifestyle in the Non-place. *Cultural Studies*, 23(1): 129–148.

Stevens, G. A. and Burley, J. 1997. 3,000 Raw Ideas = 1 Commercial Success! *Research Technology Management*, 40(3): 16–27.

Witt, M. A., Kabbach de Castro, L. R., Amaeshi, K., Mahroum, S., Bohle, D. and Saez, L. 2017. Mapping the Business Systems of 61 Major Economies: A Taxonomy and Implications for Varieties of Capitalism and Business Systems Research. *Socio-Economic Review* 2018, 16(1): 35–38.

2 Africapitalism: A Management Idea for Business in Africa?

Kenneth Amaeshi and Uwafiokun Idemudia

BACKGROUND

Africapitalism, a term coined by the Nigerian entrepreneur, Tony O. Elumelu CON, is an economic philosophy that embodies the private sector's commitment to the economic transformation of Africa through investments that generate both economic prosperity and social wealth.[1] Elumelu argues that 'Africa's renaissance lies in the confluence of the right business and political action.'[2] The concept is fast becoming a buzzword in Africa and is expected to gain recognition even beyond the continent. It has continued to attract significant attention in both business and policy circles. For instance, on an invitation to a panel chaired by the UN Secretary General Ban Ki-moon (9 April 2014), Elumelu shared his views on Africapitalism with the UN General Assembly and Economic and Social Council (ECOSOC).[3] *The World in 2015*, a key publication by *The Economist*, featured a piece on 'The Rise of Africapitalism'.[4] The Tony Elumelu Foundation has also established the Africapitalism Institute,[5] a research-based think tank to mainstream the understanding and practice of Africapitalism.

One of the projects funded by the Africapitalism Institute is the Edinburgh Project.[6] This, amongst its other goals, aims to rethink

---

[1] This chapter is a slightly amended version of a publication in the *Africa Journal of Management*, 1(2): 2015. The Open Access published journal version of this paper can be freely downloaded from www.tandfonline.com/doi/pdf/10.1080/23322373.2015.1026229.

[2] http://tonyelumelufoundation.org/africapitalisminstitute/driving-africas-renaissance -africapitalism/.

[3] www.heirsholdings.com/tonyelumelu/tony-elumelu-addresses-the-un-general-assembly.

[4] www.economist.com/news/21631956-entrepreneurs-will-transform-africa-says-tony -elumelu-chairman-heirs-holdings-and.

[5] www.tonyelumelufoundation.org/africapitalisminstitute/.

[6] www.business-school.ed.ac.uk/blogs/research-news/2014/09/22/africapitalism-afri can-business-leaders-and-africas-development/.

capitalism in Africa by focusing on the role of business leaders, inves-
tors and entrepreneurs in Africa's development. It was a four-country
study – Côte d'Ivoire, Kenya, Nigeria and South Africa – with an
international partnership involving nine universities: Pan Atlantic
University, Lagos Business School (Nigeria); Strathmore Business
School (Kenya); University of Loughborough (UK); University of
Nottingham (UK); University of Durham (UK); York University
(Canada); University of Cape Town (South Africa); and University of
Grand-Bassam (Côte d'Ivoire); with the University of Edinburgh (UK)
overseeing the entire project.

In this chapter, we seek to provide insight about this concept
that, as explained above, has seen the birth of a dedicated institute and
the commencement of a continent-wide research project. We link
Africapitalism to the broader literature on business and society, and
critically interrogate and explore it as a possible management idea for
business in Africa in response to the onslaught of global capitalism.
Coincidentally, the literature on the role of business in society often
takes context for granted. When it does take context into consideration, it often adopts an (historical) institutional perspective, which
tends to focus more on *why* firms behave the way they do, rather than
on *how* firms *ought* to behave, especially in weak institutional contexts. This neutrality, arguably, reflects a dominant paradigm within
the social sciences, which have had enormous influence on the field of
business in society scholarship. Stepping out of this neutrality, we
argue that Africapitalism, i.e., the need for the private sector in Africa
to commit to the socio-economic development of Africa, is both an
imaginative *management idea* and a creative moral-linguistic artefact
that embodies a new space for appropriating and re-moralising capitalism in Africa. We situate Africapitalism in the broader conversation
on global capitalism and highlight some of the salient principles that
make it simultaneously an aspect of global capitalism but uniquely
different in its situated contextualisation. In so doing, we try to rein-
state the sense of place and belonging in the economic globalisation
discourse as a form of economic patriotism, and we argue that this is

the quintessential distinctiveness of Africapitalism in the global, economic world order. We also highlight emerging issues for further research and seek to ignite a continuing discussion on this theme.

INTRODUCTION

Africa has a long and chequered history of colonialism, bad governance and poverty. In addition, the continent suffers from weak institutions and distressed civil societies. Resuscitating Africa from near economic and social collapse has continued to remain a thriving business for multinational institutions, foreign governments, aid agencies, international NGOs and international donors. Regrettably, some of these actors have also proven to be Africa's Achilles' heel. The latest to arrive among this foray of helpers are multinational corporations, which often (are forced to) take on public responsibilities in the form of Corporate Social Responsibility (CSR). Predictably, none of these has become the panacea to the myriad of challenges confronting the continent (see Idemudia, 2014); rather, most of them continue to flounder at the margins. The crisis of 'development' in Africa and the failure of either the state or the market to deliver has, in recent years, led to a call for better collaboration and partnership between the state, business and civil society, if developmental challenges in the region are to be addressed (see Garforth et al., 2007; Idemudia, 2014; Richey and Ponte, 2014).

While the 1980s and 1990s were generally seen as the 'lost decades' for development in most parts of the region, Africa is now supposedly on the rise (see *The Economist*, 2011, 2013; Carmody, 2008). This rise is largely driven by natural resources extraction, export of primary commodities and the global market's recent rediscovery of Africa as the last frontier of capitalism. This re-discovery and recognition has been intensified in the wake of the global financial crisis. Implicated in this rise are entrepreneurs who push the boundaries and explore new and innovative opportunities in the continent. The emergence of successful African entrepreneurs has also contributed to the new narrative of Africa rising. Recognising the power of the market for development and the key role of entrepreneurs as economic development change agents in unfettered markets, the nouveau economic elites in Africa have sought to engage with the sustainable development of the continent in a number of ways. One such attempt is the emergence of Africapitalism as a possible economic and management idea in Africa and beyond.

Elumelu's Africapitalism is an idea that emphasises the obligations of the private sector towards the socio-economic development of Africa and assumes the feasibility of such an undertaking. As an economic idea, it will require efficient economic coordination by diverse actors, such as the state, civil society and markets. In order to do so, it will need to tap into the moral psychology of the actors (moral agents) and hypothesise human behaviours and needs. This may be contrary to the starting point of neo-classical economic thinking of the *homo economicus*, who is primarily driven by self-interest. Indeed, an Africapitalism perspective that is rooted in the values of Ubuntu sees the purpose of management as neither to benefit one *collection of individuals*, as the shareholder theory would suggest, nor to benefit many collections of individuals, as the stakeholder theory proposes. Instead, its purpose is to benefit the community as well as the larger communities of which it is a part (Lutz, 2009). As such, the *common good* becomes the principal target of managers (ibid.). This is an entirely different perspective and will have implications for how the business-society relationship is understood in Africa.

The significance of Africapitalism stems from both the enormity of the developmental and governance challenges confronting Africa (see Mbaku, 2004) and the fact that the continent requires a customised economic philosophy and business model that better allows it to meet its needs. This is particularly the case given what Ekeh (1990) has referred to as the 'tyranny of borrowed paradigm,' in which African realities are either ignored in theoretical debates or made to fit into Western constructs. Consequently, while Lutz (2009) notes that theories that were created within and for individualistic cultures are often not at home within communal cultures, Blunt and Jones (1997) assert that Western approaches to management and leadership are often incompatible with the cultural context of Africa. Similarly, Zoogah (2008) has argued that there is a need for a contextualised approach to management theory that incorporates the African context and the lived experience of its people in its theorising and modelling (see also Edoho, 2001). In addition, Lutz (2009) suggested that such a theory is needed not only in the interest of moral integrity and social stability, but also in the interest of economic productivity.

After considering a variety of alternatives, Zoogah and Nkomo (2013) see research on africa that is strong in differentiating Africa yet still highly similar to the West, i.e., that advocates for balanced identity as the most optimal space via which African management research can maintain its unique African identity while still contributing to global management theories. They assert that this is consistent with strategic balance theory, which suggests that a balance between differentiation and conformity leads to better outcomes. This is where Africapitalism comes in as a hybrid notion (i.e., a management idea – a 'fairly stable body of knowledge about what managers ought to do' (Kramer, 1975: 47)) that is potentially an alternative to the status quo. Africapitalism seeks to avoid cultural romanticism that seems to see African culture as the panacea to solve African problems and Western universalist discourse that ignores subtle contextual particularities by reasserting the sense of place, culture and emotion in capitalism. However, if Africapitalism is to be a meaningful idea and not to be conflated with other similar ideas (i.e., a CSR-esque phenomenon) and its true transformational potential is to be realised both in terms of management theory and practice in Africa, then there needs to be a clarification of its philosophical foundation and the underpinning associative ideas.

It is against this background that this chapter seeks to propose a series of associated ideas that might underpin the notion of Africapitalism as a basis for the socio-economic governance role of business and a management idea. It considers its implications for business and society relationships in Africa. The chapter starts by exploring the nature of global capitalism before dovetailing to the quintessential characteristics of Africapitalism as both a moral and a linguistic project.

GLOBAL CAPITALISM: PROSPECTS, PROBLEMS AND PARADOXES

Capitalism is one of the most creative inventions of mankind. Arguably, capitalism as a mode of economic coordination is fundamentally anchored on the principles of freedom (liberty), individuality (self-interest), diligence (thrift and self-discipline), rights (private property) and equity (fairness). Where each of these fundamentals or a combination of them is out of kilter, capitalism limps, wobbles and could become dangerously wild, if unchecked. The recent global financial crisis, which has been described as a crisis of capitalism, is a case in point. The different societal pathologies created by entrepreneurs and enterprises – for example, global warming, labour exploitation, inequality, pollution, human rights infringements, etc. – are manifestations of unguarded capitalism. Nonetheless, capitalism in its completeness ought to be a force for good, driving human innovation for a progressive world.

In other words, capitalism is primarily a moral project, both as a process and as an outcome (Dunning, 2003, 2005; Lundan, 2011; Judge et al., 2014), underpinned by a 'moral or ethical ecology' (Dunning, 2005: 138) or what Donaldson and Dunfee (1999) characterise as a set of 'hypernorms'. At the heart of capitalism is the moral question of 'what is produced, in what ways it is produced, and who benefits from the goods (and bads) created' (Dunning, 2005: 136). Reinforcing the moral foundation of capitalism, Novak (1982: 56) argues that 'each age of capitalism requires its own specific moral culture which nurtures the virtues and values on which its existence depends'. Unfortunately, '[f]or too long capitalism, its institutions and morality have been kept separate from each other' (Dunning, 2005:

149), and the resultant successes and failures of capitalism have been treated as matters of mere technicalities (Hayek 1979).

That said, capitalism has strong cultural influences and undertones (Hall and Soskice, 2001). The Continental-European form of capitalism is different from the Anglo-Saxon variant. While the former is socially oriented, the latter is highly economistic in outlook and orientation. These varieties are informed by distinct socio-cultural philosophies. The emergence of capitalism in China, for instance, is unique, given the role of the state in furthering economic advancement. What are seen today as mere expressions of markets are historical products of well-articulated socio-political philosophies. In most advanced capitalist societies, the state is instrumental in the shaping of the different forms of capitalism in these societies. For instance, French capitalism is different from both the UK and German forms of capitalism (Kang and Moon 2012). Capitalism in these countries is a function of historical and cultural antecedents leading to what has been characterised as a 'methodological national' (Smith 1979) approach to the study of capitalism. As Offe states:

> If there is anything distinctive about the 'European' model of capitalism, it is the insight, congealed in a myriad of economic institutions and regulatory arrangements, that the interest of 'all of us' will be served well if the pursuit of the interest of 'each of us' is to some extent constrained by categorical status rights.
>
> *(Offe, 2003: 444)*

Nonetheless, the study of capitalism assumes strong institutional contexts and actors – for example, strong governments, civil society, effective or efficient regulations and governance. However, nation-states and governments in Africa are weak. This weakness makes it difficult for the states and governments to play effectively the roles of protecting lives and properties, as well as ensuring social well-being, infrastructure development and the development of enabling institutions for the production and consumption of goods and services within Africa. In addition, and unfortunately, the benefits of capitalism are unevenly, some may say, unjustly distributed, partly due to structural and power imbalances in the global polity and partly as a result of weak local (national) governance systems. Capitalism requires effective government, market, and civil society to yield good societal outcomes. Where one or more of these are missing, the tendency of capitalism leading to societal pathologies is magnified. Thus, reflecting on the benevolence and malevolence of capitalism, Dunning writes:

> I would assert that capitalism, although possibly the best economic system currently known to man to create wealth, is sub-optimal. In its current state, it is perceived to result in, or continue to allow, an unacceptable level of poverty and social injustice, insufficient participation and a lack of democracy. It is also frequently associated with corporate malfeasance, misuse of economic and political power by governments, and a cavalier attitude by supranational entities towards environmental, security and cultural related issues.
>
> *(Dunning, 2005: 138)*

Consequently, Newell (2008) stated that we are now at a critical crossroads, where we must choose between a laissez-faire approach to capitalism and regulated capitalism that would serve broader social and environmental goals, such as social justice and sustainability. In response, those that accept the realities of economic globalisation and liberalisation on ideological grounds, as well as on the market efficiency arguments, have called for capitalism with a human face as a strategy to deal with the contradictions of capitalism (Leisinger, 2007). For instance, while Bill Gates has called for creative capitalism,[7] drawing on his notion of embedded liberalism, John Ruggie has also suggested principled pragmatism (United Nations, 2006). In contrast, proponents of regulated capitalism argue that economic globalisation and liberalisation have altered the balance of

---

[7]   Through which business, especially the big ones, can improve the lot of the poor by better aligning their self-interest with the good of society (O'Laughlin 2008).

rights and obligations that structure corporate behaviour (Chang, 2001). Indeed, while firms now enjoy enormous amount of freedom and protection of their rights, essentially secured by what Stephen Gill has labelled the 'new constitutionalism' (2003), there seems to be a commensurate decline in their responsibility and obligations to society at large. These scholars thus argue that self-regulation, as espoused in the laissez-faire approach to capitalism, is unlikely to deliver in terms of addressing the contradictions of capitalisms without stronger regulations (see Utting, 2005, 2008; Newell, 2001, 2008; O'Laughlin, 2008). However, McBarnet (2007) has also pointed out that the corporate accountability movement may be asking more of the law than the law can deliver, as corporations are very adept at circumventing regulatory control and creatively complying with legal requirements.

This laissez-faire approach to capitalism versus the regulated capitalism debate has been particularly insightful, especially as it highlights the strength and limitations of both sides to the debate. However, Crouch (2010) points out that the unintended consequence of this debate has been the tendency to neglect business as a fundamental institution in socio-economic governance. He argues that it is 'essential that analysis of policy and politics of development takes full account of giant corporations as a form of governance in its own right'. This is because, in the present context, the corporate hierarchies of big business are a major source of governance that rival both the state and the market. Thus, there is a need for attention to turn to the role of firms as political actors, rather than simply being entities to be regulated by public policy (Crouch, 2010). It is therefore not surprising that, in the context of Africa, the discourse of Africapitalism has recently emerged as one way of engaging with the potential socio-economic governance role that business can play in Africa's development. This is particularly important given that the discussions about the changing role of business in development in Africa are only just emerging (see Idemudia, 2014). However, while recent works (see Geelhoed et al., 2014; Carney and Freeland, 2014;

Anyansi-Archibong and Anyansi, 2014) on Africapitalism have been insightful, they have either tended to conflate it with other similar ideas like philanthro-capitalism – and thus undermine the innovative fresh perspective that the notion can bring to the analysis of business and society relationship in Africa (e.g., Anyansi-Archibong and Anyansi 2014) – or use it in an unspecified manner that belies its transformative possibilities.

AFRICAPITALISM AS AN IMAGINATIVE MORAL-LINGUISTIC PROJECT

Africapitalism is an attempt to re-imagine entrepreneurship and reunite capitalism with its moral roots in Africa. This chapter takes the commitment of Africapitalism seriously and considers the necessary principles or values foundational to such a commitment. It identifies four possible principles: sense of progress, sense of parity, sense of peace and sense of place, which are arguably rooted in the Ubuntu worldview. In this regard, Africapitalism implies the restoration of African-ness in capitalism, reflecting the economic and social practices implicit in African culture and tradition. To realise its goals, Africapitalism must bring its moral intuitions and principled commitments into alignment with modern economic practices. Here, the notion of Ubuntu[8] or African traditional humanism comes to mind. In economic terms, it is a kind of humanism that does not proscribe self-enrichment, but requires the affluent to improve their community (Lutz, 2009; Littrell et al., 2013). In this kind of voluntary wealth distributivism, one's economic and social power is measured by his or her economic empowerment of others.

Thus, if self-identity in traditional Africa is a relational and transactional category, then a person is a creative articulation of his

---

[8]   Ubuntu is simultaneously the foundation and edifice of African philosophy, and its direct relevance to management theory and practice is covered extensively in the literature (see Lutz 2009; Prinsloo 2000; Mbigi and Maree 1995; and Karsten and Illa 2005).

or her individuality within the matrix of the social community. In a fundamental sense, the community shapes identity. As such, an Africapitalism perspective sees the firm not as a mere collection of individuals, but as a community (Karsten and Illa, 2005; McFarlin et al., 1999). 'In a community the individual does not pursue the common good *instead* of his or her own good; rather pursues his or her own good *through pursuing* the common good' (Lutz, 2009). This is because the values of Ubuntu are able to hold the paradoxical relationship of individual and community in dynamic and interdependent tension by proposing the abrogation of the twin dangers of the subjugation of the individual to the collective, and the detached superordinacy of the individual (Littrell et al., 2013). Hence, drawing on the Ubuntu emphasis on group solidarity and relationship building, Africapitalism offers an alternative corporate culture that allows firms to strive for profit-making – but not the sort of profit-making at any cost that allows for the exploitation of human beings – because the ultimate goal of self-enrichment is to use it for the improvement of the community (Lutz, 2009; Prinsloo, 2000). At its core, the values of Ubuntu that might underpin the notion of Africapitalism include respect for the dignity of others, group solidarity, participation, sharing, the spirit of harmony and interdependency (see Mbigi, 2002; Makhudu, 1993). As mentioned above, we see the following four points as its cardinal values of Africapitalism: (1) sense of progress and prosperity, (2) sense of parity, (3) sense of peace and harmony and (4) sense of place and belonging.

Sense of Progress and Prosperity

Africapitalism is predicated on the creation of social wealth in addition to the pursuit of financial profitability. Wrapped around both social wealth and financial profitability is a sense of progress and prosperity that goes beyond just material accumulation to also include psycho-social human well-being. In this regard, progress and prosperity are not just the absence of poverty, but the presence of conditions that make life more fulfilling (e.g., access to quality education, health, social capital, democratic institutions, etc.) (Brundtland, 1994). Accordingly, Brundtland stated:

> Prosperity is more than the absence of poverty, pressing though that
> is. It means addressing sustainable development and careful
> husbandry of the world's resources, while recognising the rights of
> developing countries to break out from poverty. It means addressing
> population growth which leads to famine, destabilisation and war.
> It means quality of life achieved through education, employment,
> social justice and social security ... True world prosperity will
> remain a distant goal unless we pursue policies based on the concept
> of global solidarity.
>
> *(Bruntland 1994: 57)*

This sense of progress and prosperity is nowhere more needed than in Africa, a continent riddled with extreme negative human conditions.

Sense of Parity

The benefits of progress and prosperity need to be equitably shared. It is very easy for the accumulation of wealth to be lopsided. Most liberal economies have also led to high inequality (Piketty, 2014). Inequality has become the new scourge and burden of success and the new poverty. Inequality in Africa is not necessarily created by liberalism, but the absence of it and the entrenchment of crony capitalism and corruption. Africapitalism is driven by a counter-current of progressivism, which recognises that growth needs to be inclusive. In other words, it promotes a form of entrepreneurship that strives to create financial and social wealth for all stakeholders and not just for shareholders.

Sense of Peace and Harmony

Capitalism can be very innovative, and at the heart of contemporary capitalism is the Schumpeterian quest for creative destruction. Framed as such, capitalism presents an arena of continuous struggles and contestations between the incumbents and the emergent, between old and new regimes and between places and spaces. This quest for creative destruction is often underpinned by the logic of self-interest (Adam Smith), which creates enormous rewards for firms and entrepreneurs, and has been proven to be one of the best drivers of entrepreneurial activities. Yet, it is riddled with imperfections – e.g., excessive inequality and market failure (Crouch, 2011).

The quest for 'investments that generate both economic prosperity and social wealth', which is at the heart of Africapitalism, is a quest for balance, harmony and peace. It is a recognition of the tendency of liberal market capitalism to lead to some form of socio-environmental imbalance, which is often dangerous to humanity. This sense of balance, which is expressed as the balance between economic prosperity and social wealth, can be further stretched to include the need to create a balance between the impacts of consumption and production on the ecology, environment, society and economy. In this regard, Africapitalism shares similar values of balance and harmony with the sustainability movement (Schwartz and Carroll, 2008), which can be summed up as the quest for peace and security: 'a process of achieving human development ... in an *inclusive, connected, equitable, prudent,* and *secure* manner' (Gladwin et al., 1995: 878, emphasis in original). Africapitalism is also underpinned by a stakeholder orientation insofar as it not only sees the creation of private wealth in the form of profits for shareholders, but strives to create social wealth for all stakeholders. It is a re-enactment of the modern management philosophy of harmony and balance (Kramer, 1975).

Sense of Place and Belonging

The sense of place and belonging is at the heart of the Africapitalism agenda. It is a direct response to globalised capitalism, which often takes place for granted and prioritises cost instead. Consequently, it is easy to outsource and for capital to follow the least cost-tolerant path. Arguably, therefore, globalisation trivialises place and promotes 'placelessness'. It reduces place to a mere resource, to the extent that the economic value of a place determines its situation in the scheme of things. Place is consumed, and place is fluid. Globalisation reduces place to space, which, according to Gieryn (2000: 465), 'is what place becomes when the unique gathering of things, meanings, and values are sucked out'. Lamenting the impact of globalisation on place, Escobar wrote:

> Place has dropped out of sight in the 'globalization craze' of recent years, and this erasure of place has profound consequences for our understanding of culture, knowledge, nature, and economy. It is perhaps time to reverse some of this asymmetry by focusing anew – and from the perspective afforded by the critiques of place themselves – on the continued vitality of place and place-making for culture, nature, and economy.
>
> *(Escobar 2001: 141)*

The focus on cost and not place renders the global economic order placeless, and this placelessness has implications for managerial framing of costs and opportunities. As such, Africapitalism is underpinned by the value of sense of place and rootedness (Tuan, 1977). It strives to restore in managerial decision making the link between place and economics on the one hand, and between place and self-identity on the other hand. Economic transactions are emplaced in place, and place is intrinsically bound with self, for 'there is no place without self and no self without place' (Casey, 2001: 684). In other words, Africapitalism becomes an expression of *topophilia* (Tuan, 1974) – 'the effective bond between people and place' (Duncan and Duncan, 2001: 41).

The sense of place and belonging can also manifest itself as an expression of patriotism, which 'attributes an intrinsic moral value to the defence of the homeland, even if it does not specify its boundaries' (Clift and Woll, 2012: 314) and 'entails a significant degree of loyalty to one's country and an associated disposition to take pride in it, to be subject to emotions closely connected with one's perception of its well-being, and to give some degree of preference to its needs and interests over the needs and interests of other countries' (Audi, 2009: 367–368). Within the context of Africapitalism, this expression of patriotism could be classified as a form of economic patriotism, which suggests 'that economic choices should be linked with concerns for one's homeland' (Clift and Woll, 2012: 308). In this case, the focus of Africapitalism on Africa is not arbitrary since, 'economic patriotism, like economic nationalism, needs to be defined by its territorial references and its underlying conception of political economic space, not by its supposed policy content' (ibid.). And at the firm level, it could lead to corporate patriotism: 'those forms of corporate behaviour which contribute to the national welfare of citizens and elicit the supportive behaviour of consumers and other stakeholders' (Puncheva-Michelotti et al., 2014: 1–2). As such, Africapitalism is, arguably, an exercise in, and an acceptance of, economic and political pragmatism given that 'economic patriotism is a universal phenomenon endemic within interdependent markets and economic jurisdictions' (Clift and Woll, 2012: 309).

As a linguistic project, Africapitalism jolts conventional wisdom and repositions the development of Africa in the world firmly as an indigenous project in which Africans will play significant, active roles. We see this glimmer of audacious hope across the continent, whether engaging with business leaders in Lagos, Nairobi, Accra or Johannesburg. The message and the sentiments it evokes are unique. The emotive power of Africapitalism is not necessarily a new phenomenon in economic history. Economic patriotism and nationalism played significant roles in the rebuilding of Western Europe after World War II, for instance. The same could be seen in the contemporary rise of China as an economic world power. This highlights the view that economic development is both a rational and an emotional project. As such, the resurgence of the behavioural perspective of economics and finance at the wake of the recent global financial crisis is not surprising. The behavioural turn emphasises the role of emotions, sentiments and sometimes crass irrationality on the rational person of neoclassical economics – including entrepreneurs. And herein lies the distinctiveness of Africapitalism as a powerful emotional economic tool for Africa's sustainable development. Since '[to] live is to live locally, and to know is first of all to know the places one is in' (Casey, 1996: 18; see also Escobar, 2001), the emotive force of Africapitalism, which is embedded in the sense of place and belonging, lends it the ability to connect with the African identity in a way that is not easily reflected in the broad view of capitalism.

EMERGING ISSUES AND FUTURE RESEARCH

It is important to emphasise that this chapter merely seeks to highlight the foundational ideas that might underpin the notion of Africapitalism. It is not an attempt to establish an Africapitalism theory of management. Hence, there are three main emerging issues. First, clarifying these foundational issues stems from the fact that Africapitalism shares the ethos of *doing good to do well* with other, similar ideas like Corporate Social Responsibility, corporate citizenship (CC), bottom of the pyramid and triple bottom line. Yet, Africapitalism is sufficiently different from these concepts, in the sense that while these concepts attempt to address the problems of owner-wealth maximisation theories of the firm without addressing the root of the problem (i.e., individualism) (Lutz, 2009), Africapitalism takes on this challenge by suggesting that the firm can be seen as a community (i.e., sense of belonging) rooted in a sense of place. Consequently, Africapitalism creates a space to challenge what Blowfield (2005) has labelled 'the non-negotiable value of capitalism', where concepts such as CSR or CC are taken for granted. The implication thus is that although Africapitalism might share the ameliorative potential of concepts like CSR or philanthropy, potentially it offers a much more transformative agenda.

Second, by reasserting the role of *place* and *emotion* in capitalism, Africapitalism offers an alternative basis for the socio-economic governance role of business that goes beyond the often limited business case argument that underpins many other concepts in the field of business and society. Crucial here is the fact that Africapitalism is not just an African-only project; rather, it is a mentality that is inclusive of different agents and actors that share the emotional attachment to the place. Third, the discrepancy between traditional African cultures and theories taught to African managers and future managers remains a serious problem (Lutz, 2009). Similarly, Zoogah (2008) has pointed out that it has been suggested that Africans lack the confidence to generate meaningful, significant and unique management knowledge. Africapitalism offers a potential space to begin to address these challenges.

There is a need, then, to further clarify what Africapitalism might mean as a *management idea* (Birkinshaw and Moles, 2008; Kramer, 1975) in practice and the need to formulate hypotheses that can be tested using empirical data. This chapter is an attempt to spark a debate in this area. There is a need for other scholars with an interest in Africa to join the debate and subject the concept to more rigorous analyses that might spur further innovation.

CONCLUSION

Africapitalism is capitalism by African-oriented entrepreneurs for Africa. It allows for a space to re-appropriate the discourse of capitalism in a manner that puts Africa, its culture and people front and centre of any possibility of capitalist development in the region. Articulated as such, it comes across as a force for good. It is a creative and novel way of domesticating and unleashing the power of capitalism in Africa. It is a concept that can easily unleash the emotive imagination of Africans and refocus their minds on what it means to be African in Africa. In this regard, Africapitalism becomes an expression of economic patriotism.

Africapitalism is a creative push back on the disadvantages of globalisation. It is an entrepreneurial quest and mindset that challenges the conventional win-lose mentality of entrepreneurs and businesses in Africa to create shared value (i.e., win-win outcomes) in and for Africa instead. The idea of capturing national governments for personal gains, which seems rather prevalent in the continent, is anachronistic, unfair to African society and ultimately unsustainable. Economic patriotism, which is at the core of Africapitalism, is una-shamedly good for Africa, and should be promoted within and for the continent.

Africapitalism without a strong philosophy behind it runs the risk of being hollow and ungrounded. Entrepreneurs and firms are at the very heart of capitalism. Any change in the way capitalism runs today should involve these actors. For Africapitalism to succeed, it needs to permeate the entrepreneurial mindset and the boardroom. Given its normative base, it also needs supporting governance mechanisms. Africapitalism requires Africa-consciousness and a form of re-imagined Afrocentricism that places the interests of Africa and Africans at the epicentre of business decisions, and that will guide Africa's renaissance. Afri-consciousness is a socio-mental awareness of Africa, putting Africans before the market. The sudden characterisation of the continent as the last frontier of capitalism bears the hallmarks of the exploitative form of capitalism, which will not be good for the continent. Afri-consciousness helps to neu-tralise the onslaught of globalisation and redirects the positive energy of capitalism in Africa to meeting the genuine development needs of African people.

However, Africapitalism can only thrive in a politically stable and environmentally sustainable Africa. It should be open to the natural and unnatural contingencies of the modern market and robust enough to carve a separate and distinct niche for itself in the face of globalisation and globalised Western capitalist market structures. Furthermore, Africapitalism can be both secular and non-secular in orientation. It can be informed by the ethos of both indigenous and non-indigenous religions in Africa. That said, African entrepreneurs must work creatively with the different governments to achieve this goal. This is where responsible business-government relations become a critical strategic option for businesses in Africa. Yet, Africapitalism can potentially serve as the common discourse for collective action and a space to redress the imbalance in management research and theory on Africa. This is particularly important given that Zoogah and Nkomo (2013) have indicated how the predominance of Western epistemology in the production of management knowledge about Africa has led to the exclusion of African voices.

REFERENCES

Agnew, J. A. 1987. *Place and Politics: The Geographical Mediation of State and Society*. London: Allen and Unwin.

Anyansi-Archibong, C. and Anyansi, P. M. 2014. African Entrepreneurs and Their Philanthropies: Motivations, Challenges and Impacts. In *Handbook of Research on Entrepreneurs Engagement in Philanthropy Perspectives*. Edited by M. Taylor, R. J. Strom and D. O. Renz, 267–297. Cheltenham and Northampton: Edward Elgar Publishers.

Audi, R. 2009. Nationalism, Patriotism, and Cosmopolitanism in an Age of Globalization. *Journal of Ethics*, 13: 365–381.

Birkinshaw, J., Hamel, G. and Mol, M. 2008. Management Innovation. *Academy of Management Review*, 33: 825–845.

Blowfield, M. 2005. Corporate Social Responsibility: Reinventing the Meaning of Development? *Journal of International Affairs*, 81(3): 515–524.

Blunt, P. and Jones, M. L. 1997. Exploring the Limits of Western Leadership Theory in East Asia and Africa. *Personnel Review*, 26(1/2): 6–23.

Brundtland, G. H. 1994. What Is World Prosperity? *Business Strategy Review*, 5: 57–69.

Carney, D. and Freeland, C. (eds.). 2014. Making Capitalism More Inclusive: Selected Speeches and Essays from Participants at the Conference on Inclusive Capitalism, 27 May, London:

Carmody, P. 2008. Exploring Africa's Economic Recovery. *Geography Compass*, 2 (1): 79–107.

Casey, E. 1993. *Getting Back into Place: Toward a Renewed Understanding of the Place-World*. Bloomington: Indiana University Press (cited in Escobar 2001).

Casey, E. 1996. 'How to Get from Space to Place in a Fairly Short Stretch of Time. Phenomenological Prolegomena'. In *Senses of Place* 27. Edited by S. Feld and K. Baso, 14–51. Santa Fe, NM: School of American Research.

Casey, E. S. 2001. Between Geography and Philosophy: What Does It Mean to Be in the Place World? *Annals of the Association of American Geographers*, 91(4): 683–693.

Chang, H. J. (2001) Breaking the Mould: An Institutionalist Political Economy to Neoliberal Theory of the Market and the State. Program Paper (SPD) No. 6. Geneva: UNRISD.

Clift, B. and Woll, C. 2012. Economic Patriotism: Reinventing Control over Open Markets. *Journal of European Public Policy*, 19(3): 307–323.

Crouch, C. 2010. CSR and Changing Modes of Governance: Towards Corporate Noblesse Oblige. In *Corporate Social Responsibility and Regulatory Governance: Towards Inclusive Development*. Edited by P. Utting and J. C. Marques, 26–49. London: Palgrave Macmillan.

Crouch, C. 2011. *The Strange Non-Death of Neoliberalism*. Cambridge: Polity Press.

Donaldson, T. and Dunfee, T. W. 1999. *Ties That Bind: A Social Contracts Approach to Business Ethics*. Boston, MA: Harvard Business School Press.

Duncan, J. and Duncan, N. 2001. Sense of Place as a Positional Good: Locating Bedford in Place and Time. In *Textures of Place: Exploring Humanist Geographies*. Edited by P. C. Adams, S. Hoelscher and K. Till, 41–54. Minneapolis: University of Minnesota Press.

Dunning, J. H. 2003. *Making Globalization Good: The Moral Challenges of Global Capitalism*. Oxford University Press.

Dunning, J. H. 2005. Is Global Capitalism Morally Defensible. *Contributions to Political Economy*, 24(1): 135–151.

Dunning, J. H. 2008. Corporate Social Responsibility: An Institutional Perspective. In *Corporate Governance and International Business: Strategy, Performance and Institutional Change*. Edited by R. Strange and G. Jackson, 168–195. Basingstoke: Palgrave Macmillan.

Edoho, F. M. 2001. Management in Africa: The Quest for a Philosophical Framework. In *Management Challenges for Africa in the Twenty-First Century: Theoretical and Applied Perspectives*. Edited by F. M. Edoho, 73–90. Westport, CT: Praeger.

Ekeh, P. 1990. Social Anthropology and Two Contrasting Uses of Tribalism in Africa. *Comparative Studies in Society and History*, 34(4): 660–700.

Escobar, A. 2001. Culture Sits in Places: Reflections on Globalism and Subaltern Strategies of Localization. *Political Geography*, 20: 139–174.

Garforth, C. Philips, C. and Bhatia-Panthaki, S. 2007. The Private Sector, Poverty Reduction and International Development. *Journal of International Development*, 19: 723–734.

Geelhoed, J. Samhoud and Smolders, I. 2014. *Creating Lasting Value: How to Lead, Manage and Market Your Stakeholder Value*. London: Kogan Page.

Gieryn, T. 2000. A Space for Place in Sociology. *Annual Review of Sociology*, 26: 463–496.

Gill, S. 2003. *Power and Resistance in the New World Order*. Basingstoke: Palgrave Macmillan.

Gladwin, T., Kennelly, J. and Krause, T. 1995. Shifting Paradigms for Sustainable Development: Implications for Management Theory and Research. *Academy of Management Review*, 20(4): 874–907.

Hall, P. A. and Soskice, D. (eds.). 2001. *Varieties of Capitalism: The Institutional Foundations of Comparative Advantage*. Oxford: Oxford University Press.

Hayek, F. 1979. *Law Legislation and Liberty*, Vol. 3. London: Routledge and Kegan Paul.

Idemudia, U. 2014. Corporate Social Responsibility and Development in Africa: Issues and Possibilities. *Geography Compass*, 8/7: 421–435.

Judge, W. Q., Fainshmidt, S. and Brown III, J. L. 2014. Which Model of Capitalism Best Delivers Both Wealth and Equality? *Journal of International Business Studies*, 45: 363–386.

Kang, N. and Moon, J. 2012. Institutional Complementarity between Corporate Governance and Corporate Social Responsibility: A Comparative Institutional Analysis of Three Capitalisms. *Socio-Economic Review*, 10: 85–108.

Karsten, L. and Illa, H. 2005, Ubuntu as Key African Management Concept: Contextual Background and Practical Insights for Knowledge Applications. *Journal of Managerial Psychology*, 20(7): 607–620.

Kramer, H. 1975. The Philosophical Foundations of Management Rediscovered. *Management International Review*, 15(2–3): 47–55.

Leisinger, K. M. 2007. Capitalism with a Human Face: The UN Global Compact. *Journal of Corporate Citizenship*, 28: 113–132.

Littrell, R. F., Wu, N.H., Nkomo, S., Wanasika, I., Howell, J. and Dorfman, P. 2013. 'Pan-Sub-Saharan African Managerial Leadership and Values of Ubuntu'. In *Management in Africa: Macro and Micro Perspectives*. Edited by T. R. Lituchy, B. J. Punnett, and B. B. Puplampu, 232–248. New York: Routledge.

Lundan, S. M. 2011. An Institutional Perspective on the Social Responsibility of TNCs. *Transnational Corporations*, 20(3): 61–77.

Lutz, D. W. 2009. African Ubuntu Philosophy and Global Management. *Journal of Business Ethics*, 84: 313–328.

Makhudu, N. 1993. Cultivating a Climate of Co-operation through Ubuntu. *Enterprise*, 68(August), 40–42.

Mbaku, J. M. 2004. *Institutions and Development in Africa*. Trenton, NJ: Africa World Press.

Mbigi, L. 2002. The Spirit of African Leadership: A Comparative African Perspective. *Journal for Convergence*, 3(4): 18–23.

Mbigi, L. and Maree J. 1995. *Ubuntu, the Spirit of African Transformation Management*. Randburg: Knowledge Resources.

McBarnet, D. 2007. Corporate Social Responsibility beyond the Law, through Law, for Law: The New Corporate Accountability. In *The New Corporate Accountability: Corporate Social Responsibility and the Law*. Edited by D. McBarnet, A. Voiculescu and T. Campbell, 9–56. Cambridge: Cambridge University Press.

McFarlin, D. B., Coster, E. A. and Mogale-Pretorius, C. 1999. South African Management Development in the Twenty-First Century. *Journal of Management Development*, 18(1): 63–78.

Murton, B. 2012. Being in the Place World: Toward a Maori 'Geographical Self'. *Journal of Cultural Geography*, 29(1): 87–104.

Newell, P. 2001. Managing Multinationals: The Governance of Investment for the Environment. *Journal of International Development*, 13(7): 907–919.

Newell, P. 2008. CSR and the Limit of Capital. *Development and Change*, 39(6): 1063–1078.

Novak, M. 1982. *The Spirit of Democratic Capitalism*. Lanham, MA and New York: Madison Books.

Offe, C. 2003. The European Model of 'Social' Capitalism: Can It Survive European Integration? *Journal of Political Philosophy*, 11(4): 437–469.

O' Laughlin, B. 2008. Governing Capital? Corporate Social Responsibility and the Limits of Regulation. *Development and Change*, 39(6): 945–957.

Piketty, T. and Ganser, L. J. 2014. *Capital in the Twenty-First Century*. Cambridge, MA: Harvard University Press.

Prinsloo, E. D. 2000. The African View of Participatory Business Management. *Journal of Business Ethics*, 25: 275–286.

Puncheva-Michelotti, P., McColl, R., Vocino, A. and Michelotti, M. 2014. Corporate Patriotism as a Source of Corporate Reputation: A Comparative Multi-Stakeholder Approach. *Journal of Strategic Marketing*, 22(6): 471–493.

Richey, L. A. and Ponte, S. 2014. New Actors and Alliances in Development. *Third World Quarterly*, 35(1): 1–21.

Schwartz, M. and Carroll A. B. 2008. Integrating and Unifying Competing and Complementary Frameworks: The Search for a Common Core in the Business and Society Field. *Business and Society*, 47: 148–186.

Smith, A. D. 1979. *Nationalism in the Twentieth Century*. Oxford: Martin Robertson.

The Economist. 2011. The Hopeful Continent: Africa Rising. Available at www .economist.com/node/21541015/print. Accessed 1 December 2014.

The Economist. 2013. The Hopeful Continent: Africa Rising. Available at www .economist.com/node/21572377/print. Accessed 1 December 2014.

Tuan, Y. F. 1974. *Topophilia: A Study of Environmental Perception, Attitudes, and Values.* Englewood Cliffs, NJ: Prentice Hall.

Tuan, Y. F. 1977. *Space and Place: The Perspective of Experience.* Minneapolis, MN: University of Minnesota Press.

United Nations. 2006. *Promotion and Protection of Human Rights: Interim Report of the Special Representative of the Secretary-General on Issues of Human Rights and Transnational Corporation and Other Business Enterprise* (UN Document No. E/CN.4/2006/97) Commission on Human Rights, 22 February. New York: United Nations Economic and Social Council.

Utting, P. 2005. Corporate Responsibility and the Movement of Business. *Development in Practice,* 15(3/4): 375–388.

Utting, P. 2008. The Struggle for Corporate Accountability. *Development and Change,* 39(6): 959–975.

Zoogah, D. B. 2008. African Business Research: A Review of Studies Published in the *Journal of African Business* and a Framework for Enhancing Future Studies. *Journal of African Business,* 9(1): 219–255.

Zoogah, D. B. and Nkomo, S. 2013. Management Research in Africa: Past, Present and Future. In *Management in Africa: Macro and Micro Perspectives.* Edited by T. R. Lituchy, B. J. Punnett and B. B. Puplampu, 9–31. New York: Routledge.

3 Business Elites to the Rescue! Reframing Capitalism and Constructing an Expert Identity

Implications for Africapitalism

George Ferns, Adun Okupe and
Kenneth Amaeshi

> One of the main casualties has been trust – in leaders, in institutions, in the free-market system itself.
>
> Yet, in a world that is more networked than ever, trust is harder to earn and easier to lose.
>
> So the big question is: how can we restore and sustain trust?

> Christine Lagarde (2014), Managing Director, International Monetary Fund
> Conference on Inclusive Capitalism, 27 May, 2014, London

INTRODUCTION

It is no secret that capitalism is facing a legitimacy crisis (du Gay and Morgan, 2013; Muller, 2013). Recurring protests and riots seeking to disrupt dominant economic and political institutions are a vivid illustration of disapproval aimed toward, amongst others: Wall Street greed (Van Gelder, 2011), the privatisation of public goods such as water (Simmons, 2015) and environmental degradation caused by capitalism's externalising function (Böhm et al., 2012; Klein, 2014). Arguably, the recent 2008 financial crisis, which resulted in the global collapse of financial markets and the liquidation of several major financial institutions, acted as a pivotal turning point for the irrefutable hegemony enjoyed by modern-day 'casino capitalism' (Strange, 2015). In addition, as the schism between the rich and poor widens, concerns with inequality continue to fuel popular discontent with capitalism (Piketty, 2014).

This is also the case in developing countries where capitalism often turns 'wild' – stimulating corruption, cronyism and rent-seeking behaviour (Taylor, 2012; Acemoglu and Robinson 2008).

Importantly, withering trust regarding the virtues of capitalism is associated with increased disapproval for economic elites: the minority group owning a disproportionate share of global wealth "in positions to make decisions having major consequences" (Mills, 1956: 3). In particular, whether as heads of industry, occupants of the professions or as key advisors to governments, elites' *expertise* is increasingly being 'put on trial' (Morgan et al., 2015). As the Edelman Trust Barometer (2016) fittingly shows, trust in CEOs for instance has not recovered since the financial crisis, hovering just below the 50 per cent rate. Christine Lagarde's quote above, taken from her keynote speech at the 2014 Conference on Inclusive Capitalism, further illuminates concern with society's distrust of economic elites. This sentiment chimes with Zald and Lounsbury's (2010: 964) proposition to 'look behind the metaphorical curtain in the Emerald City to demystify the wizardry of experts'. In this chapter, we answer their call, and focus on the *language* of elites as they uphold their identity as experts in the context of capitalism's legitimacy crisis.

We contend that elites are not static bystanders in light of critique waged against capitalism. Instead, elites proactively adapt in accordance with evolving cultural trends whilst also expending significant resources shaping those trends (Hartmann, 2007). Accordingly, as Bourdieu (1996) suggests, it is not necessarily the control of material resources that defines elites as influential, but the dynamic ways by which elites effectively mobilise cultural and symbolic capital to secure their interests. This includes the ways in which elites aptly redefine and incorporate critique into their own structures (Boltanski and Chiapello, 2008). Any critique of capitalism thus stems as much from civil society and ordinary people as it does from the discursive activity of elites themselves. Yet, despite discourse and language being central to organisational studies literature on economic elites (Helfen, Schüßler and Botzem, 2015; Schmidt, 2008), few studies explore the specific discursive strategies employed by elites as they engage with critiques of capitalism, including the effect of such discursive activity on identity construction. Instead, scholars have predominantly been concerned with differentiating elites based on, for instance, embeddedness within different 'varieties of capitalism' (Morgan, 2015), varying backgrounds in terms of education and class (Maclean et al., 2012, 2014) and the heterogeneity of their cultural capital (Spence et al., 2016). Notwithstanding, the emphasis on discourse and identity is particularly important because it underscores how elites utilise symbolic capital to reproduce their positions of power, including how they construct their own identity as experts: 'elites derive their power from the discursive formation of signifying and legitimating' (Scott, 2008: 32).

To address this, we examine economic philosophies composed and promoted by four economic elites, chosen based on their attempt to address and respond to the shortcomings of capitalism, and also for the traction they have been able to garner. These include Tony Elumelu's recent vision of *Africapitalism*; John Mackey and Raj Sisodia's higher-purpose approach to business through *Conscious Capitalism*; Lynn Forester de Rothschild's notion of *Inclusive Capitalism*; and Al Gore and David Blood's call for paradigmatic reforms to the financial industry as illustrated by *Sustainable Capitalism*. We are particularly interested in the 'interpretive schemas', or frames (Benford and Snow, 2000; Goffman, 1974), through which elites define their economic philosophies. This is because these frames are based on broader cultural values that are comprised to form the 'central organizing idea or story line that provides meaning' to each economic philosophy (Gamson and Modigliani, 1987: 143). Moreover, framing is used to simplify otherwise complex phenomena, or, as Goffman notes, frames are used as a way 'to locate, perceive, identify and label a seemingly infinite number of concrete occurrences defined in its terms'. As such, frames not only help individuals make sense of their environments, but also play an important role in constructing their roles and identities (Lefsrud and Meyer, 2012; Tajfel, 1981).

Our frame analysis draws from Snow and Benford (1988), who identify three core framing tasks. The first is *diagnostic* framing, which concerns defining the problem and those responsible for creating the problem. In our case, this entails how elites define capitalism in terms of its faults. The second task is *prognostic* framing and regards proposed solutions to identified problems. Here, we examine the suggestions offered by elites in terms of what to do concretely about fixing capitalism as evidenced through their philosophy. The third task is *motivational framing*, which entails offering a 'call to action' in the form of compelling and emotive vocabularies that also provide a sense of identity. In this regard, we examined the outcomes, both financial and societal, as promised by the elites upon adopting their economic philosophy. Overall, we address two research objectives: (1) to explore the frames that elites use as a way to respond and shape critiques of capitalism and (2) to investigate how such responses help elites construct an identity as trusted experts.

This chapter is structured as follows. We first describe each economic philosophy, including a synthesis of the philosophies and their progression since conception. Next, we present our findings by illustrating the main frames that elites draw on in forming their economic philosophies. In addition, we discuss how, through their framing activities, elites construct an identity as 'trusted experts'. Finally, we conclude with a discussion of our findings, including, as per the theme of this edited book, lessons for Africapitalism.

Overview of Economic Philosophies

Zealous and self-assured, the elites featured in this study insist, rather counterintuitively, on changing the very system responsible for their success. As such, elites argue that unfettered free-market thinking must be reconsidered. But instead of aiming to overthrow capitalism per se, the four economic philosophies propose *redirecting* capitalism and initiating change from within. The following sections will highlight their philosophies.

Africapitalism

Founded by Nigerian banker and entrepreneur Tony Elumelu, Africapitalism is an economic philosophy that hinges on the power of the private sector as a vehicle for long-term, sustainable value creation (Elumelu, 2013). Africapitalism is therefore a call for business people across Africa to instil a mentality of 'doing well as a business, by doing good within the community' (Nurse and Dougherty, 2013). Elumelu, who is also one of Africa's wealthiest individuals (Forbes, 2015), coined the term in 2011 and has spearheaded the movement through high-profile media engagements, participation at transnational summits such as the World Economic Forum and through a self-created pan-African think tank, The Africapitalism Institute, which was founded in 2014. Elumelu has, in addition, founded The Tony Elumelu Entrepreneurship Programme, which promotes Africapitalism by furthering young entrepreneurs' business ideas through seed capital. A unique emphasis is placed on the transformative potential of Africans investing in Africa (Edwards, 2013; Elumelu, 2013). Africapitalism therefore sets itself apart from other 'new capitalisms', given it incorporates a sense of economic patriotism – designed to motivate and incite a sense of entrepreneurialism 'that generate[s] both economic prosperity and social wealth' (Amaeshi and Idemudia, 2015: 210). Conversely, it is similar to other new capitalisms given that it seeks to combine both financial and social benefits that stem from business activity. According to the Africapitalism manifesto (Elumelu, 2013), the philosophy is based on three main principles:

Wealth Creation: The private sector in Africa – both foreign multinationals as well as African business leaders – must break free from the historical tendencies of exploitation and extraction of wealth (i.e., rent-seeking), and instead focus on generating profit through wealth creation.

Funding Entrepreneurship: Leveraging private enterprise to solve problems must be a core area of focus not just for investors, but also for NGOs and philanthropists.

Transparent Competitive Markets: Governments are not responsible for running industries; they are responsible for providing a supportive environment for businesses to thrive, in markets that are fair, transparent and open.

Conscious Capitalism

Although the origin of the term 'Conscious Capitalism' is not clear, it has recently gained popularity within both public and business discourse. Arguably, Rothman and Scott's (2003) book, *Companies with a Conscience*, was a pioneering effort toward conceptually and empirically developing Conscious Capitalism. However, Conscious Capitalism is more commonly attributed to its most avid proponents: John Mackey (CEO of Whole Foods Market) and Raj Sisodia (co-founder and co-chairman of Conscious Capitalism, Inc). As such, Conscious Capitalism's take-off can be attributed to the release of John Mackey and Raj Sisodia's (2014) book: *Conscious Capitalism: Liberating the Heroic Spirit of Business*. The term loosely refers to some form of 'enlightened' business practice, or the idea that a company should transcend the traditional conception of business as solely for generating profits. Therefore, a focus is businesses finding an intrinsic *purpose*, which is 'far more effective and powerful than extrinsic financial incentives' (Mackey and Sisodia, 2014: 55).

Since its conception, Conscious Capitalism has created significant buzz in popular press outlets including books and business press articles. Most notably, business news sources such as *Fast Company* (Shane, 2013) and *Fortune* (Schawbel, 2013) continue to extensively report on the progress of Conscious Capitalism as a concept and business practice. However, with the exception of the *California Management Review* (O'Toole and Vogel, 2011), Conscious Capitalism has attracted little serious scholarly attention. Nevertheless, an impressive list of companies, including Whole Foods, Trader Joe's, Southwest Airlines, Starbucks, Patagonia, The Container Store and Unilever, have remarked that Conscious Capitalism (to varying degrees) fits with their sustainable business philosophy. At its core, Conscious Capitalism proposes that business transcend its obsession with short-term profits and do more. Conscious Capitalism describes several other tenets that make up the philosophy:

> *Higher Purpose*: Recognising that every business has a purpose that includes, but is more than, making money.
>
> *Stakeholder Orientation*: Recognising that the interdependent nature of life and the human foundations of business, a business needs to create value with and for its various stakeholders.
>
> *Conscious Leadership*: Human social organisations are created and guided by leaders – people who see a path and inspire others to travel along the path.
>
> *Conscious Culture*: This is the ethos – the values, principles, practices – underlying the social fabric of a business, which permeates the atmosphere of a business and connects the stakeholders to each other and to the purpose, people and processes that comprise the company.

SUSTAINABLE CAPITALISM

Sustainable Capitalism is defined as 'a framework that seeks to maximise long-term economic value creation by reforming markets to address real needs while considering all costs and integrating environmental, social, and governance metrics into the decision-making process' (Gore and Blood, 2012: 6). The philosophy was conceived by Al Gore – former US vice-president turned Nobel Prize–winning climate activist – with ex-Goldman Sachs partner, David Blood. The philosophy forms part of the grounding vision of their investment bank – Generation Investment Management – which was launched in 2004 and is headquartered in London. The firm focuses on investing in what they refer to as 'sustainable business models'. Elaborated on in a manifesto released in 2012, Sustainable Capitalism is tailored specifically to the financial sector and was inspired, in particular, by the events that led up to the financial crisis (Gore and Blood, 2011).

Sustainable Capitalism's primary emphasis is on long-term thinking that takes into consideration sustainably metrics, which the creators argue '[do] not represent a trade-off with profit maximisation but instead actually fosters superior long-term value creation' (Gore and Blood, 2012: 1). Although this might not seem particularly novel, the global financial industry's fixation with the short term is what Gore and Blood argue is harming societies and the natural environment, and something that is unsustainable. In fact, that the global financial crisis did not result in a large-scale system 'shock' further highlighted the need for an alternative philosophy to investment banking. In this respect, Gore famously remarked of the crisis and sustainability that 'the conversation about sustainability has if anything gone backwards' (The Economist, 2012). Despite this lack of progress, Sustainable Capitalism places considerable emphasis on the fiduciary duty of financial actors to take into account environmental, social and governance (ESG) issues when investing their clients' money. Their manifesto outlines the following five factors as being necessary for Sustainable Capitalism to be achieved by 2020:

Identify and incorporate risks from stranded assets – to quantify the impact of stranded assets and the subsequent implications for assessing investment opportunities until a fair price on externalities forces a change in valuation methodologies.

Mandate integrated reporting – integrated reporting is to be mandated for publicly listed companies by the appropriate regulatory agencies and the encouragement of voluntary action by these companies in the short term to provide integrated reports until such regulation comes to pass.

End the default practice of issuing quarterly earnings guidance – bringing together a significant group of CEOs who have already stopped providing quarterly earnings guidance with others who pledge to stop doing so as a catalyst for change around this practice and to stimulate long-term thinking.

Align compensation structures with long-term sustainable performance – compensation structures for both executives and asset managers should be revised so that they are aligned with long-term financial and ESG performance.

Encourage long-term investing with loyalty-driven securities – companies issue loyalty-driven securities that are only paid to investors who have held stock for more than three years.

INCLUSIVE CAPITALISM

The notion of capitalism as 'inclusive' dates back to debates on self-interest which conceive of capitalism as exclusive, at least in the writing of Thomas Hobbes and later Adam Smith. Perhaps more contemporary uses of the term can be attributed to C. K. Prahalad, who opens his book *The Fortune at the Bottom of the Pyramid: Eradicating Poverty Through Profits* with the question of 'Why can't we create Inclusive Capitalism' (Prahalad, 2003: xv). Prahalad questions whether capitalism can become more inclusive of those populations that do not have the means and access to necessarily benefit from capitalism itself and are often subjugated by capitalism.

Initiated by Lady Lynn Forester de Rothschild and a large cohort of economic and political elites, including Prince Charles and Bill Clinton, Inclusive Capitalism's purpose is 'to restore capitalism as an engine of broadly shared prosperity' (Coalition for Inclusive Capitalism, 2015a). Its organising body, the Coalition for Inclusive Capitalism, organises yearly meetings – 'its guest-list ... estimated to hold one-third of the world's investable assets' (Brooks-Pollock, 2014) – to discuss ways of making current models of capitalism more socially and environmentally responsible. In particular, the purpose of Inclusive Capitalism is to redesign capitalism to benefit everyone, not only a small minority. It is thus concerned with issues pertaining to global inequality. Inclusive Capitalism places specific focus on the need for corporate leaders to rethink their approach to doing business and making money. Accordingly, many of its adherents are heads of large multinational companies such as Siemens' Joe Kaeser and Andrew Liveris of the Dow Chemical Company. Similar to Sustainable Capitalism, Inclusive Capitalism operationalises its philosophy through encouraging firms – and especially CEOs – to incorporate ESG factors into their decision-making. However, the philosophy clearly seeks to distance itself from both philanthropy and corporate social responsibility arguing that Inclusive Capitalism is not about how 'a firm spends some of the money it makes, it's about how it makes its money' (Coalition for Inclusive Capitalism 2015: 149). The Coalition for Inclusive Capitalism thus adheres to the following principles:

Metrics – We see Integrated Reporting and sustainability accountancy standards as some of the most powerful emerging corporate practices available to support and embed Inclusive Capitalism.

Investing for the long term – By embracing Inclusive Capitalism practices, investors can signal that they are focused on the long term, and corporations can attract more value-oriented, duration investors. The pressure to sacrifice the future to the quarter will be reduced.

CEOs leading by example – Inclusive Capitalism embraces the best practices of CEOs that demonstrate the ethics of stewardship, stakeholder engagement and responsibility.

Ownership-based governance – Inclusive Capitalism is about maximising stakeholder value not just shareholder value.

SYNTHESIS OF ELITES' ECONOMIC PHILOSOPHIES

These economic philosophies share several similarities but also differ in certain aspects. Three key points are worthy of discussion. First, shared amongst all four philosophies is that their founders, or those who spearhead the philosophy, are economic elites (Useem, 1980): (1) they have, either by themselves, or through family lineage, acquired a disproportionate amount of wealth relative to occupying a small proportion of the population;[1] (2) they have done so primarily though commercial, as opposed to political or military, means; and (3) they share close ties with a network of other business elites, as manifested through interlocking board directorships (Davis 1991). Second, all elites call for a change to the way capitalism is practised.

---

[1] According to Forbes (2014), each of the four new capitalisms' leaders net worth surpasses $100,000,000.

Their philosophies are grand theories of change and not concerned with merely tinkering with the status quo. Therefore, their message is rather similar: 'while the present form of capitalism has proven its superiority, it is nevertheless abundantly clear that some of the ways in which it is now practised do not incorporate sufficient regard for its impact on people and the planet' (Gore and Blood, 2012: 5). Third, all philosophies not only insist that commercial and non-commercial interests can be combined without any trade-off, but that economic, social and environmental concerns are mutually reinforcing and therefore beneficial when considered together.

There are however certain differences between philosophies. First, although there is a slight overlap between Inclusive Capitalism and Sustainable Capitalism in terms of both advocating long-term thinking and consideration for ESG issues, each economic philosophy has carved out its own unique focus. Africapitalism and Conscious Capitalism are most starkly contrasted as the former is geographically focused and emphasises entrepreneurialism, whereas the latter's purpose is addressing existential questions. Sustainable Capitalism is also unique as it concentrates specifically on the financial industry. The least 'focused' is arguably Inclusive Capitalism. This is likely because it resembles a club whose members stem from a widely expansive set of fields. Second, the various economic philosophies have experienced different levels of success and have accordingly disseminated at different speeds and to different audiences. Tracking their evolution over time is difficult because no clearly set trajectory is evident. Moreover, the principles they purport are value-based and therefore not easily measurable in terms of uptake. The only exception might be Sustainable Capitalism, which bases its success on financial returns based on ESG metrics. In this regard, Sustainable Capitalism has done relatively well given that Generation Investment Management has outperformed other base-line indices year on year (Scott, 2014). In order to illustrate this heterogeneity, we now turn to the different framing strategies utilised by elites to construct their philosophies.

FRAMES AND IDENTITY CONSTRUCTION

Economic elites draw from three frames: *capitalism unleashed, short to long* and *holism* (see Table 3.1 for overview). The following section compares and contrasts these frames by illustrating how each economic philosophy uses different strategies related to Snow and Benford's (1988) framework: identifying the problem (diagnostic), stating what to do about the problem (prognostic) and a call to action (motivation mobilisation). Finally, we highlight how, by appealing to *authority* and *solidarity*, elites' framing activity constructs an identity as 'trusted expert'.

Frame 1: 'Capitalism Unleashed'

Elites feel that capitalism is trapped in a symbolic prison, and that only by setting capitalism free can it truly reach its potential. What exactly hinders capitalism, however, differs between philosophies. Most commonly, elites ask that business transcend its obsession with short-term profit maximisation, which is, with the exception of Sustainable Capitalism, a tenet of all economic philosophies. For example, Conscious Capitalism (Mackey and Sisodia 2014: xi), which arguably draws most explicitly from this frame compared to the other philosophies, frequently refers to capitalism having 'gone off the rails the past quarter century' resulting in business now being constrained by a lack of purpose. In fact, Conscious Capitalism (2016a) bases its entire philosophy on 'the idea that business is about more than making a profit. It's about a higher purpose'. Inclusive Capitalism (2014: 13) shares the idea of capitalism being hampered, but attributes 'market fundamentalism' as the obstruction, which 'is breaking down a basic social contract'. Africapitalism (2013: 16) takes a somewhat different approach by problematising capitalism as stuck in a logic based on 'centralised governments managing basic industries', which is attributed to the 'well-meaning but misguided global development finance institutions'.

Elites' prognostic framing emphasises enlightening businesses and unshackling capitalism from whatever is restricting its potential.

TABLE 3.1 *Summary of the framing, call to action and expert identity construction for each of the philosophies*

		Diagnostic framing	Prognostic framing	Call to action	Expert identity construction
Africapitalism	Frame 1: *Capitalism unleashed*	Historic embeddedness in 'old' development logic	Self-reflection and inward focus	Social and financial returns	**Authority:** international organisations
	Frame 2: Short to long	Short-term, rent-seeking behaviour	Investing rational shift to long term	Poverty alleviation and nation-building	**Solidarity:** narratives of success
	Frame 3: *Holism*		Community	Prosperity for both community and company	
Conscious Capitalism	Frame 1: *Capitalism unleashed*	Lack of purpose	Rediscovery of business purpose	'Higher' social and financial returns	**Authority:** business gurus
	Frame 2: Short to long	Short-term gains	Mindset shift away from speculation	Sustained financial performance	**Solidarity:** shared struggles
	Frame 3: *Holism*	Reductionism	Stakeholder approach	Business leadership	

TABLE 3.1 (cont.)

		Diagnostic framing	Prognostic framing	Call to action	Expert identity construction
Inclusive Capitalism	Frame 1: *Capitalism unleashed*	Market fundamentalism	Broadening of business environment	Shareholder returns and regaining trust	**Authority:** science and research
	Frame 2: Short to long	Short-term profits	Longer-term performance measurement	Environmental sustainability and generational equity	**Solidarity:** togetherness
	Frame 3: *Holism*	Business become too isolated	Stakeholder approach	Extend benefits of capitalism to everyone	
Sustainable Capitalism	Frame 1: *Capitalism unleashed*	n/a	n/a	Long-term shareholder returns	**Authority:** science and research
	Frame 2: Short to long	Short termism	Market and regulatory reform	Intergenerational justice	**Solidarity:** n/a
	Frame 3: *Holism*	Metrics not considering negative externalities	Integrating ESG measures	Improved long-term performance	

Elites stress several ways to do so. For example, Africapitalism (Elumelu 2013: 7) suggests that for businesses to 'break free from the historical tendencies of exploitation and extraction of wealth', they must realise their own potential: 'Africans themselves need to build the kinds of companies that make the products we buy, adding value within the continent for Africa's own benefit.' Conscious Capitalism (Mackey and Sisodia 2014: 33) also suggests rediscovery of sorts by underscoring the need for a reflection regarding a 'deeper consciousness about why businesses exist and how they should be organised and led'. Inclusive Capitalism (Coalition for Inclusive Capitalism 2015) concerns not so much a rediscovery as an expansion: 'taking a broader view of the firm – its purpose, products, people and planet'. In doing so, the private sector will be able to 'restore trust from all members of society'.

Elites' call to action highlights the significant commercial and social benefits that could be realised if capitalism is unleashed from that which stymies its advancement. The types of motive vocabularies are therefore predominantly focused on gain, accumulation and performance. Inclusive Capitalism (Coalition for Inclusive Capitalism 2015) in particular underscores how 'companies that follow inclusive and sustainable standards perform better for their shareholders than those that do not'. In a similar vein, Africapitalism accentuates the 'tremendous commercial and social returns' that can be achieved as businesses 'open their eyes to the growing opportunity to profit from wealth creation'. Conscious Capitalism is not as direct in terms of asserting financial gains but does indicate broader benefits that can be achieved when business reaches its higher purpose: to 'create lasting value as the world evolves to even greater levels of prosperity, helping billions of people flourish and lead lives infused with passion, purpose, love and creativity' (Mackey and Sisodia, 2013).

Frame 2: 'Short to Long'

The second frame utilised by the elites regards capitalism's temporal dimensions, including amongst others, inter-generational sustainability issues, quarterly reporting cycles and/or the short-term focus of financial markets. Sustainable Capitalism (Gore and Blood 2012: 2) in particular draws from this frame in its diagnosis of the problem: 'remarkably, even after enduring the global financial crisis – caused in significant part by short-term, unsustainable strategies . . . – many of us are still content to embrace short-termism in nearly all aspects of our lives'. In a similar way, Africapitalism (Elumelu 2013: 7) attributes 'short-term', 'rent-seeking', 'short-sighted', 'extractive' and/or 'speculative' activities to worsening socio-economic conditions of Africans by 'misallocating capital away from wealth creation'. Focusing specifically on the effects of short-termism on businesses, Conscious Capitalism (Mackey and Sisodia 2014: xii) vividly illustrates that 'the drive for short-term gains has led to the destruction of many great companies like General Motors and Sears and the bankruptcies of Enron, WorldCom, Kmart, and Kodak'.

Elites accordingly suggest that business shift its focus to value creation with a long-term outlook. This is framed differently, however, by each philosophy. Africapitalism, for instance, proposes advancing entrepreneurship initiatives that have positive social impacts and long-term horizons. In doing so, the 'focus and rationale for investment' (Elumelu 2013: 14) changes alongside the evolving 'nature of the opportunity'.

Sustainable Capitalism emphasises the need to engage in market and regulatory reforms, related to, for example, ending the default practice of quarterly earnings reports, encouraging compensation schemes that reward long-term sustainable performance and discouraging high-frequency trading that causes market volatility. In a chapter called 'Patient, Purposeful Investors', Conscious Capitalism (Mackey and Sisodia 2014: 99) suggests a mindset shift away from speculation toward thinking of investing and long-term business as synonymous and inseparable. In other words, although short-term investments might sometimes pay off for a single individual, speculative investments cannot sustain themselves in the long run, and are, therefore, unsustainable.

Calls to action that draw from the 'go-long' frame concern the perceived benefits of long-term approaches – e.g., related to improving the 'human endeavour' to ensure 'prosperity over the long term' (Coalition for Inclusive Capitalism 2015a). The latter, which Sustainable Capitalism (Gore and Blood 2012: 12) refers to as 'generational responsibility', is frequently associated with environmental sustainability and the need to address climate change in order to preserve a planet for future generations. Accordingly, as professed by the Bank of England Governor Mark Carney (2014: 3) in his keynote speech at the 2014 Conference on Inclusive Capitalism in London: 'a long term perspective is required to [align] incentives across generations, [if unsuccessful] systems designed and enjoyed by previous generations may prove, absent reform, unaffordable for future ones'. The benefits to the human condition of a long-term investment approach are likewise hailed by Africapitalism (Elumelu 2013: 13) as these sorts of investments 'build up communities, create opportunities to emerge from extreme poverty, while also creating brand awareness and customer loyalty, solving problems and delivering sustainable returns'.

Frame 3: Holism

All economic philosophies draw from the idea that capitalism has somehow resulted in business becoming detached from society and its ills. As such, capitalism is not only problematised for its inability to solve global issues such as inequality, but criticised in terms of mismanaging external stakeholder relations. For example, Inclusive Capitalism (Coalition for Inclusive Capitalism 2014: 5) is grounded in the idea that business has become too isolated as a bystander in the shadows of global issues: 'A good deal of the problems we are facing can be traced back to the idea that business is somehow separate from society, rather than being a core element.' Conscious Capitalism

(Mackey and Sisodia 2014: 18) attributes such segmentation to the tendency for capitalism to engage in reductionism, which results in businesses failing 'to recognize the significant impacts they have on the environment, on other creatures that inhibit the planet, and the physical health and psyches of team members and consumers'. Sustainable Capitalism (Gore and Blood 2012: 12) focuses primarily on how metrics used by the financial industry and economists, especially GDP, as a proxy for 'progress' do not consider negative externalities, and are thus inadequate for addressing issues such as climate change: 'The quality, not simply the quantity, of growth should be valued.'

The suggested solutions that draw from the holism frame are principally focused on businesses becoming more inclusive and aware of their environments. Accordingly, engaging with stakeholders is frequently proposed. Three philosophies adopt a stakeholder focus, whilst Africapitalism instead opts for a subtler emphasis on community engagement. Inclusive Capitalism (Coalition for Inclusive Capitalism 2014: 16) on the other hand places the concept of stakeholder engagement at the centre of its approach – after all: 'In today's interconnected world, our challenges are so great and so complex that no single organisation can address them alone.' As such, businesses are urged to incorporate concerns of multiple actors into their decision-making thereby recognising 'that their actions do not merely affect their personal rewards, but also the legitimacy of the system in which they operate' (Carney, 2014: 8). Similarly, by quoting naturalist John Muir who said 'when you tug at a single thing in nature, you find it attached to the rest of the world', Conscious Capitalism stresses the need to consider the entire ecosystem within which it is embedded. In doing so, businesses begin to 'recognize that, without employees, customers, suppliers, funders, supportive communities and a life-sustaining ecosystem, there is no business' (Conscious Capitalism, 2016b). Notably, besides its stakeholder focus, Sustainable Capitalism also suggests that companies engage with quantifiable environmental, social and governance (ESG) indicators and report on their progress accordingly. As such, businesses should consider *all* costs when making decisions – including environmental costs and the effect on stakeholders.

The reward of such activity is presented in terms of businesses being able to make better, well-informed choices, which Inclusive Capitalism (Coalition for Inclusive Capitalism 2015) argues can help 'extend the opportunities and benefits of our economic system to everyone'. This, of course, is deemed beneficial for both commercial reasons and social ends. Conscious Capitalism (2016), for example, argues that holistic approaches are especially useful for development of business leadership: 'Their higher state of consciousness makes visible to them the interdependencies that exist across all stakeholders, allowing them to discover and harvest synergies from situations that otherwise seem replete with trade-offs.' Indeed, Sustainable Capitalism (Gore and Blood 2012: 7) similarly proposes that incorporating social and environmental concerns into decision-making, coupled of course with financials, produces long-term value – 'since they have a more holistic understanding of the material issues affecting their business'. Africapitalism (Elumelu 2013: 13), which frequently refers to development benefits, draws from the holism frame to stress the benefit of creating a 'positive cycle of company and community prosperity'.

SYNOPSIS: CONSTRUCTING A 'TRUSTED EXPERT' IDENTITY

By reframing capitalism in line with the above frames, elites do more than merely make suggestions. When reading through the manifestos, one cannot help but feel a certain sense of trust in what they are saying, as if they *know*. Each framing task produces this effect: elites know what the problem is; they claim to have the necessary knowledge needed to solve it, and that, by following their philosophy in particular, significant benefits will be attained. Together, this constructs an identity as an expert. In this section, we illustrate two examples of how this is achieved as elites make appeals to *authority* and *solidarity*.

In regard to authority, reference is made to other authority types – e.g., people, laws, organisations – and then 'transferred' through association with the elite's own person, and economic philosophy. Although this practice is pervasive amongst all philosophies, each philosophy appeals to different authority types. For example, Sustainable Capitalism (Gore and Blood 2012: 13) favours authority of research and science, commonly referencing trusted government organisations such as the UN and the Bank of England, including other experts such as Morgan Stanley, the audit firm PWC and the consulting firm McKinsey:

> we needed to identify and better understand the obstacles we faced. To achieve this, we collaborated with McKinsey in the summer of 2010 to convene a range of experts and practitioners in the Sustainable Capitalism field.

Interestingly, Africapitalism only occasionally draws from African authorities (e.g., Rwanda's president Paul Kagame or the African Development Bank); preferring instead internationally renowned non-African figures such as the World Bank, Monitor Group, *The Economist* or the Harvard professor Michael Porter. Conscious Capitalism also associates with certain business gurus who, they argue, somehow represent their philosophy. For example, Conscious Capitalism (2014: 198) states that conscious business is 'asking yourself questions like, "What would Warren Buffett do in this situation?"' Using its esteemed list of members and speakers, Inclusive Capitalism (2015a) often uses authority figures not even associated with economics or business, but who have high levels of perceived trust: 'His Holiness Pope Francis was pleased to be informed of the Second International Conference on Inclusive Capitalism and he sends cordial greetings.'

Second, elites construct themselves as trusted experts through the use of narratives that infer a sense of solidarity. Africapitalism does so by drawing from emotive appeals related to remarkable success story of its founder Tony Elumelu (2013: 5): 'This type of story is being repeated every day, in all kinds of industries, all over Africa – East to West, and North to South.' In addition, such narratives are buttressed with vivid imagery of being in unison for change: 'We welcome you to stand with us, in the shining light of Africa's new dawn.' Similarly, Conscious Capitalism (Mackey and Sisodia 2014: 2) evokes a sense of trust by appealing to overlapping struggles shared by both elite and non-elites. Speaking about his own success, John Mackey reminisces: 'Despite working many eighty-plus-hour weeks, Renee [his partner] and I initially took salaries of only about $200 a month and lived in the office above the store.' This emphasis on solidarity can also be recognised with other philosophies, for instance in terms of Inclusive Capitalism's (Coalition for Inclusive Capitalism 2015: 8) frequent referencing to 'a deep and real sense of solidarity', highlighting that 'we are all in this together' as 'partners for life' – all 'members of a global community'. Sustainable Capitalism contrasts most significantly from the other philosophies by forgoing emotive appeals to solidarity, and instead relying on their expert identity, as described about, to establish trustworthiness.

CONCLUSION AND PROPOSITIONS

This chapter began by describing capitalism's legitimacy crisis, prompted by an increasing emphasis on capitalism's apparent negative outcomes such as inequality and environmental harm. However, instead of exploring the 'usual suspects' – e.g., social movements and left-wing radicals – we focused on a small group seemingly least likely to impose a critique of capitalism: economic elites. Notwithstanding, as this research illustrates, there are clear cases in which elites *do* actively engage in criticising the very system responsible for their success. One could of course argue that the idea of economic elites 'fixing' capitalism is contradictory, and even ludicrous, and that elites are engaged in a large-scale public relations campaign merely aimed at strengthening their image. This would, however, be a grave simplification. It would be difficult to imagine a networked society, persistently suspicious of the elite, being totally duped by elite messages. In addition, furthering capitalism's destructive tendencies would work against the interests of the elite. This is supported by the fact that inequality and environmental degradation threaten economic stability (Stern, 2007), global health (McMichael et al., 2007) and food/water security (Schmidhuber and Tubiello, 2007), which, in turn, could stir social unrest and thereby hinder elites continuing their very existence as elites (Scheffran, Brzoska and Brauch, 2012; Zhang, et al., 2007).

Indeed, elites are by no means passive bystanders. Their dynamic nature in terms of managing symbolic capital allows them to adapt to broader changes in society and even stimulate such changes themselves. By recognising this agentic capability, we have explored the different discursive strategies economic elites use in their attempts to reframe capitalism. This way, economic elites are able to address their own views on the perceived shortcomings of capitalism, whilst concurrently being able to defend capitalism from critique. Our findings suggest that elites draw from a variety of different frames that they utilise to construct their own revised philosophy of capitalism. A 'capitalism unleashed' frame was used to express how certain shortcomings constrain capitalism of reaching is true potential; urging for a rediscovery of purpose through both inward reflection ('what does capitalism mean for me?') and outward expansion ('how can capitalism work for others?). Elites also used a 'go-long' frame which suggested that the focus of investment should change in order to address serious concerns with short-termism. Lastly, a 'holism' frame was employed in various ways to emphasise the need for capitalism to become more inclusive of its broader environment and consider the wider impacts of business on all stakeholders.

We also demonstrated how elites' reframing of capitalism consequentially constructs an identity as 'expert' by appealing to *authority* and *solidarity*. This is important, we argue, for two reasons. First, elites must be able to (re)establish credibility. By appealing to authority, they reinforce a connection to other reputable actors and ultimately their own ability and knowledge. The strong emphasis on science and research further highlighted how elites reinforce their appreciation for rational thinking, which, in turn adds to their identity as experts (Walton, 2010). Second, given events such as the financial crisis, coupled with concerns surrounding the virtues of capitalism, being a trusted expert relies on a sense of trust (Crane, 2012). Arguably, as Christine Lagarde's quote in the beginning of this chapter illustrated, trust has been negatively affected in recent years. Moreover, a lack of trust is transferred to elites because of the close association between economic elites and an ensuing crisis (Misztal, 2013). Here, the construction of *solidarity* plays an important role. As illustrated, solidarity is frequently emphasised by economic elites in this study as a means to gain trust by appealing to common, overlapping struggles between elite and non-elite. These findings have particular implications for elites' projects at reframing capitalism. As such, in light of this book's focus on Africapitalism, we below reflect on two propositions for the Africapitalism project, and conclude with a general proposition for all philosophies.

PROPOSITION I: WALKING THE TALK

Africapitalism clearly has a unique focus compared to the other three philosophies – its geographical emphasis. Whereas other philosophies maintain a global presence, Africapitalism uses its locality as an advantage. However, despite Africapitalism specifying that the international development community hinders capitalism from flourishing in Africa – given, for instance, an emphasis on aid – the philosophy seems itself to be stuck in a Western mindset. By this, we mean that Africapitalism draws so prolifically from non-indigenous ideas and sources that it occasionally seems to reproduce certain Western ideas about capitalism. For example, the very organisations criticised for hampering the development of a uniquely African variety of capitalism – e.g., the World Bank and IMF – are relied upon to support the bulk of claims made in the Africapitalism manifesto. In addition, the work of Western consultants such as McKinsey and Michael Porter is frequently cited, which forgoes focusing on African scholars. In a similar vein, when African thinkers *are* quoted they occupy space only on the side of the page and not front and centre. We accordingly suggest to 'walk the talk' – an Africapitalism needs

African examples, including African researcher, thinkers and entrepreneurs to lead the way.

PROPOSITION 2: CHALLENGE FROM OUTSIDE THE BOX

Overwhelmingly, Africapitalism relies on the transformational power of the private sector to stimulate social progress. This seems adequate, given that entrepreneurship is at the heart of its philosophy. However, evident within all other philosophies, and somewhat missing from Africapitalism, is an explicit emphasis on building stakeholder partnerships with organisations such as civil society organisations. Indeed, Africapitalism is by no means dismissive of NGOs, yet seems to consider civil society in a supportive, rather than in a partnership role. Notwithstanding, as evidenced with other philosophies, civil society often helps to legitimate a philosophy given the credibility attributed to an unlikely friendship, and trust placed in NGOs. As such, we encourage Africapitalism to think outside the box and develop means of fostering partnerships that are not limited to for-profit businesses. Fortunately, Africapitalism portrays governments as potentially strong partners. However, Africapitalism does seem to negate the power of the state's legal arm, which stems probably from the often weak legal institutions that persist in certain African regions, coupled with a history of corruption. This differs substantially from other philosophies that draw from governments to help regulate businesses where necessary. For example, Sustainable Capitalism 9 stresses using the regulatory vehicle of governments to help companies price environmental cost and mandate EGS reporting. This highlights instances where governments impose regulations without necessarily overburdening the private sector. As such, Africapitalism should preferably help African states rebuild trust amongst publics, as opposed to proposing removal of regulation.

PROPOSITION 3: BETTER TOGETHER

Evident throughout this chapter is the lack of unity, particularly *between* economic philosophies. Urging for collectiveness in this regard would be considered utopian if economic elites espoused starkly different framing strategies. However, as our analysis demonstrated, despite the framing tasks of each capitalism differing, there exists a considerable overlap in terms of their purposes and goals. Accordingly, we propose that elites build on the communality of established framing strategies and, in addition, create a shared identity. This does not necessarily mean that existing organisations need to abandoned, but that elites, for instance, should form a conglomerate of organisations with similar intensions. Thereby each elite can pursue his/her own objectives, but be governed by a larger overarching purpose. Furthermore, creating a shared identity will likely be beneficial in terms of making better use of each new capitalism's recourses. Drawing from their dense networks, coordinated action amongst new capitalisms would arguably simulate sharing platforms and synergies. Such behaviour would arguably be key in stimulating a collective identity and transform economic philosophies from being mere individual projects to collective action.

REFERENCES

Acemoglu, D., Johnson S. and Robinson J. 2002. An African Success Story: Botswana. CEPR Discussion, Paper 3219.

Ahmed, N. 2014, May 28. Inclusive Capitalism Initiative Is Trojan Horse to Quell Coming Global Revolt. *The Guardian*.

Amaeshi, K. and Idemudia, U. 2015. Africapitalism: A Management Idea for Business in Africa? *Africa Journal of Management*, 1(2): 210–223.

Amsden, A. H., DiCaprio, A. and Robinson, J. A. 2012. *The Role of Elites in Economic Development*. Oxford: Oxford University Press.

Benford, R. D., and Snow, D. A. 2000. Framing Processes and Social Movements: An Overview and Assessment. *Annual Review of Sociology*, 26(1974): 11–39.

Bishop, M. and Green, M. 2010. *Philanthrocapitalism: How Giving Can Save the World*. New York, NY: Bloomsbury Publishing USA.

Boltanski, L. and Chiapello, E. 2008. *The New Spirit of Capitalism*. London: Verso.

Bourdieu, P. 1996. *The State Nobility: Elite Schools in the Field of Power*. Cambridge: Polity Press.

Brooks-Pollock, T. 2014, July 24. 'Inclusive Capitalism' Conference Ends in High Court Battle between Organisers. *The Telegraph*.

Carney, M. 2014. Inclusive Capitalism: Creating a Sense of the Systemic. Speech, Bank of England.

Clarke, G. and Sison, M. 2003. Voices from the Top of the Pile: Elite Perceptions of Poverty and the Poor in the Philippines. *Development and Change,* 34(2): 215–242.

Coalition for Inclusive Capitalism. 2014. *Making Capitalism More Inclusive.* Edited by D. F. Carney and C. Freeland. Available at www.global-economic-symposium .org/knowledgebase/The-Future-of-Social-Impact-Investing/virtual-library/mak ing-capitalism-more-inclusive-selected-speeches-and-essays-from-the-confer ence-on-inclusive-capitalism-1/at_download/file. Accessed 25 January 2018.

Coalition for Inclusive Capitalism. 2015a. About Us. Available at www.inc-cap.co m/conferences/conference-2016/general/. Accessed 20 May 2009.

Coalition for Inclusive Capitalism. 2015b. The Pathway to Action. Thoughts from the 2015 Conference on Inclusive Capitalism. Available at www.inc-cap.com/ wp-content/uploads/2015/07/Book-2.pdf. Accessed 25 January 2018.

Conscious Capitalism. 2016. Purpose. Available at www.consciouscapitalism.org/ purpose. Accessed 20 June 2017.

Conscious Capitalism. 2016. Stakeholder Orientation. Available at www.con sciouscapitalism.org/stakeholder. Accessed 20 June 2017.

Conscious Capitalism. 2016. The Conscious Capitalist Credo. Available at www .consciouscapitalism.org/node/4005. Accessed 20 June 2017.

Crane, L. 2012. Trust Me, I'm An Expert: Identity Construction and Knowledge Sharing. *Journal of Knowledge Management,* 16(3): 448–460.

Davis, G. F. 2009. *Managed by Markets: How Finance Re-shaped America.* New York, NY: Oxford University Press.

De Swaan, A. 1988. *In Care of the State: Health Care, Education, and Welfare in Europe and the USA in the Modern Era.* Oxford: Oxford University Press

du Gay, P. and Morgan, G. 2013. Understanding Capitalism: Crises, Legitimacy, and Change through the Prism of the New Spirit of Capitalism. In *New Spirits of Capitalism?: Crises, Justifications, and Dynamics.* Edited by P. du Gay and G. Morgan, 45–66. Oxford: Oxford University Press.

The Economist. 2012. Sustainable Capitalism Blood, Gore and Capitalism.

Edelman. 2016. *Edelman Trust Barometer.* Available at www.edelman.com/insights/ intellectual-property/2016-edelman-trust-barometer/. Accessed 20 June 2017.

Edwards, R. 2013, 12 July. Can Africapitalism Save the Continent? *The Guardian.* Available at www.theguardian.com/world/2013/jul/12/africa-africapitalism-ton y-elumelu. Accessed 25 January 2018.

Elumelu, T. 2013. *Africapitalism: Path to Economic Prosperity and Social Wealth.* Lagos: Africapitalism Institute.

Engelen, E., Ertürk, I., Froud, J., Johal et al. 2012. Misrule of experts? The Financial Crisis as Elite Debacle. *Economy and Society*, 41(3): 360–382.

Forbes. 2015. Africa's 50 Richest. Available at www.forbes.com/africa-billionaires/list/#tab:overall. Accessed 17 February 2016.

Gamson, W. A., and Modigliani, A. 1987. The Changing Culture of Affirmative Action. In *Research in Political Sociology*. Edited by R. G. Braungart and M. M. Braungart, 137–177. Greenwich, CT: JAI Press.

Goffman, E. 1974. *Frame Analysis: An Essay on the Organization of Experience*. Boston, MA: Northeastern University Press.

Gore, A. and Blood, D. 2011, 14 December. A Manifesto for Sustainable Capitalism. *Wall Street Journal*.

Gore, A. and Blood, D. 2012. *Sustainable Capitalism*. London: Generation Investment Management LLP.

Hartmann, M. 2007. *The Sociology of Elites*. London: Routledge.

Helfen, M., Schüßler, E. and Botzem, S. 2015. Legitimation Strategies of Corporate Elites in the Field of Labor Regulation: Changing Responses to Global Framework Agreements. In *Elites on Trial: Research in the Sociology of Organizations*. Edited by G. Morgan, S. Quack and P. Hirsch, 243–268. Bingly, UK: Emerald Group Publishing Limited.

Hossain N. and Moore M. 1999. Elite Perceptions of Poverty: Bangladesh, *IDS Bulletin*, 30(2).

Klein, N. 2014. *This Changes Everything: Capitalism vs. the Climate*. New York, NY: Simon and Schuster.

Lagarde, C. 2014. Economic Inclusion and Financial Integrity. Speech, London. Conference on Inclusive Capitalism.

Lefsrud, L. M., and Meyer, R. E. 2012. Science or Science Fiction? Professionals' Discursive Construction of Climate Change. *Organization Studies*, 33(11): 1477–1506.

Mackey, J. and Sisodia, R. 2013, 14 January. 'Conscious Capitalism' Is Not an Oxymoron. *Harvard Business Review*. Available at https://hbr.org/2013/01/cultivating-a-higher-conscious. Accessed 25 January 2018.

Mackey, J. and Sisodia, R. 2014. *Conscious Capitalism: Liberating the Heroic Spirit of Business*. With a New Preface by the Authors. Cambridge, MA: Harvard Business Review Press.

Maclean, M., Harvey, C. and Chia, R. 2012. Reflexive Practice and the Making of Elite Business Careers. *Management Learning*, 43(4): 385–404.

Maclean, M., Harvey, C. and Kling, G. 2014. Pathways to Power: Class, Hyper-Agency and the French Corporate Elite. *Organization Studies*, 35(6): 825–855.

McMichael, A. J., Campbell-Lendrum, D. H., Corvalan, C. F., Ebi, K. L., Githeko, A. K., Scheraga, J. D. and Woodward, A. 2007. Climate Change and Human Health. *Population and Development Review*, 23(1): 205.

Mills, C. W. 1956. *The Power Elite*. New York, NY: Oxford University Press.

Misztal, B. 2013. *Trust in Modern Societies: The Search for the Bases of Social Order*. Hoboken, NJ: John Wiley & Sons.

Morgan, G. 2015. Elites, Varieties of Capitalism and the Crisis of Neo-Liberalism. In *Elites on Trial: Research in the Sociology of Organizations*. Edited by G. Morgan, S. Quack and P. Hirsch, 55–80. Bingly, UK: Emerald Group Publishing Limited.

Morgan, G., Quack, S., and Hirsch. M, 2015. *Elites on Trial: Research in the Sociology of Organizations*. Bingly, UK: Emerald Group Publishing Limited.

Muller, J. 2013. Capitalism and Inequality. *Foreign Affairs*, 92(2): 30–51.

Nurse, E., and Dougherty, J. 2013, November 12. Tony Elumelu: The 'Africapitalist' who wants to Power Africa. Available at http://www.cnn.com/2013/11/12/africa/gallery/tony-elumelu-africapitalist-africa/index.html. Accessed 28 November 2017.

O'Toole, J. and Vogel, D. 2011. Two and a Half Cheers for Conscious Capitalism. *California Management Review*, 53(3): 60–76.

Piketty, T. 2014. *Capital in the Twenty-First Century*. Cambridge, MA: Harvard University Press.

Prahalad, C. 2003. *The Fortune at the Bottom of the Pyramid – Eradicating Poverty through Profits*. Upper Saddle River, NJ: Pearson.

Reis, E. P. and Moore, M. 2005. *Elite Perceptions of Poverty and Inequality*. New York, NY: Zed Books.

Rothman, H. and Scott, M. 2003. *Companies with a Conscience: Intimate Portraits of Twelve Firms That Make a Difference*. Old Main, PA: Pennsylvania State University.

Schawbel, D. 2013, John Mackey: Why Companies Should Embrace Conscious Capitalism. *Forbes*. January 15.

Scheffran, J., Brzoska, M. and Brauch, H. 2012. *Climate Change, Human Security and Violent Conflict: Challenges for Societal Stability*. Dordrecht, The Netherlands: Springer Science & Business Media.

Schmidhuber, J. and Tubiello, F. N. 2007. Global Food Security under Climate Change. *Proceedings of the National Academy of Sciences of the United States of America*, 104(50): 19703–19708.

Schmidt, V. 2008. Discursive Institutionalism: The Explanatory Power of Ideas and Discourse. *Annual Review of Political Science*, 11(1): 303–326.

Scott, J. 2008. Modes of Power and the Re-conceptualization of Elites. *Sociological Review*, 56(1): 25–43.

Scott, M. 2014. Blood and Gore: 'Capitalism is in Danger of Falling Apart.' *Financial Times*. July 2.

Sebudubudu, D. 2010. The Impact of Good Governance on Development and Poverty in Africa: Botswana: A Relatively Successful African Initiative. *African Journal of Political Science and International Relations*, 4(7): 249–262.

Shane, S. 2013, 7 October. Beyond Bogus Corporate Responsibility: It's Time to Get Your Hands Dirty. *Fast Company*. Available at www.fastcompany.com/3013985/beyond-bogus-corporate-responsibility-its-time-to-get-your-hands-dirty. Accessed 25 January 2018.

Simmons, E. S. 2015. Market Reforms and Water Wars. *World Politics*, 68(1): 37–73.

Snow, D. A. and Benford, R. D. 1988. Ideology, Frame Resonance, and Participant Mobilization. *International Social Movement Research*, 1: 197–218.

Spence, C., Carter, C., Husillos, J., and Archel. 2016. Taste Matters: Cultural Capital and Elites in Proximate Strategic Action Fields. *Human Relations*, 70(2): 211–236.

Stern, N. 2007. *Stern Review: The Economics of Climate Change. Stern Review: The Economics of Climate Change*. London: HM Treasury.

Strange, S. 2015. *Casino Capitalism*. Oxford: Oxford University Press.

Tajfel, H. 1981. *Human Groups and Social Categories: Studies in Social Psychology*. Cambridge: Cambridge University Press.

Taylor, S. D. 2012. *Globalization and the Cultures of Business in Africa: From Patrimonialism to Profit*. Bloomington, IN: Indiana University Press.

UNCT 2008. *World Economic Situation and Prospects*. New York, NY: United Nations Publications.

Useem, M. 1980. Corporations and the Corporate Elite. *Annual Review of Sociology*, 6(1): 41–77. Available at www.jstor.org/stable/10.2307/2946004.

Van Gelder, S. 2011. *This Changes Everything: Occupy Wall Street and the 99% Movement*. San Francisco, CA: Berrett-Koehler Publishers.

Walton, D. 2010. Appeal to Expert Opinion: Arguments from Authority. University Park, PA: Penn State Press.

Zald, M. N. and Lounsbury, M. 2010. The Wizards of Oz: Towards an Institutional Approach to Elites, Expertise and Command Posts. *Organization Studies*, 31(7): 963–996.

Zhang, D. D., Brecke, P., Lee, H. F., He, Y.-Q., and Zhang, J. 2007. Global Climate Change, War, and Population Decline in Recent Human History. *Proceedings of the National Academy of Sciences of the United States of America*, 104(49): 19214–19219.

4 Africapitalism and Corporate Governance

Emmanuel Adegbite, Franklin Nakpodia, Konan Anderson Seny Kan and Olorunfemi Onakoya

INTRODUCTION

The pursuit of accelerated economic advancement across the globe was crucial to the development of the United Nations Sustainable Development Goals, aimed at ending poverty, fighting inequality and injustice, and tackling the effects of climate change. Many countries have substantially adopted this intervention, especially in Africa, where considerable challenges remain, albeit amidst a record of moderate gains. Striving towards a higher goal, Africa deserves more economic interventions, especially those intended to stimulate the rethinking of the business-society relationship (Amaeshi and Idemudia, 2015).

Taylor's (2014) review of capitalism in Africa concluded that the cultural background of most African nations prevents the full adoption of Western capitalism. While acknowledging the modest successes of businesses at some levels, Taylor (2014) sought to understand whether the business and the value system upon which capitalism rests have a social basis in Africa. Chua (2004) argued that capitalism in Africa faces a backlash that undermines its private sector, as foreign firms and foreign-dominated interests characteristically influence its practice. Chua (2004) further contended that the inculcation of a social basis for African capitalism demands a variety of interactions and influences, which are Afrocentric. Equally, Olutayo and Omobowale (2007) asserted that underdevelopment amongst Third World nations was provoked when its majority adopted capitalism, whose origin is traceable to the West. The foregoing concerns highlight the necessity for the development of a brand of local capitalism that acknowledges the uniqueness of the institutional environment in Africa. Here, the underlying conceptual assumption is post-colonial in essence. As such, Africa's capitalism has to develop its own semantic universe that demonstrates its originality and distinctive features from the colonial literature on development in Africa (including its economies and management of its organisations). This provides the context for embracing the Africapitalism philosophy.

Africapitalism, a word coined by Mr. Tony O. Elumelu CON,[1] a Nigerian banker and economist, is an approach to capitalism and a management philosophy, which explores how the private sector can contribute to Africa's development through ventures that create both economic and social positive outcomes. It is intended to promote sustainable organisations which can support its relevant stakeholders over the long term and proposes a possible route to Africa's sustainable development (Amaeshi and Idemudia, 2015; Elumelu, 2012). However, the success of Africapitalism lies in its capacity to address the challenges and weaknesses confronting corporations operating in Africa. These challenges include weaknesses in the capital markets, legal institutions, state and democratic institutions, human rights institutions, as well as negative socio-cultural pressures (Amaeshi and Idemudia, 2015). Indeed, prior attempts to develop an endogenous management model which addresses Africa's production challenges have failed to be usable (Seny Kan, Apitsa and Adegbite, 2015). Africapitalism may represent a novel approach to considering the inter-relationship between corporations in Africa and the society within which they operate. In this manner, it represents a reflection of how production has to be organised in a way that meets different stakeholders' demands.

Traditionally, the organisation of corporate production, to meet stakeholders' expectations, in the modern economy and in the management literature has been framed within the lens of corporate gov-

---

[1]   'CON' is a national honour, 'Commander of the Order of the Niger'.

ernance. In their 'actor-centred' model of corporate governance, for instance, Aguilera and Jackson (2003) define corporate governance as a relationship between various stakeholders in the process of decision-making and control over firm resources. Africapitalism on the other hand, speaks directly to how firms use their resources and influences in creating financial and social wealth for their direct and indirect stakeholders. As such, corporate governance is an integral part of the exercise of Africapitalism. In other words, Africapitalism, as a management philosophy, needs a corporate governance framework to make it practicable. In essence, while the Africapitalism principle will inform the corporate governance model of the firm, the latter also presents the structure and medium of expression for Africapitalism.

In addition, corporate governance is contextual (Adegbite and Nakajima, 2011), and context matters to Africapitalism (Amaeshi and Idemudia, 2015). The existence of different national institutions means that increased global competition, as well as the integration of financial markets, will not express themselves in the same ways in different national governance systems. As different systems of capitalism typically produce different responses to similar pressures, a one-size-fits-all approach to the firm's governance is unattractive (Aguilera and Jackson, 2003). Following this position, the Africapitalist corporate governance model articulated in this chapter presents itself as an important structure for conceptualising, understanding and committing to the private sector's participation in Africa's socio-economic development. Therefore, defining and articulating the principles of this Africapitalist corporate governance model represents the main objective and contribution of this chapter. Drawing insights from Africa's leading economies (South Africa and Nigeria), our discussions facilitate the emergence of a workable, practical and useful corporate governance model, which in turn promotes the Africapitalism project.

The rest of this chapter proceeds by undertaking a review of relevant literature and theory. It then discusses the corporate governance challenges and regulatory responses in Africa. It subsequently proposes an Africapitalist corporate governance model, highlighting its key principles and practices to achieve the objectives of Africapitalism. The chapter ends by presenting some concluding remarks and recommendations for future research.

LITERATURE REVIEW AND THEORY

The variety of underlying perspectives shows corporate governance as a polysemy (e.g., Turnbull, 1997). Tricker (2015) reinforces this in the various perspectives of corporate governance definitions provided. In this chapter, we focus on agency theory, stakeholder theory and institutional theory perspectives on corporate governance – theories predominantly explored in corporate governance, especially in weak institutional contexts such as in Africa (e.g., Andreasson, 2011; Rwegasira, 2000). More importantly, we indicate how these theories fail to offer a comprehensive frame of production activities and capitalism in the African setting.

Agency theory is one of the core theories in the extant corporate governance literature. It attempts to explain elements of organisational behaviour through an understanding of the relationships between shareholders (the principal) and managers (the agent) (Jensen and Meckling, 1976). This is because a conflict may exist between the actions undertaken by agents in furtherance of their self-interest, and those required to promote the interests of the principal. This is possible due to the separation of the firm's ownership from its control (a feature of the modern firm) and the information advantages that managers have over shareholders. These put managers in a position to maximise their wealth without being detected (Fama and Jensen, 1983), thus creating an agency problem. Sison (2007: 471) provided an underlying driver for the dominant 'agency theory' orientation towards corporate governance in firms:

> A firm is formed by people called 'owners'. They put in the funds, through which the firm is able to operate, and in exchange, society

recognizes their right to call the shots and their interests protected. So despite the boss's self-sufficient airs, he is a mere stand-in for the real boss, the owners ... Owners put their money in the firm expecting rewards. They do not do so out of selflessness, love of neighbour or some other lofty ideal. They expect to earn more money after a given time. That in a nutshell is the logic of investment.

The above quote suggests that shareholders own the firm and its profits/resources in their entirety. In this manner, corporate governance becomes an instrument for resolving the agency problem between the principal stakeholders in an organisational structure, i. e., the principal and the agent. As shareholders require assurance for their investments, the agency theory literature puts shareholder primacy at the core of corporate governance.

However, the view that corporate governance predominantly involves shareholders and the firm underestimates the implicit and explicit relationships between the corporation and its employees, creditors, suppliers, customers, local communities and government and the interrelationships among these constituencies (Adegbite and Nakajima, 2012). This is the basis of the stakeholder theory. The stakeholder model presents a broader framework, to align the interests of managers with those of all relevant stakeholders (Donaldson and Preston, 1995; Freeman, 2010). As a result, the stakeholder theory takes into context a wider group of constituents rather than focusing only on shareholders (Mallin, 2013). However, this model also suffers from the near impossibility of meeting large and different stakeholders' objectives and fails to provide any mechanism that gives certainty to companies that they will survive their social obligations (Maher and Andersson, 2000).

The limitations inherent in the agency and stakeholder theories have encouraged the emergence of other theoretical arguments. The institutional approach to corporate governance takes into account the dynamics between the micro-institutions of the organisations and the external institutional stakeholders (Choi and Dow, 2008). In fact, the institutional constraints for corporate accountability in Africa and the consequent international pressures for improved governance structures by the IMF/World Bank are making it imperative for developing countries to adopt prescribed corporate governance structures. Adegbite, Amaeshi and Nakajima (2013) noted that while this may serve as an incentive for attracting Foreign Direct Investment (FDI), for instance, corporate governance guidelines which mirror the peculiarities of the West may undermine local initiatives aimed at corporate governance structures and processes which identify and attempt to address local challenges. This is particularly important, as corporate governance issues begin to assume prime importance in Africa, owing to the strengthening private sector. Despite the prospects of a substantial private sector impact, corporate governance and accountability in Africa remain marred by significant challenges (Okike, Adegbite, Nakpodia and Adegbite, 2015), which institutional perspectives have highlighted but have made only limited attempts to address precisely.

Inculcating Africapitalism principles in a corporate governance framework represents a re-construction that infuses value beyond the requirements of shareholder primacy and differing stakeholder demands and tests the expendability at which organisational practices respond to societal circumstances or demands (Selznick 1996). In this regard, Africapitalism represents a voice of resistance to the culture and limitations of short-sightedness, which has been the consequence of allowing shareholder primacy to have a pernicious effect on the dominant perception of corporate governance in Africa (Adegbite and Nakajima, 2012), even within the purview of institutional explanations. This is particularly important in Africa, where the institutional protections for stakeholders, including minority shareholders, are weak, and managers, who are majority owners, and are a large recipient of unfettered powers, drive firms. The literature on corporate governance and responsibility in Africa has argued that many weak capitalist economies are marred by the lack of vibrant capital markets, weak states, legal environments and civil societies, which may undermine the attempts to hold firms accountable to their non-majority shareholding stakeholders (Amaeshi, Adegbite and Rajwani, 2016).

Understanding these challenges helps in articulating the contributions of an Africapitalism mindset in addressing them. Africapitalism is a philosophy that believes that the private sector has a significant role to play in the development of Africa by creating economic prosperity as well as social value (Amaeshi and Idemudia, 2015). It deviates from the good old-fashioned capitalism that has been practised for years on the African continent, as it seeks to blend 'doing well financially and doing good socially' (Ahmad and Ramayah, 2012). Africapitalism entails a long-term investment approach in key sectors, especially infrastructure and agribusiness, while African governments should focus on 'capacitising the private sector' and creating the right environment for the emergence of a new crop of Africapitalist entrepreneurs (Elumelu, 2014). The right environment for Africapitalism includes an effective corporate governance model for the firm to have a medium of expression for creating social and economic prosperity. Africapitalism, despite its laudable and emotive philosophical lure, will fail without such. Indeed, Africapitalism is a management idea revolving around considering the firm as a community with an awareness of the context it belongs to (Amaeshi and Idemudia, 2015). This management idea consists in balancing four cardinal values: sense of progress and prosperity, sense of parity, sense of peace and harmony and sense of place and belongingness. We therefore proceed to highlight some significant corporate governance challenges in Africa, and the limitations of current regulatory responses. This allows us to explore how the Africapitalism philosophy can inform a better corporate governance system on the one hand, and how this governance system can then present the expressive structure for the practice of Africapitalism, on the other.

CORPORATE GOVERNANCE CHALLENGES AND REGULATORY RESPONSES IN AFRICA

The challenges of corporate governance in Africa have been widely reported (see Okeahalam, 2004; Okpara, 2010; Seny Kan, 2013;

Adegbite, 2015). In this section, citing examples from Africa's largest economies (South Africa and Nigeria), we identify four major challenges and the consequent regulatory responses to them. We also highlight the limitations of these regulatory responses, in creating a background for the potential contributions of Africapitalism, as a management philosophy.

Weak Disclosure

Corporate disclosure and transparency are key to good corporate governance (Mallin, 2002). For example, Farvaque, Refait-Alexandre and Saidane (2011) identified the benefits of corporate disclosure to include value creation and better firm governance, amongst others. However, corporate disclosure in Africa remains a problem. Okeahalam (2004) argued that the absence of an efficient disclosure in corporate governance systems across the African continent poses a major challenge. In the foremost corporate governance codes (for example, The UK Corporate Governance Code and Sarbanes Oxley Act), the pursuit of full and transparent disclosure is identified as the foundation for the relative success and reputation of these codes (Jungmann, 2006; Coates, 2007; Kim, 2016). However, Africa has lagged in relation to its corporate disclosure practices, owing to a number of factors. For instance, Al-Bassam, Ntim, Opong and Downs (2015) indicated that an increase in block ownership significantly stifles corporate governance disclosure. Ahunwan (2002) also reported evidence of a narrow concentration of corporate ownership in the Nigerian business environment and the implications for disclosure. Furthermore, Adegbite (2015) suggested that cultural differences explain the variations in attitudes to corporate disclosures amongst countries. The resulting opacity undermines Africa's access to foreign investments and undermines the continent's competitiveness for global trade and finance. For example, Mangena and Tauringana (2007) argued that foreign investors seek investments in companies with less information asymmetry and high disclosure practices, which explains the low patronage of foreign investors in Zimbabwe.

Weak Shareholder Activism

In examining another major challenge to good corporate governance in Africa, Bourveau and Schoenfeld (2015) explained that weak disclosure decreases the likelihood of shareholder activism. In other words, the low degree of corporate disclosure in Africa may result in ineffective shareholder activism. Shareholder activism increases corporate efficiency, by acting as a check on the behaviour of management (Sarkar and Sarkar, 2000). Similarly, Gow, Shin and Srinivasan (2014) demonstrate that shareholder activism is associated with greater accountability. In developed economies, Dhir (2006) indicated that shareholder-initiated proposals occupy a unique place in corporations, arguing that they offer shareholders an instrument with which they can initiate corporate action, as against merely reacting to management performance. However, evidence (Sarkar and Sarkar, 2000) suggests that shareholder activism does not command similar influence in many African countries. For instance, Teoh, Welch and Wazzan (1999) observed that shareholder activism in South Africa is very low, such that the announcement of shareholder pressure or voluntary corporate divestment had little discernible effect on the South African financial markets. Similarly, Adegbite, Amaeshi and Amao (2012) demonstrate how unhealthy politics and management control frustrate shareholder activism in Nigeria. Therefore, weak shareholder activism implies that factors outside the control of shareholders determine management accountability. This can potentially increase agency costs especially in regions such as Africa. Prior literature has identified the weakness in shareholder activism and its implications for corporate governance (see Amao and Amaeshi, 2008; Adegbite et al., 2012), recent findings (Uche, Adegbite and Jones, 2016) also reveal low-level shareholder activism, suggesting that the problem persists.

Weak Board Independence

Boards constitute an important governance mechanism (Claessens and Yurtoglu, 2013) and the extent of board independence represents a key driver for good corporate governance (Filatotchev and Nakajima, 2010). Langevoort (2000) states that board independence expresses a willingness to entrench a high degree of rigour, scrutiny and objectivity to the evaluation of company's management. Indeed, contrary to the insider directors who may play as the pawns of CEOs, independent directors are meant to balance the power between shareholders and the management (Joseph, Ocasio and McDonnell, 2014). The arguments for board independence have been built on various factors notably the separation of the CEO and Chairman positions. Filatotchev and Nakajima (2010) noted that consolidating the roles of the CEO and the Chairman into a single position generates an undue concentration of power and influence in one individual, and consequently jeopardises board independence. In addition, board independence affects the performance of board committees such as the audit committee. The implications of board independence in African firms have been attracting attention. For example, Mahadeo and Soobaroyen (2016) show that the degree of board independence has become increasingly important for matters such as board composition, board committees and Corporate Social Responsibility (CSR). However, board independence remains a concern across the continent. Findings in Adegbite (2015) revealed that many CEOs in Nigeria, upon retirement, assume the Chairmanship position of their organisations and continue to retain strong influence on their successors. This helps further consolidation of power and influence in key individuals, who are then only accountable to themselves and their cronies.

Absence of Large Local Institutional Investors

The presence of foreign (large) institutional shareholders and the absence of local ones confront corporate governance in Africa. The literature has acknowledged the importance of institutional investors as a force for good corporate governance (see Gillan and Starks, 2003; Ingley and van der Walt, 2004). For instance, Black (1992) stated that institutional investors restrained managerial appetite for value-destroying mergers and acquisitions. However, many foreign investors, who have limited knowledge of the economic and social environment in which these firms operate, occupy the African corporate space for institutional investments. With the presence of local institutional investors holding significant shareholding power, firms are in a better position to respond to the demands of their environment and play a more constructive role in society. The outcomes in Vaughn and Ryan (2006) underscore the need for domestic institutional investors to be at the forefront of explaining, advocating and monitoring corporate governance practices.

However, rather than also advocating for local investments, many African governments only actively seek FDI, which has resulted in a growing number of foreign institutional investors on the African continent. Indeed, Malherbe and Segal (2001) reported that South Africa's institutional investors are, relative to the size of its economy, among the largest in the developing world. Consequently, Fremond and Capaul (2003) indicated that South Africa's domestic institutional investors take a passive attitude towards corporate governance; they actually do not publicly intervene in corporate governance affairs. The case is no different in Nigeria, as Adegbite (2015) noted that local institutional investors are playing limited roles in the corporate governance of public companies, typically reflected in their lack of courage to challenge executive corruption (see also Uche, Adegbite and Jones 2016).

Regulatory Responses

The foregoing has motivated policy makers in Africa to develop legislation and other policy initiatives aimed at addressing these problems. Ntim and Osei (2011) report that the many challenges relating to board independence among South African corporations were crucial to the development of the King (I and II) Reports. The inauguration of a committee mandated by the Securities and Exchange Commission (SEC) in Nigeria to develop a corporate governance guideline for public companies triggered corporate governance regulatory consciousness in 2002.

The result was the introduction of the SEC Code for Corporate Governance in 2003 (revised in 2011). To promote the practice of corporate governance in Nigeria, several corporate governance codes have emerged. These codes include the Code of Corporate Governance for Banks in Nigeria – issued by the Central Bank of Nigeria (CBN) in 2006; the Code of Corporate Governance for Insurance companies – issued by the insurance regulator (NAICOM) in 2008; and the Code of Corporate Governance for Pension Operators – issued by the Nigerian Pension Commission (PENCOM) in 2011.

Following the introduction of these codes, Nigeria has witnessed a gradual but consistent improvement in its corporate governance practices, especially in the banking sector (Onuoha, Ogbuji, Ameh and Oba, 2013). However, the overall impact of the positive strides in corporate governance practices in the financial sector is isolated, as similar improvements in the non-financial sector have not been noted. Inyang (2009) explained that capacity constraints and costs had hampered the impact of regulatory interventions in the non-financial sectors of the economy. Consequently, cases of corporate misgovernance are still reported, evidenced by the financial scandals in Lever Brothers Nigeria (Ahunwan, 2002), Cadbury Nigeria (Okike and Adegbite, 2012) amongst others.

Whereas the corporate governance system in Nigeria has, and continues to encounter significant problems, the South African corporate governance system has been identified as both the best on the African continent and as a model for many developing countries (Vaughn and Ryan, 2006; Waweru, 2014). The King Report III in South Africa, which operates on an 'apply and explain' basis, provides some general principles bordering on ethical leadership as well as principles of good governance, which relates to the performance of boards and executives. A major feature of the King Report III is its broadness in terms of organisations to which the code applies. Unlike the SEC Code (2011) in Nigeria, which focuses on publicly listed companies, the principles entrenched in the King Report III apply to all forms of organisations, irrespective of the manner and form of the corporation. As a result, despite the significant presence of SMEs, the King Report has ensured that small businesses understand and seek compliance with the provisions stated in the code. These commendable strides notwithstanding, South Africa has experienced its share of corporate governance scandals. For instance, First Strut violated ethical practices resulting in multiple financing of single assets, VAT fraud, dodgy invoicing and bribes, amongst others (de Wet, 2013). In addition, Joffe (2015) reported how the unethical governance practices in South Africa's largest electricity supplier, Eskom, have raised doubts regarding the perpetual succession potentials of the corporate giant. These developments reinforce the challenges faced by many economies in Africa with respect to their corporate governance systems.

Regulatory Limitations

The limitations (and the inability) of the corporate governance codes to substantially address corporate governance challenges in African economies have encouraged policy makers to seek other initiatives. For instance, to drive corporate governance among firms in the African continent two organisations, African Peer Review Mechanism (APRM) and Pan African Consultative Forum on Corporate Governance (PACFCG), were established. The APRM is a country self-assessment mechanism, which fosters the adoption of policies, standards and practices that promote stability, high economic growth, sustainable development and accelerated sub-regional and continental economic integration through sharing of experiences and reinforcement of successful and best practices on governance, including corporate governance. The PACFCG, for its part, raises awareness of the significance of corporate governance by forging consensus on concepts and methods of corporate governance, developing action plans for the implementation of good corporate governance standards, and contributing to and learning from the global policy dialogue on corporate governance, amongst others.

In addition, in order to promote good governance practices, collaborations were created; for instance, the Commonwealth Association for Corporate Governance (CACG), the Department for International Development (DFID – UK), the Organisation for Economic Cooperation and Development (OECD) amongst others have collaborated with African countries to promote corporate governance reforms. These efforts have also deepened at the regional level, with research and advocacy organisations increasing in scope. This has facilitated the emergence of several organisations such as the Africa Governance Monitoring and Advocacy Project (AfriMAP), the African Institute of Corporate Citizenship (AICC) and the Corporate Governance Initiative, all committed to promoting good corporate governance practices in Africa.

The emergence of non-regulatory approaches to corporate governance effectiveness is due to the increasing understanding of the limitations of hard regulation and laws in promoting sustainable economic behaviour. Often, rules can be circumvented, especially in the presence of weak enforcement, corruption, regulatory incompetence and weak civil societies (Nakpodia, Adegbite, Amaeshi and Owolabi, 2016). While we have discussed some key challenges of corporate governance in Africa and identified the variety of regulations and policy initiatives developed to tackle these challenges, Africa still grapples with numerous corporate governance problems. The weaknesses in the political system, non-functional institutional frameworks, the power and influence of elites, among others have intensified these challenges. The limitations of the regulatory interventions have therefore necessitated calls for alternatives to corporate regulation that are principle-based and speak directly to a culturally relevant spirit of accountability. The emergence of Africapitalism is not only a response to this call but also represents a significant departure from existing reforms.

ADDRESSING CORPORATE GOVERNANCE CHALLENGES
THROUGH AFRICAPITALISM

In the previous section, some major problems confronting corporate governance in Africa were highlighted (weak disclosure, weak shareholder activism, the absence of large local institutional investors and weak board independence), thus indicating that Africa lacks the necessary governance mechanism to foster the development of a robust Africapitalism philosophy. This implies that for Africapitalism to succeed, especially given its normative foundation, supporting governance mechanisms must reinforce its practices (Amaeshi and Idemudia, 2015). To this end, we argue that the Africapitalism philosophy will benefit from the development of an Africapitalist corporate governance model, which essentially implies the integration of Africapitalism principles in a corporate governance framework. In this sense, we emphasise how Africapitalism can promote corporate governance practices in Africa. Africapitalism principles are based on four cardinal values (sense of parity and inclusion, sense of progress and prosperity, sense of peace and belongingness and sense of peace and harmony) that are intended to create social wealth and to entrench financial profitability (Amaeshi and Idemudia, 2015). Africapitalism would be an innovative response to the ills of Western capitalism. It compels a change of paradigm, away from viewing business from a win-lose mentality of entrepreneurs and businesses in Africa to the creation of shared value (i.e., win-win outcomes) in and for Africa (Amaeshi and Idemudia, 2015).

First, a major problem associated with corporate governance in Africa is a lack of full and transparent disclosure. It signifies a deliberate attempt to conceal information, thereby making it difficult to determine if organisational benefits are distributed equitably. Cramton and Dees (1993) indicated that concealing information is a deceptive tactic when the concealment is intended to create or support a false belief, thereby enhancing the difficulty in ascertaining if corporate benefits are fairly allocated. The foregoing reinforces the view that information enhances market efficiency (see efficient market hypothesis). This problem is consistent with the need for a *'sense of parity'*, which demands that the benefits of progress and prosperity be equitably shared, considering that wealth accumulation across the African continent is lopsided (Ameshi and Idemudia, 2015). A dominant feature of such capitalism is inequality, but an Afrocentric capitalism philosophy (Africapitalism) espouses a counter-current of progressivism, which appreciates that growth needs to be inclusive and transparently reported. Weak disclosure frustrates this expectation as it ensures that uneven distribution of social and financial wealth among stakeholders goes undetected and unreported (Adegbite, 2015). The implication is the lack of legitimacy pressures, which ought to subject corporations to some form of societal expectations and control.

Second, another cardinal value of Africapitalism is the *'sense of place and belongingness'*, which not only represents a direct reaction to globalised capitalism, but emphasises the importance of customising practices to address local challenges. In the literature review and theory section of this chapter, we argued that the lack of recognition of the distinctiveness of its institutional environment is a challenge to capitalism in Africa. The influx of foreign institutional investors – who continuously seek to adopt governance practices in Africa best suited to their home countries – only serves to intensify the problem. As a result, we witness the erosion of the economic value of 'place' (see Gieryn, 2000; Escobar, 2001). This development highlights the necessity to develop a framework wherein corporate governance practices are locally adapted. In furtherance of the foregoing, Adegbite (2015) suggested that foreign institutional investors' effective contribution to Africa's development would become evident only if their board member representatives possess substantial knowledge of the business terrain in Africa, in order to promote local content in their policies and operations. Partnerships with local institutional investors will also be a useful medium to engage with the continent. This strengthens Casey's (2001: 684) observation that 'there is no place without self and no self without place'.

Sense of place and belongingness, as a paradigm of Africapitalism, also expresses patriotism, which is evident in the commitment to defend the homeland (Amaeshi and Idemudia, 2015). There is a dearth of large local institutional investors on the African continent owing to problems such as unfriendly business environments and discriminatory governmental policies, which favour foreign investors at the expense of their local counterparts, amongst others. However, Africans are beginning to confront this problem. For instance, Aliko Dangote, a Nigerian entrepreneur while commissioning a state-of-the-art integrated cement plant in Masaiti district, Zambia, acknowledged that Africa is gradually taking its destiny in its own hands. Africapitalism will spur similar efforts, especially considering the exposure of Africa to dangers inherent in capital flight over the years (Ndikumana and Boyce, 2011). Ali Dangote exemplifies the possibility for local investors to partake in Africapitalist corporate governance, by providing a space for negotiation and dialogue. Africapitalism also grants legitimacy to the recognition and insertion of local governance practices into corporate governance frameworks in Africa.

Third, board independence concerns, especially with one individual occupying both the CEO and Chairmanship position is another challenge to corporate governance in Africa. This leads to the possession of excessive influence and power, thus creating self-interest concerns. Adegbite (2015) states that a board needs the benefit of two individuals to administer the responsibilities of the CEO and the Chairman. Brickley, Coles and Jarrell (1997) also note that separating the titles will reduce agency costs in corporations and improve performance. Unlike when both positions are fused, separation of the functions not only acts as a check and balance mechanism but also enhances board accountability and responsibility. Independent directors can respond more appropriately to the concerns of non-shareholding stakeholders (Ayuso and Argandona, 2009). Ibrahim, Howard and

Angelidis (2003) similarly contended that outside board members tend to be more sensitive to society's needs, which contributes to promoting a mutually beneficial co-existence between organisations and their environment. This engenders harmony within and outside the organisation, as against when there is a fusion of both roles, which can create an excessively powerful management (Fulcher and Scott, 2011). Africapitalism, in this respect, helps to promote a *'sense of peace and harmony'*. While this allows for a separation of power and responsibilities, a stakeholder orientation that accommodates decision-making inputs from other members of the organisation reinforces this concept.

Fourth, the overriding aim of Africapitalism is the clamour for social wealth and financial profitability, which connects with the *'sense of progress and prosperity'*. Furthermore, the increasing capacity of African entrepreneurs and the desire to invest in the African continent links with the *'sense of progress and prosperity'*. The focus of Africapitalism is to trigger economic progress and prosperity amongst African states (Oseni and Oseni, 2015), which is predicated on systematically increasing the number of Africans who are equipped with the resources to provoke investment drive on the continent, in order to create opportunities that encourage Afrocentric investments. Besides, the *'sense of progress and prosperity'* also addresses the establishment of conditions that promote corporate well-being. However, the pursuit of this objective links with the freedom with which investors and shareholders can interrogate the activities of their directors. As previously noted, shareholder activism is low in Africa, thus providing directors with an opportunity to engage in practices that maximise their wealth. Africapitalism, as a driver of progress and prosperity, would improve access to quality education and democratisation, among others, which are key to the emergence of a robust shareholder activism framework. We do not propose that shareholder activism is only possible via local investors, and we accept that foreign investors also drive shareholder activism in Africa, with sufficient knowledge and appreciation of the local context. In other words,

Africapitalism can inform and shape the context of shareholder activism and, indirectly, the administration of corporate governance.

Africapitalism principles can help promote better corporate governance given the cultural support and legitimacy it draws from African society, norms and value systems. For example, the corporate culture in South Africa, which acknowledges the Ubuntu philosophy (Nkomo, 2003), may have informed the improvements in the corporate governance system in South Africa. The philosophy fosters an environment of inclusion, collaboration and integrity. The philosophy has also prompted the relative robustness of the main corporate governance legislation in South Africa, i.e., the King Report III. For instance, an important element of the code is the admonition of directors to embrace Ubuntu as the core governance ethic of their companies. As a result, corporations in South Africa are championing a new model of capitalism, by balancing the profit concerns with social and environmental goals (Vaser, 2014). The embracement of Africapitalism across corporate Africa will encourage the administration of corporate governance in a way that benefits shareholders and stakeholders alike. We capture our discussions in Table 4.1.

CONCLUSION

In the main, this chapter reviewed some key corporate governance challenges in Africa and the efforts to address them. Discussions show that despite the standardised policy interventions, there are opportunities to reconsider attempts aimed at better governance, from a normative philosophical perspective. In response, we explored how Africapitalism as a socio-economic philosophy could support good governance practices across the continent. In doing this, we explored how an Africapitalist corporate governance model could sustainably connect businesses to society within Africa. This chapter reveals how the cardinal values associated with Africapitalism can help in shaping good corporate governance practices.

This is an exploratory chapter, opening discourse on corporate governance and Africapitalism. There is a need for future research to

TABLE 4.1 *Africapitalism solutions to corporate governance problems in Africa*

Challenges	Consequences	Africapitalism solution	Africapitalism principle
Weak disclosure	Negatively affecting African companies' access to foreign investments and their competitiveness on a global scale	Africapitalism as an inclusive management philosophy can foster usefulness of sharing necessary information among stakeholders.	Sense of parity
Weak shareholder activism	Negatively affecting efficiency-accountability of companies	Africapitalism seeks to balance the creation of social wealth in addition to the pursuit of financial profitability. Thus commitment of shareholders to the companies could be the norm and not the exception.	Sense of progress and prosperity
Weak board independence	Greater concentration of both managerial and control power	Africapitalism as a re-enactment of the modern management philosophy of harmony and balance can mitigate the ongoing power concentration tendency.	Sense of peace and harmony

TABLE 4.1 (cont.)

Challenges	Consequences	Africapitalism solution	Africapitalism principle
Absence of local large institutional investors	Negatively affecting companies' ability to respond to local demands	Africapitalism as a vehicle of rootedness can strive to infuse a form of patriotic commitment towards the economic dynamism.	Sense of place and belongingness
Regulatory limitations /regulatory pressures	Complication of the regulatory frame to corporate governance rendering their enforcement inefficient	From the right balance of the four cardinal values underpinning the Africapitalism, a comprehensive environment where good practices can easily be spread may emerge.	Sense of parity; progress and prosperity; peace and harmony; place and belongingness

consider how to translate the Africapitalist 'solutions' to corporate governance weaknesses proposed in this chapter into practice. For example, will initiatives based on an Africapitalism corporate governance framework imply and promote the appointment of women and civil society representatives on boards, or the setting up of board ethics (Africapitalism) committees? Another initiative that deserves exploration is the implementation of Africapitalism impact shares (which government, philanthropists, NGOs could purchase) and the consequent impact on corporate governance. We also suggest the development of an Africapitalism governance index/scorecard, which provides some reputational benefits for pursuing Africapitalism. The extent, to which these suggestions help put Africapitalism in practice and the different configurations they need to take, is a useful pathway to progress discussions in this space.

REFERENCES

Adegbite, E. 2015. Good Corporate Governance in Nigeria: Antecedents, Propositions and Peculiarities. *International Business Review*, 24(2): 319–330.

Adegbite, E., Amaeshi, K. and Amao, O. 2012. The Politics of Shareholder Activism in Nigeria. *Journal of Business Ethics*, 105(3): 389–402.

Adegbite, E., Amaeshi, K. and Nakajima, C. 2013. Multiple Influences on Corporate Governance Practice in Nigeria: Agents, Strategies and Implications. *International Business Review*, 22(3): 524–538.

Adegbite, E. and Nakajima, C. 2011. Institutional Determinants of Good Corporate Governance: The Case of Nigeria. In *Firm-Level Internationalisation, Regionalism and Globalisation*. Edited by E. Hutson, R. Sinkovics and J. Berrill, 379–396. London: Palgrave Macmillan.

Adegbite, E. and Nakajima, C. 2012. Institutions and Institutional Maintenance: Implications for Understanding and Theorizing Corporate Governance in Developing Economies. *International Studies of Management and Organization*, 42(3): 69–88.

Aguilera, R. V. and Jackson, G. 2003. The Cross-National Diversity of Corporate Governance: Dimensions and Determinants. *Academy of Management Review*, 28(3): 447–465.

Ahmad, N. H. and Ramayah, T. 2012. Does the Notion of 'Doing Well by Doing Good' Prevail among Entrepreneurial Ventures in a Developing Nation? *Journal of Business Ethics*, 106(4): 479–490.

Ahunwan, B. 2002. Corporate Governance in Nigeria. *Journal of Business Ethics*, 37 (3): 269–287.

Al-Bassam, W. M., Ntim, C. G., Opong, K. K. and Downs, Y. 2015. Corporate Boards and Ownership Structure as Antecedents of Corporate Governance Disclosure in Saudi Arabian Publicly Listed Corporations. *Business & Society*: 1–43. Available at https://doi.org/10.1177/0007650315610611. Accessed 25 January 2018.

Amaeshi, K., Adegbite, E. and Rajwani, T. 2016. Corporate Social Responsibility in Challenging and Non-Enabling Institutional Contexts: Do Institutional Voids Matter? *Journal of Business Ethics*, 134(1): 135–153.

Amaeshi, K. and Idemudia, U. 2015. Africapitalism: A Management Idea for Business in Africa? *Africa Journal of Management*, 1(2): 210–223.

Amao, O. and Amaeshi, K. 2008. Galvanising Shareholder Activism: A Prerequisite for Effective Corporate Governance and Accountability in Nigeria. *Journal of Business Ethics*, 82(1): 119–130.

Andreasson, S. 2011. Understanding Corporate Governance Reform in South Africa Anglo-American Divergence, the King Reports, and Hybridization. *Business & Society*, 50(4): 647–673.

Ayuso, S. and Argandoña, A. 2009. Responsible Corporate Governance: Towards a Stakeholder Board of Directors?: IESE Business School Working Paper No. 701.

Black, B. S. 1992. Institutional Investors and Corporate Governance: The Case for Institutional Voice. *Journal of Applied Corporate Finance*, 5(3): 19–32.

Bourveau, T. and Schoenfeld, J. 2015. Shareholder Activism and Voluntary Disclosure. Available at http://papers.ssrn.com/sol3/papers.cfm?abstract_id=2668304. Accessed Retrieved 16 August 2016.

Brickley, J., Coles, J. and Jarrell, G. 1997. Leadership Structure: Separating the CEO and Chairman of the Board. *Journal of Corporate Finance*, 3: 189–220.

Casey, E. S. 2001. Between Geography and Philosophy: What Does It Mean to Be in the Place-World? Annals of the Association of American Geographers, 91(4): 683–693.

Choi, J. J. and Dow, S. 2008. *Institutional Approach to Global Corporate Governance: Business Systems and Beyond*. Vol. 9. Bingley, UK: Emerald Group Publishing.

Chua, A. 2004. World on Fire: How Exporting Free Market Democracy Breeds Ethnic Hatred and Global Instability. New York, NY: Anchor Books.

Claessens, S. and Yurtoglu, B. B. 2013. Corporate Governance in Emerging Markets: A Survey. *Emerging Markets Review*, 15: 1–33.

Coates, J. C. 2007. The Goals and Promise of the Sarbanes–Oxley Act. *Journal of Economic Perspectives*, 21(1): 91–116.

Cramton, P. C. and Dees, J. G. 1993. Promoting Honesty in Negotiation: An Exercise in Practical Ethics. *Business Ethics Quarterly*, 3(04): 359–394.

De Wet, P. 2013. First Strut: '20 Years of Mega Fraud'. Available at http://mg.co.za/article/2013-08-08-00-mind-boggling-fraud-is-one-for-the-books. Accessed 23 August 2016.

Dhir, A. A. 2006. Realigning the Corporate Building Blocks: Shareholder Proposals as a Vehicle for Achieving Corporate Social and Human Rights Accountability. *American Business Law Journal*, 43(2): 365–412.

Donaldson, T. and Preston, L. E. 1995. The Stakeholder Theory of the Corporation: Concepts, Evidence, and Implications. *Academy of Management Review*, 20(1): 65–91.

Elumelu, T. O. 2012. The Path to Economic Prosperity and Social Wealth. Available at www.heirsholdings.com/wp-content/uploads/2013/04/Africapitalism-Path-to-Economic-Prosperity-and-Social-Wealth.pdf. Accessed 27 January 2016.

Elumelu, T. 2014. Africapitalism. In *Transforming the Relationship between Business and Society in Africa and Beyond. Making Capitalism More Inclusive*. London: Coalition for Inclusive Capitalism. 92–97.

Escobar, A. 2001. Culture Sits in Places: Reflections on Globalism and Subaltern Strategies of Localization. *Political Geography*, 20(2): 139–174.

Fama, E. F. and Jensen, M. C. 1983. Separation of Ownership and Control, *Journal of Law and Economics*, 26: 301–325.

Farvaque, E., Refait-Alexandre, C. and Saïdane, D. 2011. Corporate Disclosure: A Review of Its (Direct and Indirect) Benefits and Costs. *International Economics*, 128(4): 5–31.

Filatotchev, I. and Nakajima, C. 2010. Internal and External Corporate Governance: An Interface between an Organization and Its Environment. *British Journal of Management*, 21(3): 591–606.

Freeman, R. E. 2010. *Strategic Management: A Stakeholder Approach*. Cambridge: Cambridge University Press.

Frémond, O. and Capaul, M. 2003. Report on the Observance of Standards and Codes (ROSC), Corporate Governance Country Assessment – Republic of South Africa. Available at http:///www.worldbank.org/ifa/SouthAfricaCG.pdf. Accessed 12 August 2016.

Fulcher, J. and Scott, J. 2011. *Sociology*. Oxford: Oxford University Press.

Gieryn, T. F. 2000. A Space for Place in Sociology. *Annual Review of Sociology*, 26: 463–496.

Gillan, S. L. and Starks, L. T. 2003. Corporate Governance, Corporate Ownership, and the Role of Institutional Investors: A Global Perspective. *Journal of Applied Finance*, 13(2): 4–22.

Gow, I. D., Shin, S.-P. S. and Srinivasan, S. 2014. Consequences to Directors of Shareholder Activism. Harvard Business School, Working Paper 14–071, 1–60.

Ibrahim, N. A., Howard, D. P. and Angelidis, J. P. 2003. Board Members in the Service Industry: An Empirical Examination of the Relationship between Corporate Social Responsibility Orientation and Directorial Type. *Journal of Business Ethics*, 47(4): 393–401.

Ingley, C. and Van der Walt, N. T. 2004. Corporate Governance, Institutional Investors and Conflicts of Interest. *Corporate Governance: An International Review*, 12(4): 534–551.

Inyang, B. J. 2009. Nurturing Corporate Governance System: The Emerging Trends in Nigeria. *Journal of Business Systems, Governance and Ethics*, 4(2): 1–13.

Jensen, M. C. and Meckling, W. H. 1976, Theory of the Firm: Managerial Behaviour, Agency Costs, and Ownership Structure. *Journal of Financial Economics*, 3: 305–350.

Joffe, H. 2015. SA Pays Price of Eskom's Disastrous Governance. Available at www .bdlive.co.za/opinion/columnists/2015/03/25/sa-pays-price-of-eskoms-disastrous-g overnance. Accessed 17 August 2016.

Joseph, J., Ocasio, W. and McDonnell, M. 2014. The Structural Elaboration of Board Independence: Executive Power, Institutional Logics, and the Adoption of CEO-Only Board Structures in U.S Corporate Governance. *Academy of Management Journal*, 57(6): 1834–1858.

Jungmann, C. 2006. The Effectiveness of Corporate Governance in One-Tier and Two-Tier Board Systems – Evidence from the UK and Germany. *European Company and Financial Law Review*, 3(4): 426–474.

Kim, Y. H. 2016. Effectiveness of the Sarbanes Oxley Act on Corporate Governance: Evidence from Executive Turnover. *Journal of Applied Business Research*, Forthcoming.

Langevoort, D. C. 2000. Human Nature of Corporate Boards: Law, Norms, and the Unintended Consequences of Independence and Accountability. *Georgetown Law Journal*, 89: 797–832.

Mahadeo, J. D. and Soobaroyen, T. 2016. A Longitudinal Study of the Implementation of the Corporate Governance Code in a Developing Country: The Case of Mauritius. *Business & Society*, 55(5): 738–777.

Maher, M. and Andersson, T. 2000. Corporate Governance: Effects on Firm Performance and Economic Growth. Available at http://papers.ssrn.com/sol3/Papers.cfm?abstract_id=218490. Accessed 15 December 2015.

Mallin, C. 2002. The Relationship between Corporate Governance, Transparency and Financial Disclosure. *Corporate Governance: An International Review*, 10 (4): 253–255.

Mallin, C. A. 2013. *Corporate Governance*. 4th edn. Oxford: Oxford University Press.

Malherbe, S. and Segal, N. 2001. Corporate Governance in South Africa. Development Centre Discussion Paper.

Mangena, M. and Tauringana, V. 2007. Disclosure, Corporate Governance and Foreign Share Ownership on the Zimbabwe Stock Exchange. *Journal of International Financial Management & Accounting*, 18(2): 53–85.

Nakpodia, F., Adegbite, E., Amaeshi, K., & Owolabi, A. (2016). Neither principles nor rules: Making corporate governance work in Sub-Saharan Africa. Journal of Business Ethics, 1–18. https://doi.org/10.1007/s10551-016-3208-5

Ndikumana, L. and Boyce, J. K. 2011. Capital Flight from Sub-Saharan Africa: Linkages with External Borrowing and Policy Options. *International Review of Applied Economics*, 25(2): 149–170.

Nkomo, S. M. 2003. Teaching Business Ethically in the 'New' South Africa. *Management Communication Quarterly*, 17(1): 128–135.

Ntim, C. G. and Osei, K. A. 2011. The Impact of Corporate Board Meetings on Corporate Performance in South Africa. *African Review of Economics and Finance*, 2(2): 83–103.

Okeahalam, C. C. 2004. Corporate Governance and Disclosure in Africa: Issues and Challenges. *Journal of Financial Regulation and Compliance*, 12(4): 359–370.

Okike, E. and Adegbite, E. 2012. The Code of Corporate Governance in Nigeria: Efficiency Gains or Social Legitimation? *Corporate Ownership and Control*, 95 (3): 262–275.

Okike, E. N. M., Adegbite, E. A., Nakpodia, F. A. and Adegbite, S. 2015. A Review of Internal and External Influences on Corporate Governance and Financial Accountability in Nigeria. *International Journal of Business Governance and Ethics*, 10(2): 165–185.

Okpara, J. 2010. Perspectives on Corporate Governance Challenges in a Sub-Saharan African Economy. *Journal of Business and Policy Research*, 5(1): 110–122.

Olutayo, A. O. and Omobowale, A. O. 2007. Capitalism, Globalisation and the Underdevelopment Process in Africa: History in Perpetuity. *Africa Development*, 32(2): 97–112.

Onuoha, B. C., Ogbuji, C. N., Ameh, A. A. and Oba, U. O. 2013. Strategies for Improving Corporate Governance by Organizations in Nigeria. *International Business and Management*, 7(2): 26–31.

Oseni, J. E. and Oseni, E. 2015. Theoretization of Africapitalism Concept. Available at http://papers.ssrn.com/sol3/papers.cfm?abstract_id=2638419. Accessed 14 May 2016.

Rwegasira, K. 2000. Corporate Governance in Emerging Capital Markets: Whither Africa? Corporate Governance. *An International Review*, 8(3): 258–267.

Sarkar, J. and Sarkar, S. 2000. Large Shareholder Activism in Corporate Governance in Developing Countries: Evidence from India. *International Review of Finance*, 1(3): 161–194.

Selznick, P. 1996. Institutionalism 'Old' and 'New'. *Administrative Science Quarterly*, 41(2): 270–277.

Seny Kan, K. A. 2013. Des pistes de réflexion pour la construction d'un cadre structurant des economies en développement: apport de la recherche en gouvernance d'entreprise. *African Management Studies*, 1(2): 1–37.

Seny Kan, K. A., Apitsa, S. M. and Adegbite, E. 2015. 'African Management': Concept, Content and Usability. *Society and Business Review*, 10(3): 258–279.

Sison, A. (2007). Enron - pride comes before the fall. In W. Zimmerli, C, K. Richter & M. Holzinger (Eds.), *Corporate ethics and corporate governance* (pp. 129-136). Berlin, Germany: Springer.

Taylor, S. 2014. *Capitalism and African Business Cultures*. World Institute for Development Economics Research (WIDER) Working Paper 2014/054, United Nations University.

Teoh, S. H., Welch, I. and Wazzan, C. P. 1999. The Effect of Socially Activist Investment Policies on the Financial Markets: Evidence from the South African Boycott. *Journal of Business*, 72(1): 35–89.

Tricker, B. 2015. Corporate Governance: Principles, Policies and Practices. 3rd edn. Oxford, UK: Oxford University Press.

Turnbull, S. 1997. Corporate Governance: Its Scope, Concerns and Theories. *Corporate Governance: An International Review*, 5(4): 180–205.

Uche, C. O., Adegbite, E. and Jones, M. 2016. Institutional Shareholder Activism in Nigeria: An Accountability Perspective. *Accounting Forum*, 40(2): 78–88.

Vaser, W. 2014. Setting the Global Agenda for Ubuntu Capitalism. Available at www.waynevisser.com/wp-content/uploads/2012/04/chapter_wvisser_ubuntu _capitalism.pdf. Accessed 12 January 2016.

Vaughn, M. and Ryan, L. V. 2006. Corporate Governance in South Africa: A Bellwether for the Continent? Corporate Governance: *An International Review*, 14(5): 504–512.

Waweru, N. 2014. Determinants of Quality Corporate Governance in Sub-Saharan Africa: Evidence from Kenya and South Africa. *Managerial Auditing Journal*, 29(5): 455–485.

5 Rethinking Human Capital Development in Africa

Towards an Africapitalism Perspective

Aminu Mamman, Ken Kamoche and
Hamza B. Zakaria

INTRODUCTION

Experts have argued that the political economy of Africa does not suit its social, cultural and economic contexts (see Andreasson, 2005; Hope 1997; Kraus, 2002). Hence, there have been many calls for a more 'appropriate' model or at least a more appropriate philosophy that fits the African socio-economic environment (Amaeshi and Idemudia, 2015; Andreasson, 2005; Hope 1997; Kamoche, 2011; Kamoche and Harvey, 2006; Mbaku, 2004; Newenham-Kahindi et al., 2013). One of the economic philosophies that is receiving significant traction of late is the notion of Africapitalism. This is 'an economic philosophy that embodies the private sector's commitment to the economic transformation of Africa through investments that generate both economic prosperity and social wealth' (Amaeshi and Idemudia, 2015: 210). Like Ubuntu, Africapitalism is premised on the notion that the community and the business are in a symbiotic relationship. Hence, investment that builds economic and common good is good business. It can be argued that Africapitalism is a hardnosed economic philosophy with a social conscience, which is very much in tune with the African psyche of communalism (Lutz, 2009; Makhudu, 1993; Mbaku, 2004; Mbigi, 2002; Mbigi and Maree, 2005).

Whichever economic model or philosophy Africa adopts, it will need the appropriate human capital to transform the idea into practice. Therefore this chapter focuses on how economic actors and stakeholders can be co-sponsors and co-producers of the human capital needed to operationalise the philosophy of Africapitalism. To achieve this aim, the chapter adopts the four cardinal values of Africapitalism (Amaeshi and Idemudia, 2015) to articulate how Africa's human capital can be developed under this philosophy. While we acknowledge the merits of focusing on the provision of education and skills as the main components of human capital, we critique the neoclassical and neoliberal assumptions of Human Capital which underpins Africa's approach to human capital development (Fafunwa and Aisiku, 1982; White, 1996; Woolman, 2001). Therefore, we propose a new approach. Using Africapitalism underpinned by Ubuntu philosophies, we argue for a collaborative 'architecture' that binds international investors, public, private and NGO sectors as sponsors and co-producers of human capital in Africa. The following sections elaborate on this idea, starting with a brief review of the philosophies of Africapitalism and Ubuntu. The philosophies will be used to advance a case for a more appropriate approach to human capital development in Africa.

AFRICAPITALISM AND UBUNTU PHILOSOPHY: AN OVERVIEW

Africapitalism is a term coined by Tony O. Elumelu, an African-born banker, economist, entrepreneur and successful businessman who felt the need to articulate a new economic philosophy for Africa (Amaeshi, 2015; Amaeshi and Idemudia, 2015). Africapitalism is an economic philosophy that embodies the private sector's commitment to the economic transformation of Africa through investments that generate both economic prosperity and social wealth (Amaeshi and Idemudia, 2015: 210).

Central to Africapitalism is the notion that the private sector has obligations for the socio-economic development of Africa. This obligation is not necessarily for altruistic but for business motives. The socio-economic development will ensure the sustainability of the private sector. Underlining this argument is also the idea that all economic actors (both local and international) have a stake in the socio-economic development of Africa and therefore should collaborate to find an efficient way to coordinate their economic activities rather than pursue the 'survival of the fittest winner-takes-all' economic philosophy which, some have argued, has been detrimental to Africa's social and economic progress (Amaeshi and Idemudia, 2015). However, applying the new economic philosophy requires the modification or adjustment of neoclassical economic thinking to reflect the role of business in society underpinned by enlightened self-interest on the part of economic actors (Amaeshi and Idemudia, 2015). This approach is perhaps best captured by the notion of society-minded-entrepreneurship (Amaeshi, 2015), where the entrepreneurs are:

> not only success-driven, but also impactful and purpose-driven. They seek to positively address the ills and challenges of society through their enterprises. Like success-driven entrepreneurs, they are innovative and imaginative. However, unlike the former, they are driven by enlightened self-interest. They recognize the societal challenges and risks around them, but are never deterred by them. Instead, they see them as opportunities. In that regard, one can argue that they are optimistic and courageous, because they can see opportunities where others see risks and frustrations. They have a positive image of themselves and try to be the change they want to see in Africa. They are long-term-oriented and patient.
>
> *(Amaeshi, 2015)*

Amaeshi and Idemudia (2015: 215) argued that where the fundamentals of capitalism 'or a combination of them is out of kilter, capitalism limps, wobbles, and could become dangerously wild if unchecked'. The economic challenges of many African countries today can partly be attributed to the scenario described by Amaeshi and Idemudia. Therefore, Africapitalism is an attempt to 'reunite capitalism with its moral roots in Africa' (Amaeshi and Idemudia, 2015: 215). How can this be achieved? The following cardinal values of Africapitalism provide the guiding principles for addressing the inconsistencies and misalignments between profit motive and societal well-being.

The first cardinal value of Africapitalism is the *Sense of Progress and Prosperity*. The aim of this value can be described as achieving what Parsons (1971) calls social equilibrium where economic pursuit does not conflict with social peace and order. Indeed without social order and peace capitalism will not thrive (Alesina and Perotti, 1996; Hall and Soskice, 2003). In fact, Africa is widely acknowledged as one of the regions with present and potential social conflicts which hinder economic progress (Salehyan et al., 2012). An economic philosophy that encourages the accumulation of wealth for psycho-social human well-being should contribute to the elimination of present and potential social conflict and ensure economic development and fulfilling lives for all (Amaeshi and Idemudia, 2015; Zahra et al., 2009). Hence this cardinal value advocates the creation of social wealth in addition to the pursuit of profit. The implications of this cardinal value for human capital development in Africa will be discussed later. Suffice it to say, based on this cardinal value, the accumulation of human capital should not be for only selfish economic gain but for wider societal benefit.

The second cardinal value of Africapitalism is the *Sense of Parity*. This value focuses on the issue of inequity stemming from liberal capitalism (Amaeshi and Idemudia, 2015). Inequity in a society has long-term negative consequences for all (Alesina and Perotti, 1996; Persson and Tabellini, 1994). In fact, the idea of trickledown economics where the market allocates resources and wealth has been debunked by many experts (Aghion and Bolton, 1997). This is because research evidence has shown that many people have been left behind despite economic growth experienced in many countries (Datt and Ravallion, 2002). Market imperfection, crony capitalism, corruption and misapplication of economic liberalism have been blamed for the rampant inequity (Amaeshi and Idemudia, 2015; Gyimah-Brempong, 2002). Therefore, the cardinal value of *sense of parity* advocates that 'the benefits of progress and prosperity need to be equitably shared' (Amaeshi and Idemudia, 2015: 216). Inequity has been a feature of market liberalism around the world (Baliamoune-Lutz, 2007;

Persson and Tabellini, 1994) but the African region has been acknowledged to be the worst affected by inequity (Deininger, and Squire, 1996). For example, inequity is reflected in many of Africa's indices of social and economic development (Gyimah-Brempong, 2002). Thus, the economic progress of Africa should be measured in terms of inclusive growth rather than GDP growth. The idea of *sense of parity* calls for the re-examination of how factors of production such as human capital are conceptualised and measured in Africa. As will be argued later, achieving equity requires addressing the mindset of economic actors through education. There should be equity in access to human capital development enabled through collaboration between the public, private and international development actors.

The third cardinal value of Africapitalism is *Sense of Peace and Harmony*. This value focuses on balancing the notion of self-interest with societal/stakeholders interest. The former is central to the philosophy of liberal market capitalism (Smith, 1952) while the latter is one of the key arguments for Africapitalism. Undoubtedly, liberal market capitalism taps into the human instinct for self-interest and self-preservation. However, liberal capitalism does not adequately acknowledge that there are many ways to achieve self-interest and self-preservation. For example, the concept of enlightened self-interest acknowledges that collaboration and cooperation in human endeavour can sometimes produce better outcomes than individualistic pursuit of self-interest (Frimer et al., 2011). Similarly, the notion of moral economy is not entirely underpinned by altruism because self-interest is embedded in group interest to ensure sustainability (Fafchamps, 1992). Therefore, Africapitalism advocates the pursuit of social wealth given that 'the tendency of liberal market capitalism *can* lead to some form of socioenvironmental imbalance, which is often dangerous to humanity (Amaeshi and Idemudia, 2015: 217). Similarly, Africapitalism advocates the pursuit of social wealth for all stakeholders rather than for one's self-interest. As we will argue later, the pursuit of social wealth for all stakeholders also implies the pursuit of human capital for all stakeholders. Perhaps the strongest argument for the pursuit of social wealth is that of achieving sustainability. It can be asked what benefit there is in any wealth that is not sustainable? Similarly, what benefit is there in any human capital that will not provide sustainable livelihood? Since *no man is an island*, sustainability will be underpinned by harmony through cooperation with the members of the society.

The final cardinal value is *Sense of Place and Belongingness*. This value focuses on addressing one of the limitations of global capitalism where cost is prioritised during investment decision-making. This cardinal value strives 'to restore in managerial decision-making the link between place and economics on one hand, and between place and self-identity on the other hand' (Amaeshi and Idemudia, 2015: 217). In other words, it is a call for economic patriotism where African economic actors are admonished to see the moral imperative and obligation in defending the economy of Africa when making decisions. Thus, Africapitalism is viewed as an emotional economic tool for Africa's sustainable development (Amaeshi and Idemudia, 2015). We would argue that this argument is not only morally right but that it also makes business sense since African economic actors cannot easily relocate to another continent if Africa becomes economically barren. The notion of economic patriotism has direct relevance to how and where human capital is used to defend and propagate the economic development of Africa. As we elaborate later, this cardinal value also has direct implications for the decision-making of international investors regarding making choices based on the availability of human capital in the region. The idea of a communal perspective on economic pursuits is further illustrated in the following discussion of Ubuntu philosophy.

Ubuntu can be described as a belief system, since belief has been argued to influence attitudes and behaviour (Damane, 2001). For example, Nussbaum (2003) described Ubuntu as a 'fountain from which actions and attitudes flow'' (p. 2). It can also be argued that Ubuntu is a philosophy as demonstrated by the following statements: 'A person is a person because of others'; Ubuntu is the quality of being human'; 'It is through others that one attains selfhood'; 'I am because we are, and since we are, therefore I am' (Mbiti, 1991; Mangaliso, 2001; Nussbaum, 2003). Ubuntu has guiding principles and behavioural expectations which we believe are apt for the application of Africapitalism philosophy. According to Ubuntu principles, humanness is supposed to be expressed through discipline, morality, altruism, self and social consciousness, responsibility and duty (Sibanda, 2014: 27). The principles that underpin Ubuntu are outlined further by one of the earlier proponents of the concept (Mbigi, 1997). Mbigi (1997) highlighted the following as the salient principles of Ubuntu: the spirit of unconditional collective contribution, solidarity, acceptance, dignity, stewardship, compassion and care. Other underlying principles of Ubuntu include fairness, interconnectedness, consensus, trust, shared understanding, harmony, respect and justice (Nussbaum, 2003).

These underlying characteristics of Ubuntu equally apply to Africapitalism. Since Ubuntu is predicated on the idea of humanness, there should be guiding principles regarding how to be 'human' as a business operator. For example, to be 'human' as a business operator is to develop a business that fits with one of the key aspirations of a society for harmony and symbiotic existence throughout all its constituent parts. The idea of social wealth advocated by Africapitalism comes to the fore here. This is because, according to Ubuntu, to be human, one has to appeal to the heart and spirit rather than to rational reasoning only (July, 2004; Sibanda, 2014). Thus, market liberalism steeped in rationality is at odds with the Ubuntu philosophy as it is with Africapitalism. To be human is to be upright, respectable and respected (Nziramasanga, 1999). Therefore, an African business enterprise should be a *humanitarian* business that is considered by the society to be 'one of us', that 'does not harm us' and that is identified with our human aspirations. Hence, a business that we can rely on not only for the goods and services it provides but a business that we are in a symbiotic relationship with because we share a common destiny.

Scholars have attempted to provide practical explanations of how Ubuntu manifests itself in making decisions that guide behaviour. For example, Metz (2007) noted two behavioural principles in his synthesis of the definitions of Ubuntu as a moral theory.

> An action is right just insofar as it positively relates to others and thereby realizes oneself; an act is wrong to the extent that it does not perfect one's valuable nature as a social being.
>
> An action is right just insofar as it produces harmony and reduces discord; an act is wrong to the extent that it fails to develop community.
>
> (Metz, 2007: 328)

Metz (2007) argues that the two principles are better reflections or characterisations of the concept because as he argues: 'a better fundamental explanation of why I ought to help others appeals not to the fact that it would (likely) be good for me, or at least not merely to this fact, but to the fact that it would (likely) be good for them' (Metz, 2007: 330). In line with this argument, organisations and investors should appreciate that being good to their host is not simply for the sake of altruistic motives, but also for developing a symbiotic relationship for the sustainability of the business and the community. For example, when international investors and companies invest directly or indirectly in the host's community human capital, they are making a hard-nosed business decision that will bring long-term returns. This is also in line with the cardinal value of the sense of *place and belongingness* (Amaeshi and Idemudia, 2015) elaborated earlier in the chapter.

The preceding discussion of Africapitalism and Ubuntu has demonstrated that there are common threads running through the two philosophies: First, the location of human activity (economic or otherwise) is within a society and there is need to judge the success and failure of such activity within the context of the society where such activity takes place: i.e., societal well-being. Thus, economic behaviour that leads to the impoverishment of the society cannot be considered a successful endeavour. Second, connected to the first point, is the recognition that the survival and progress of an individual or a business enterprise is intertwined with the fairness and harmony in the society where the individual or the business resides. Thus, there should be a symbiotic relationship between economic endeavour and societal well-being. Finally, the two philosophies are underpinned by the idea of moral obligation for societal interest. These common threads have direct implications for human capital development in Africa. At the basic level, the acquisition and use of human capital should be underpinned by the needs of the society rather than by individualistic self-interest. Also, there is a moral obligation for the acquisition and utilisation of human capital. Finally, the quality of human capital should be judged based on its contribution or potential contribution to the society not exclusively by its contribution to individualistic goals.

This chapter adopts these cardinal values and the principles of Ubuntu to demonstrate how Africapitalism can be realised in a specific area of economic development – namely human capital development. The extent to which the educational systems and curriculum in Africa inculcate the notion of *social wealth* rather than personal materialistic achievements is debatable. As we shall see later, going by the behaviour of some 'educated' public servants and business people in Africa (Mamman and Zakaria, 2016), it is difficult to make a case that some of the educated elites have been properly equipped to live up to the Africapitalism's cardinal values. Yet human capital development definitions and strategies in Africa continue to neglect what Amaeshi and Idemudia (2015: 216) call *psycho-social human well-being*. People should be encouraged to acquire knowledge and skills not only for personal materialistic achievements such as getting a job or setting up their own businesses but also for communal benefits (Mamman et al., 2015). This should also produce economic actors that can make economic decisions which are guided by a moral compass rather than by their Intelligent Quotient (IQ) only. The following section on

Africa's approach to human capital development provides a sharp contrast to what we have discussed so far.

KEY FEATURES AND APPROACH TO HUMAN CAPITAL DEVELOPMENT IN AFRICA

The genesis of the concept of human capital provides a foundation for understanding Africa's approach to human capital development. The notion of human capital can be traced back to the eighteenth century when economists underscored the role of the capacities of people in creating economic value (Marshall, 1948; Mill, 1926; Smith, 1952). Later, researchers began to determine the empirical basis of human capital theory (Fitzsimons, 2015). These researchers focused on the impact of investment in education on economic growth, wealth accumulation and personal income (Becker, 1960, 1964; Benhabib and Spiegel, 1994; Blaug, 1987; Cohn and Geske, 1990; Mincer, 1958; Sweetland, 1996). The empirical investigation of human capital theory is not restricted to the discipline of economics. Management scholars also adopted human capital theory to understand and explain why some business enterprises are more successful than others (Barney, 1991; Nyberg et al., 2014; Ployhart and Moliterno, 2011; Polyhard et al., 2009). Beyond the enterprise level, researchers on entrepreneurship also adapted human capital theory to understand and explain why some people succeed in business while others fail (Lumpkin and Dess, 1996; Wiklund and Shepherd, 2003).

More recently, development economists have perhaps made the greatest impact in espousing the adoption of human capital theory in Africa and developing countries in general (Appleton, 1995; Appleton and Teal, 1998; World Bank, 1996). Their investigations and arguments centre on explaining the variations in economic development (Lundvall and Foray, 1996). Some have concluded that countries that have higher stocks of human capital in the form of education and skills do better across the development indices (Benhabib and Spiegel, 1994; Gylfason, 2001) and are more likely to attract foreign direct investment (Noorbakhsh et al., 2001). However, others have argued that, to understand Africa's human capital development approach, it is also necessary to appreciate the impact of Africa's colonial history vis-à-vis the conception of what constitutes human capital and the system that delivers it (White, 1996; Woolman, 2001). Thus, the current discourse on human capital development in Africa is underpinned by the Western definition of what constitutes human capital – namely capacities (knowledge and skills) that have the potential to create economic value.

The notion of human capital in neoliberal Western literature is largely universalist and ahistorical and devoid of cultural perspective (Block, 1990; Fitzsimons, 2015). In fact, Fitzsimons (2015: 2) points out: 'Human capital theory, then, is an impoverished notion of capital. It is unable to understand activity other than as the exchange of commodities and the notion of capital employed is purely a quantitative one.' This criticism is partly based on the neoclassical interpretation of human capital. For example, Marshall (1948) and Smith (1952) view human capital as human capacities that can produce material wealth and income that are quantifiable. Therefore, capacities that cannot produce material wealth or income, or cannot be quantifiable are excluded from the definition of human capital (Fisher, 1906; Fitzsimons, 2015). Hence, in developing a human capital curriculum, only quantifiable knowledge, skills and abilities that can create material wealth or income are considered most relevant (Fitzsimons, 2015). We return to this point later.

Fitzsimons (2015) has also argued that the Western educational system is built on the foundation of this neoclassical theory of human capital. Similarly, White (1996) and Woolman (2001) pointed out that the colonial masters in Africa developed an educational system based on the foundation of the neoclassical theory of human capital. This point is further echoed by African scholars such as Ali Mazrui and Babs Fafunwa. They argue that the African system was established to produce the knowledge and skills required to achieve the economic goals of the colonial empire (Fafunwa and Aisiku, 1982). Yet, after de-colonialisation, the education system did not radically change to address the limitations of the neoclassical interpretation of human capital on which the African system was built (Busia, 1964; Fafunwa and Aisiku, 1982; Woolman, 2001).

What are the key features of Africa's human capital development? As stated earlier, Africa's educational system, which is aimed at developing its human capital, is anchored on the foundation of neoclassical theory bequeathed to it by the colonial masters. The focus of the educational and vocational systems in many African countries is understandably skewed towards producing graduates with knowledge and skills for the purpose of material wealth and job creation (Bloom et al., 2006; Ekeh, 1975; Omolewa, 2007). Therefore, the curriculum is largely based on assessing quantifiable achievements in subject areas that are deemed to create material wealth and ensure personal income (White, 1996). Like neoclassical theory, Africa's educational and vocational systems are steeped in the doctrine of economic rationality (Arnove, 1980). Education and vocational skills are viewed as commodities for the creation of wealth and personal income (Minnis, 2006). The basic structure of delivering the commodities are formal primary, secondary, tertiary and vocational education (Africa-America Institute, 2015; Cohn and Geske, 1990; World Bank, 2007). These are largely publicly funded and complemented by private and international organisations and non-state actors such as NGOs and faith-based organisations (Africa-America Institute, 2015; World Bank, 2007). The informal education and vocational training contribute to a significant proportion of human capital stock in Africa, although this is largely under-recognised by policy makers and some researchers (Minnis, 2006).

The second feature of African human capital development which is also anchored on neoclassical theory and the colonial legacy is the secular nature of the African educational systems (Bloom et al., 2006; Crossman, 2003). This feature ensures that human qualities that cannot be easily quantified or demonstrate material value do not feature prominently in the system

(Crossman, 2003). For example, although there is implicit recognition of the role of emotional and spiritual qualities as well as personal integrity in any human endeavour, such qualities are not key features of the educational curriculum (Ashkanasy et al., 2003; Bush, 1999; Hodge and Derezotes, 2008; Massari, 2011; Mayer et al., 2000; Mitchell and Hall, 2007; Scherer, 1997). In fact Scherer (1997) argued that emotional intelligence is a better predictor of success in life than IQ, yet such character-building skills do not feature prominently in educational curricula. However, it should be pointed out that faith-based schools have long recognised these qualities in their curriculum (Dempster and Hugo, 2006). Also, as we demonstrate below, African traditional education emphasises character building (Fafunwa and Aisiku, 1982). Similarly, a research report sponsored by the UK's Department for International Development reported:

> The over-reliance on standardised assessments of cognitive learning as a measure of quality within the human capital approach can also be problematic. Readily measurable cognitive outcomes shift from being privileged indicators of quality to defining quality. When this happens, qualitative indicators and scrutiny of processes can be overlooked.
>
> *(Tikly and Barrett, 2011: 3)*

The third feature of the human capital development approach which is also influenced by neoclassical theory and the colonial legacy is the inadequate focus on the socio-cultural context of Africa (Busia, Fafunwa and Aisiku, 1982; Jansen, 1998; Obanya, 1999). This is because neoclassical theory does not recognise the role of culture in its interpretation of human capital. As Sweetland (1996) argues, neoclassical and neoliberal perspectives see the acquisition and use of human capital from a purely rational economic point of view. Also, Fitzsimons (2015: 1) points out: 'In modern human capital theory all human behaviour is based on the economic self-interest of individuals operating within freely competitive markets. Other forms of behaviour are excluded or treated as distortions of the model.' The exclusive focus on seeing knowledge and skills as a means of acquiring material wealth and personal income has relegated the African communal perspective on knowledge and skills to the background. Although the individualistic approach can appeal to human instinct for self-interest, however, in the African context steeped in communal orientation, the communal perspective is more likely to provide sustainable benefit in the acquisition and application of human capital. This is because empirical evidence has already demonstrated the inadequacy of Africa's educational system and curriculum to benefit the cultural context of Africa (Ajayi, 1996; Dei, 2002). Also, conceptually, both Africapitalism and Ubuntu have demonstrated that human activity that is intertwined with the needs of the society is more likely to be sustainable.

In a nutshell, there are similarities and differences across the providers of human capital in Africa. The formal education system supported by state, non-state and international development partners such as UNICEF focus largely on the provision of knowledge as a foundation for building human capital (King and McGrath, 2002; Oketch, 2007; World Bank, 2007). Undoubtedly, there are many advantages of providing basic and general knowledge in preparing people for the world of work and the pursuit of economic and social goals. However, critics have argued that formal education does not prepare people with the hands-on skills to pursue economic goals. Hence, the providers of formal and informal vocational training focus largely on the provision of skills for the creation of jobs and material wealth (Haan, 2006a; ILO, 2012; Oketch, 2007; McGrath, 2011). African employers and international investors concentrate on developing the requisite human capital by focusing on knowledge and skills that are of economic value to them (Bas, 1989). The vocational approach, though laudable, is narrowly focused on individualistic economic goals rather than on social goals (Mamman et al., 2015). The similarity across the state and non-state providers of human capital in Africa is that they all view human capital as mainly skills and knowledge that generate material wealth and economic value rather than social wealth. The difference lies in the foci of the constituents of human capital rather than the goal of human capital development.

It is worth pointing out that the current economic realities of Africa and global commodification of human capital continue to reinforce the three features of the human capital development approach in Africa. For example, international development agencies such as the World Bank and ILO, as well as inter-governmental organisations such as the African Development Bank and Africa Capacity Building Foundation, encourage the acquisition of knowledge for material wealth and economic growth. Given the growing unemployment on the continent, this is understandable. However, the question is this: given the unique socio-economic context of Africa, can commodification of human capital provide sustainable solutions to Africa's social and economic challenges? To address this question, we first critique the African approach and then advance the argument for the use of Africapitalism to address some of the limitations of the current approach.

CRITIQUE OF THE KEY FEATURES OF HUMAN CAPITAL DEVELOPMENT IN AFRICA

The current approach to human capital development by state and non-state providers has its merits and weaknesses. The system of formal education by these providers has been the foundation for human capital especially for those who can acquire a good education (World Bank, 2007). In addition, the provision of formal and informal vocational education and the support provided for vocational and entrepreneurship training by international institutions has also benefited many African institutions involved in vocational training and policy formulation (Atchoarena and Delluc, 2002; Oketch, 2007). Similarly, the capacity-building support offered by international institutions has helped many African training and education providers to improve on service delivery (Atchoarena and Delluc, 2002; Oketch, 2007). However, when viewed from the economic and social challenges facing Africa today, the approach has limitations. Therefore, this section critiques Africa's approach to human capital development highlighted in the previous section.

As stated earlier, human capital development in Africa by both the state and non-state providers is underpinned by an economic rationality in which the educational and vocational system produces knowledge for individualistic material goals. Indeed, Fitzsimons (2015:1) argues that in the 'Western countries, education has been theorised under human capital theory as primarily an economic device'. Fitzsimons (2015) also argued that human capital theory is the most influential economic theory of Western education. Similarly, Woolman (2001: 28) asserts: 'Increasingly, in modern times, economism has become a dominant force influencing education policy. This occurs in highly industrialised countries as well as in the poorest developing nations. Education is regarded as the key to economic development. This impression persists in spite of the fact that economic growth usually results from complex relationships between many variables rather than any simple one-to-one interaction between schools and jobs.' In fact, some researchers have argued that a positive correlation between school enrolment and output growth should not be interpreted as an indication that human capital contributes positively to growth (Bosworth et al., 1995; Pritchett, 1996). The idea that human capital might not correlate neatly with material acquisition such as economic growth in Africa raises questions about Africa's embrace of the neoclassical theory of human capital development. It further raises questions about what should constitute human capital in an African context.

Africa's Western colonial heritage ensures that its educational system is not far removed from the Western system (Andreasson, 2005; Woolman, 2001). Given that people's behaviour is not influenced by economic rationality all the time, building an educational and vocational system on the foundation of such an assumption has limitations especially in a society where people are defined by their contribution to the society. For example, Mungazi (1996) underscores this point when he asserts that an African's place in society is determined by his contribution to the community he belongs to and that he should be trained with sensitivity to meet the needs of the community as a whole as well as those of others as individuals. Also Woolman (2001) pointed out that in Kenya and Nigeria, educational policy at independence was mostly concerned with using schools to develop manpower for economic development and Africanisation of the civil service. These accounts point to the colonial heritage of Africa's human development approach. Perhaps, more appropriately, in the African context, human capital should have communal dimension. Thus, human capital should be sought for the social value it generates, and not only for its material value. This is because the economic development of Africa will only be built on the foundation of a well-functioning society. In fact, Busia (1964:17) argues that the African ideal of socially centred human development is that which the education system should seek 'to produce men and women who were not self-centred, who put the interest of the group above personal interest'. This conflicts with the neoclassical human capital theory pursued by Africa and its international development partners today.

The previous section also highlighted secularism as a key feature of human capital development pursued by the state and non-state providers in Africa. The issue of ethics and character is seen as an exogenous factor that should not be accommodated within the economic rational model (Fitzsimons, 2015). Students are therefore oriented to acquire knowledge and skills in order to find a job and earn an income for their livelihood: hence the advocacy of *vocational emphasis in the* African education curricula even in universities known for their focus on general education (Altbach, 2004; Union, 2007). However, as Fitzsimons (2015: 2) pointed out, 'both the society and culture shape the preferences of individuals in various ways. Social factors also influence economic contractual transactions. Even contracts rest on cultural understandings and the legal framework which is itself historically determined'. In fact, even within the neoliberal model of human capital, experts argue that an educational and vocational curriculum that does not provide people the opportunity to develop emotional skills to collaborate with others is not an ideal preparation for the world of work or self-employment (Goleman, 1996; 2006).

The emphasis on secular educational system is understandable given the cultural and religious diversity on the continent. For example, Woolman (2001: 27) points out: 'Although early European nation-States evolved as the political expression of one culture, most countries today include people of many cultures. Most African states, for example, have high levels of cultural and linguistic diversity. This situation presents many challenges for schools, which are expected to cultivate a common national spirit and unity.' More so, it can be argued that one of the foci of religion is the development of psycho-social man rather than economic man. The economic challenges in Africa which have resulted in high youth unemployment also make it easier for Africa to embrace the neoclassical theory of human capital with its emphasis on a secularistic interpretation of human capital. However, emphasis on secular education has robbed Africa's educational and vocational systems of the means to produce rounded people who can pursue the acquisition of knowledge and skills for both social and economic ends (Fafunwa, 1982). In fact, in Woolman's (2001) view, in many African countries, results have not matched expectations and educational systems have, in some cases, caused new problems for nation-building.

While religion cannot and should not be central to Africa's educational system, there is room for the inclusion of some of the common human values which religions espouse. In fact, African educationists have long called for the inclusion of such values in the African educational system. For example, Fafunwa (1982) advocated the inclusion of morality and spiritual values in the educational curriculum. Fafunwa (1982: 9–10) further added: 'In old Africa ... the man who combined good character with a specific skill was adjudged to be a well-educated and well-integrated citizen of his community.' Within the African context, therefore, human capital cannot be divorced from perennial values that are required for a society to function effectively. Such values can complement the rational economic model and should enable the production of well-rounded persons who acquire knowledge and skills not only for individualistic economic goals but also for communal and societal development. The common religious values for human and societal development can be taught as secular spiritual values. We therefore advocate the inclusion of emotional and spiritual traits as part of Africa's definition of human capital (Mamman and Zakaria, 2016). The notion of emotional and spiritual intelligences emphasises connectedness, empathy, compassion and sense of belonging (Goleman, 1996, 2006; Zohar, 2005; Zohar and Marshall, 1994, 2000). We argue that conceptualising African human capital to include these traits will enable the operationalisation of Africapitalism in the context of human capital development.

The third feature of the human capital development pursued by the state and non-state providers in Africa is the inadequate regard for the socio-cultural context of Africa (Mazrui, 1978; Rwomire, 1998; Uchendu, 1979). For example, the entrepreneurship training programmes by the ILO (2012, 2014) focus on the individual entrepreneur rather than locating the programme within the context of an African philosophy of community (Mbigi, 1997; Mbiti, 1991; Nussbaum, 2003). The exclusive focus on the individual in the acquisition and utilisation of knowledge and skills for personal economic gain is not in conformity with the African philosophy of Ubuntu and Africapitalism. In fact, the Ubuntu philosophy advocates that 'It is through others that one attains selfhood'; 'I am because we are, and since we are, therefore I am' (Mbiti, 1991; Nussbaum, 2003). Therefore, to paraphrase Ubuntu, 'it is through the community that a person becomes a successful entrepreneur or craftsman'. Closely related to this is the vocational and educational curriculum that is devoid of an African philosophical context (Adeyemi and Adeyinka,

2002) which should have viewed the trainee and his/her success within the context of the community within which he/she resides rather than individualised economic pursuit typical of entrepreneurship training programmes (Haan, 2006a; Swanson, 2007).

In this regard, since African independence, experts have continued to make a case for the need to change Africa's human capital development model by reforming its educational system (Busia, 1964; Fafunwa, 1982; Mungazi, 1996). For example, Busia (1964) argues for socially centred human development while Fafunwa (1982) calls for the inclusion of social responsibility, political participation, work orientation, morality and spiritual values in the educational curriculum. Woolman (2001) has provided a clear description of human capital development in the African tradition. He argues that education is well incorporated in cultural reproduction. He maintains that African tradition integrated education with character-building and other intellectual pursuits. 'The content included all of the activities, rituals, and skills required to sustain the culture and life of the family and community. Great importance was placed on interpersonal relationships and reciprocal obligations' (Woolman, 2001: 31).

In a nutshell, our critique of the key features of human capital development in Africa has raised the following issues: What should Africa consider as human capital? What should be included in the African educational and vocational curriculum? Who should provide the support for building Africa's human capital? The following sections attempt to address these issues. First we discuss how the philosophies of Ubuntu and Africapitalism might provide answers to the challenges to human capital development on the continent. This will be followed by examples of how our suggested approach might be realised.

THE ROLE OF AFRICAPITALISM AND UBUNTU

The cardinal values of Africapitalism outlined by Amaeshi and Idemudia (2015) have some implications for human capital development in Africa, especially regarding the philosophical assumption of what should constitute human capital and the approach for complementing the state in delivering it by economic actors.

One of the cardinal values of Africapitalism advocates 'the creation of social wealth in addition to the pursuit of profitability' (Amaeshi and Idemudia, 2015: 216). The notion of a *sense of prosperity and progress* within the context of Africapitalism frowns upon exclusive accumulation of material wealth disregarding 'psychosocial human wellbeing'. This cardinal value has major implications for defining human capital for Africa's progress and prosperity. This value implies that the pursuit of knowledge should not be confined to personal achievement to the detriment of the community where the knowledge and skills will be applied. As we have argued earlier, the notion of 'communal skills and knowledge' where those who possess them do not see them as personal property but property entrusted to them for societal well-being has both philosophical and practical foundations.

In fact, in traditional African societies of the past this is how certain knowledge and skills were considered (Omolewa, 2007). People who possess them are supposed to serve the community, not just to profit from them. For example, traditional doctors, herbalists, teachers and key craftsmen were considered to be pillars of the community without whom the community would not survive and prosper. They were held in high regard because of their service not just because of the knowledge and skills they possessed (Omolewa, 2007). As Omolewa (2007: 593) pointed out, under the African traditional educational system, 'each person in the community is practically trained and prepared for his/her role in society. It is a holistic system, in which storytelling, proverbs and myths also play an important role'. If the economic philosophy of Africapitalism is to thrive, the notion of *'communal knowledge and skills'* should be integrated into the vocational and educational system and curriculum.

In advancing the value of *sense of parity*, Africapitalism advocates the idea of inclusive growth (Amaeshi and Idemudia, 2015). This is because, 'inequality has become the new scourge and burden of success and the new poverty' (Amaeshi and Idemudia, 2015: 216). To the extent that this inequality also includes that of knowledge and skills owing to the low standard of many African schools, the cardinal value of *parity* implies that economic actors, especially international investors should contribute to the elimination of such inequality of human capital within and across African countries. This should enhance the achievement of inclusive growth by enabling the capacity of Africans to have a means of livelihood through the acquisition of skills. In line with the notion of *communal knowledge and skills* advocated above, international investors and the private sector in general should not confine their contribution to the economic sector they operate in but rather collaborate with other economic actors and stakeholders to reduce the inequality in human capital across all sectors.

The third cardinal value of Africapitalism advocates the notion of *peace and harmony* (Amaeshi and Idemudia, 2015). The advocacy for the *sense peace and harmony* is based on the argument that in spite of the merits of self-interest which underpins liberal capitalism, the pursuit of self-interest is partially responsible for excessive inequality and market failure (Amaeshi and Idemudia, 2015). Hence, Africapitalism advocates the pursuit of economic prosperity and social wealth within the context of balance, harmony and peace (Amaeshi and Idemudia, 2015). We argue that peace and harmony can be achieved through the development of educational and vocational curricula that harmonise competition with collaboration in the pursuit of learning and measuring achievement through Intelligence Quotient (IQ), Emotional Quotient (EQ) and Spiritual Quotient (SQ). For example, EQ can enable people to develop the capacity to relate to each other and develop harmonious relationships in economic endeavours, given that EQ involves the 'abilities, competencies, and skills related to understanding oneself and others, relating to peers and family members, and adapting to changing environmental situations and demands' (Bar-On, 2002: 1).

Similarly, SQ will enable economic actors to develop the needed empathy and the required connectedness in economic activities and its wider impact. This is because, as Zohar (2005) argued, SQ has the following characteristics: self-awareness, spontaneity, being vision- and value-led, compassion, holism, celebration of diversity, field independence, humility, urge to ask *why* questions, ability to reframe, positive use of adversity and sense of vocation. We argue that these characteristics can be the foundation for developing human capital suitable for the implementation of Africapitalism. In fact, Zohar and Marshall (2000: 22) argue that spiritual intelligence 'is what we use to develop our longing and capacity for meaning, vision and value. It facilitates a dialogue between reason and emotion, between mind and body. It allows us to integrate the intrapersonal and the interpersonal, to transcend the gap between self and other'. Zohar and Marshall (1994: 26) in an earlier publication described spiritual intelligence as what we use to 'address and solve problems of meaning and value, the intelligence with which we can place our actions and our lives in a wider, richer, meaning-giving context, the intelligence with which we can assess that one course of action or one life path is more meaningful than another'. Therefore, we argue that human capital development should inculcate the spirit of collaboration instead of the exclusive focus on self-interest and competition which underpins the capitalist philosophy of economic development. In a nutshell, there should be a wider meaning to the acquisition of human capital by individuals.

The cardinal value of *sense of place and belongingness* (Amaeshi and Idemudia, 2015) is a critique of global capitalism where *cost* is prioritised over everything else. For example the decision to invest in a place is primarily guided by cost analysis (Amaeshi and Idemudia, 2015). We see a direct implication of this principle for human capital development in Africa. The notion of sense of place and belongingness would imply that the decision to invest in Africa could be guided by availability of cheap human capital rather than the

TABLE 5.1 *Framework of cardinal values and implications for human capital development*

Cardinal values	Human capital development implications
Sense of Progress and Prosperity: Progress should be assessed on the basis of the development of psycho-social well-being	• Reconceptualisation of what human capital means in an African context • Knowledge and skills should be acquired for individual and communal goals • The notion of *communal knowledge and skills* should be integrated into the educational and vocational system
Sense of Parity: Propagation of inclusive economic growth and reduction of inequality	• International investors to collaborate in the elimination of inequality in human capital development across the region • Human capital development should be used to achieve inclusive growth and reduce inequality • Use of communal knowledge and skills to eliminate inequality in human capital development
Sense of peace and harmony: Economic progress based on the pursuit of social wealth as opposed to self-interest	• Educational curriculum should harmonise competition with collaboration • Educational achievement measured by IQ, EQ and SQ • Use of communal knowledge and skills to operationalise the notion of social wealth
Sense of place and belongingness: Propagation of economic patriotism through de-prioritising cost and promoting 'place' in economic decisions	• Patriotic acquisition and application of knowledge and skills • Investors make investment decisions not only based on cost but also based on Africa's human capital potential • Collaboration in the development of human capital across sectors

human capital potential of Africa. Thus, rather than harnessing this potential human capital through developing it, multinational companies might decide to invest elsewhere. This would amount to commodifying and trivialising 'place' and promoting 'placelessness' (Amaeshi and Idemudia, 2015).

We argue that, multinational companies should not avoid the continent because it might lack the readily available or adequate human capital to run the enterprise or because they believe the cost of contributing to the development of Africa's human capital is too high. We argue that embracing the sense of place by developing Africa's human capital will provide multinational companies and investors with long-term economic benefits and enable them to establish themselves as true global citizens with a genuine stake in Africa's progress. In fact, the idea of globalisation suggests boundarylessness (Fukuyama, 1992; Ohmae, 2000). The notion of economic patriotism advocated by this value implies the acquisition and utilisation of human capital for the development of the continent. Economic patriotism also implies the need for the private sector to collaborate in the development of human capital across sectors for the benefit of the economy. Table 5.1 presents the framework of the cardinal values of Africapitalism and their implications for human capital development in Africa.

THE UNWITTING APPLICATION OF AFRICAPITALISM BY INTERNATIONAL COMPANIES AND DEVELOPMENT PARTNERS IN AFRICA

This section provides examples of how economic actors in Africa have unwittingly applied some aspects of the implications of cardinal values of Africapitalism. In particular, the examples echo the idea of inclusivity and collaboration in human capital development in line with some of the cardinal values of Africapitalism, i.e., *sense of parity* and *sense of place and belongingness* (see Table 5.1). The examples demonstrate the possibility of co-production of human capital as advocated in this chapter. For example, we have argued elsewhere

(Mamman et al., 2015) that for the business sector to support social and economic development in Africa, a new approach is required. The competitive winner-takes-all mentality by multinationals in Africa, and by domestic businesses themselves is unsustainable as a business philosophy. The philosophy is contributing to economic under-development and doing little to eradicate inequality and poverty (i.e., *Sense of parity*). This argument has been partly acknowledged by 'The Business Action for Africa' initiative championed by the UK's Department for International Development (DFID). Unwittingly and in line with the Africapitalism philosophy, 'The Business Action for Africa' initiative has created an idea called Business Partnerships for Development in Africa.

This initiative is in line with the cardinal value of *sense of place and belongingness.*

In line with the cardinal value of *sense of place and belongingness*, the DFID's programme director of the international leader's forum is also of the view that the relationship between the business community in the developed world and Africa must change. As he puts it, 'We have reached a tipping point in the way business sees its relationship with the developing world. A growing number of businesses, from large multinational to small-sized start-ups, are moving beyond philanthropic, risk-mitigating CSR focused activities, to find new ways to do business that benefits both the poor and their core business' (Business Action for Africa, 2014: 3). The partnerships for development in Africa adopt an 'Inclusive Business Model'. Thus, rather than competing with the domestic market throughout the value chain, the model adopts a collaborative approach with low-income producers that supply raw materials or provide business services. This approach has been advocated using spirituality and systems thinking approaches (Mamman et al., 2015). The Business Partnership for Development model has not only been adopted by multinational companies, but also by international NGOs such as Oxfam. As the chief executive of Oxfam pointed out: 'Oxfam is increasingly engaging with businesses in recognition of the critical role that the private sector plays in delivering positive development outcomes' (Business for Africa, 2014: 4). The Business for Africa programme aims to drive development through business and through partnerships. The business approach includes trading with low-income entrepreneurs in the small- and medium-sized enterprise (SME) sector; advocating for business-enabling environment reform which is targeted at low-income producers in the SME sector.

The partnership approach includes the sharing of cost and risk with low-income producers in the SME sector; building capacity and enabling access to finance for low-income producers; mentoring and institution-building that will support the SMEs; collaboration with local stakeholders and the SME sector to create input into policy formulation and implementation. There are other examples of how multinational companies have implemented the business partnership for development in Africa. For instance, Coca Cola trains SME operators in East Africa to enable them to operate the distribution of the Coca Cola product effectively. The company also supports the SMEs to access finance to start up their distribution businesses. A similar approach was used by Diageo to convince Cameroonian farmers to convert to producing sorghum, which the company needs as raw material for its product (Guinness). To achieve its objectives, the company trained local farmers and supported access for finance to enable farmers to acquire farm inputs and also start farmers' cooperatives (Business Action for Africa, 2014). These examples are in tune with the human capital development implications of the cardinal values of *sense of parity* and *sense of place and belongingness* described in Table 5.1. Further examples of human capital development implications of the cardinal values of Africapitalism as described in Table 5.1 are presented below.

In line with the *sense of place and belongingness* the IFC (2011) provides another example of how international development partners are collaborating with international NGOs, and with international and local companies to build human capital in Africa's SME sector. For example, in Rwanda, the IFC has teamed up with IBM to provide

BOX 5.1

Over the past 25 years, we have supported enterprise development in host countries as part of our commitment to support development but also as a way to support the performance of our own business. Since 2008, our enterprise development schemes have backed more than 48,000 enterprises, distributed more than USD100 m and supported more than 76,000 jobs. We started in South Africa and Chile and over the past two years, Anglo American has launched schemes in Botswana, Brazil and Peru. Zimele, our first enterprise development programme, began in 1989 in South Africa. Back then we considered the implementation of an enterprise development scheme as a commercial imperative in the complex socio-political climate of the time; we wanted to support black-owned businesses within our supply chain to develop and grow quickly to build resilience in our supply chains and to support local job creation. Over time, Zimele evolved beyond supply chains and therefore expanding the scheme to a wider pool of small and medium enterprises was an important step. Focusing too narrowly on companies that were already poised to develop as a result of the mining sector's growth would only perpetuate the inequalities in the economy, which could increase tension and ultimately affect business performance and economic growth (Business for Africa, 2016).

online training for local entrepreneurs. Similarly, in Cameroon, Ghana and Ethiopia, the IFC and the Bill Gates Foundation are training local farmers to be able to access finance and markets for their products. The final example is captured in Box 5.1.

The Business Action for Africa initiatives and the IFC (2011) are not necessarily coherent approaches that provide a blueprint or a template for the application of Africapitalism and Ubuntu philosophies. This is because the project is not coordinated across development partners, policy makers and local umbrella business

associations. However, the initiatives provide indications of the possibilities of co-production of human capital in the Africa. In line with
some of the cardinal values of Africapitalism and Ubuntu's principle
communal pursuit of economic and social goals, these examples have
demonstrated that indeed economic actors can be oriented to imbibe
the philosophy of Africapitalism and Ubuntu.

CONCLUSION

The current approach to human capital development in Africa
requires re-examination in line with the recent re-examination of
Africa's relationship with the international businesses and development partners. A new approach is required regarding the philosophy
and rationale for human capital development. The current approach is
based on a Western individualistic competitive 'winner-takes-all'
mentality. Hence, the education and training systems aim to produce
individuals who focus on personal achievement using competition
rather than collaboration or community development which Ubuntu
and Africapitalism principles advocate (Amaeshi and Idemudia, 2015;
Mamman and Zakaria, 2016; Mamman et al., 2017). We argue that
educational and vocational curriculum should be anchored in the
creation of both social wealth and financial profitability. In a poverty-
ridden African context, the pursuit of a self-interest model of human
capital development is inadequate for producing the human capital
Africa needs for sustainable development.

A more Afrocentric collaborative approach is required (i.e.,
Africapitalism). To achieve this aim, international investors, development partners, public and private sectors will need to collaborate to
produce a well-articulated vision and strategy to co-produce
a template for developing the needed human capital. The template
should be steeped in the philosophy and principles of Africapitalism
and Ubuntu discussed above. In fact, the African Development Bank's
human capital strategy has advanced a new education model centred
on a collaborative approach. It states that it will 'Engage key stakeholders in developing strong education models (parents, faculties,

universities, science academies, nongovernmental organizations, civil society and communities)' (AfDB, 2014: 15). The bank also acknowledges that the delivery of the strategy should be a collaborative effort between public and private sectors (AfDB, 2014) although international investors and NGOs did not feature prominently in the articulation of how the strategy will be delivered. Nonetheless, the AfDB's human capital development strategy appears to be an implicit admission of the need for the collaborative approach advocated in this chapter.

As an indication of how this can be achieved, there is a need to integrate policy makers and implementers in any education and vocational system. In spite of the acknowledgement of the role of policy makers and implementers in supporting skills development, the existing approach does not fully integrate them in the methodology (Mamman et al., 2017). The new approach should not only focus on technical and professional skills required for employment and self-employment, but also knowledge and skills that contribute to communal development.

To conclude, although this chapter focuses on drawing implications of Africapitalism for human capital development through the formal education and vocational systems, the application of the cardinal values has direct implications for job training and executive development of African managers. In fact, we believe that the cardinal values' implications for training and development of managers and policy makers are more important, given that managers and policy makers are the people with the most influence in transforming Africa's educational and vocational curriculum. It is in line with their significance that we advocate and call for critical and robust discussion of the nature and features of job training and executive development in Africa. The ideas advanced in this chapter can serve as a foundation or template for critiquing the nature of job training and executive development with a view to providing alternatives consistent with the philosophy of Africapitalism.

REFERENCES

Adeyemi, M. B and Adeyinka, A. A. 2002. Some Key Issues in African Traditional Education. *McGill Journal of Education*, 37(2): 223–240.

AfDB. 2014. The Bank's Human Capital Strategy for Africa. OSHD Department. Available at www.afdb.org/fileadmin/uploads/afdb/Documents/Policy -Documents/AfDB_Human_Capital_Strategy_for_Africa_2014–2018.pdf. Accessed 20 December 2015.

Africa-America Institute. 2015. *State of Education in Africa Report 2015.* http:// www.aaionline.org/wp-content/uploads/2015/09/AAI-SOE-report-2015-final.pdf. Accessed 10th August 2017.

Aghion, P. and Bolton, P. 1997. A Theory of Trickle-Down Growth and Development. *Review of Economic Studies*, 64(2): 151–172.

Ajayi, J. F. 1996. *The African Experience with Higher Education.* Athens: Ohio University Press.

Alesina, A. and Perotti, R. 1996. Income Distribution, Political Instability, and Investment. *European Economic Review*, 40(6): 1203–1228.

Altbach, P. G. 2004. Globalisation and the University: Myths and Realities in an Unequal World. *Tertiary Education and Management*, 10(1): 3–25.

Andreasson, S. 2005. Orientalism and African Development Studies: The 'Reductive Repetition' Motif in Theories of African Underdevelopment. *Third World Quarterly*, 26(6): 971–986.

Arnove, R. F. 1980. Comparative Education and World-Systems Analysis. *Comparative Education Review*, 24(1): 48–62.

Ashkanasy, N. M. and Dasborough, M. T. 2003. Emotional Awareness and Emotional Intelligence in Leadership Teaching. *Journal of Education for Business*, 79(1): 18–22.

Amaeshi, K. 2015. A New Economic Philosophy for Africa: Why Africa Needs Society-Minded Entrepreneurs, Not Glitzy Projects, and How the Economic Philosophy of Africapitalism Can Guide the Way. Available at http://ssir.org/arti cles/entry/a_new_economic_philosophy_for_africa. Accessed 20 November 2016.

Amaeshi, K. and Idemudia, U. 2015. Africapitalism: A Management Idea for Business in Africa? *Africa Journal of Management*, 1(2): 210–223.

Appleton, S. 1995. The Interaction of Poverty and Gender in Human Capital Accumulation: The Case of the Primary Leaving Examination in the Côte d'Ivoire. *Journal of African Economies*, 4(2): 192–224.

Appleton, S. and Teal, F. 1998. *Human Capital and Economic Development.* Abidjan, Côte d'Ivoire: African Development Bank Group.

Atchoarena, D. and Delluc, A. 2002. *Revisiting Technical and Vocational Education in Sub-Saharan Africa: An Update on Trends, Innovations and Challenges: New Trends in Technical and Vocational Education.* Paris: United Nations Educational, Scientific, and Cultural Organization. International Inst. for Educational Planning.

Baliamoune-Lutz, M. 2007. Globalisation and Gender Inequality: Is Africa Different? *Journal of African Economies,* 16(2): 301–348.

Barney, J. 1991. Firm Resources and Sustained Competitive Advantage. *Journal of Management,* 17(1): 99–120.

Bar-On, R. 2002. *EQ-i BarOn Emotional Quotient Inventory: A Measure of Emotional Intelligence: User's Manual.* Toronto: Multi Health System.

Bas, D. 1989. On-the-Job Training in Africa. *Internal Labour Review,* 128: 485.

Becker, G. S. 1960. Underinvestment in College Education? *American Economic Review,* 50: 346–354.

Becker, G. S. 1964. *Human Capital: A Theoretical and Empirical Analysis with Special Reference to Education.* New York, NY: National Bureau of Economic Research.

Benhabib, J. and Spiegel, M. M. 1994. The Role of Human Capital in Economic Development: Evidence from Aggregate Cross-Country Data. *Journal of Monetary Economics,* 34(2): 143–173.

Blaug, M. 1987. Rate of Return on Investment in Great Britain. In *The Economics of Education and the Education of Economist.* Edited by M. Blaug, 11–29. New York, NY: New York University Press.

Block, F. 1990. *Post Industrial Possibilities: A Critique of Economic Discourse.* Los Angeles: University of California Press.

Bloom, D. E., Canning, D. and Chan, K. 2006. *Higher Education and Economic Development in Africa.* Vol. 202. Washington, DC: World Bank.

Bosworth, B., Collins, S. M. and Chen, Y. 1995. Accounting for Differences in Economic Growth. *Brookings Discussion Papers in International Economics,* No. 115, pp. 1–63.

Bush, T. 1999. Journaling and the Teaching of Spirituality. *Nurse Education Today,* 19(1): 20–28.

Busia, K. A. 1964. *Purposeful Education for Africa.* London: Mouton.

Business Action for Africa. 2014. Business Partnerships for Development in Africa: Redrawing the Boundaries of Possibility. Available at www.acadfacility.org/down loads/news/2010/2010_article_businesspartnerships.pdf. Accessed January 2017.

Business Action for Africa. 2016. Christian Spano: Enterprise Development – 25 Years Empowering Social Visionaries. Available at http://community.business fightspoverty.org/profiles/blogs/christian-spano-enterprise-development-25-yea rs-empowering-social. Accessed January 2017.

Cohn, E. and Geske, T. G. 1990. *The Economics of Education*. Pergamon: Oxford.

Commission for Africa Report. 2005. *Our Common Interest*. London: Office of the Prime Minister.

Crossman, J. 2003. Secular Spiritual Development in Education from International and Global Perspectives. *Oxford Review of Education*, 29(4): 503–520.

Damane, M. B. 2001. Executive Commentary. *Academy of Management Executive*, 15(3): 34.

Datt, G. and Ravallion, M. 2002. Is India's Economic Growth Leaving the Poor Behind? *The Journal of Economic Perspectives*, 16(3): 89–108.

Dei, G. J. 2002. Spirituality in African Education: Issues, Contentions and Contestations from a Ghanaian Case Study. *International Journal of Children's Spirituality*, 7(1): 37–56.

Deininger, K. and Squire, L. 1996. A New Data Set Measuring Income Inequality. *World Bank Economic Review*, 10(3): 565–591.

Dempster, E. R. and Hugo, W. 2006. Introducing the Concept of Evolution into South African Schools. *South African Journal of Science*, 102 (3-4): 106–112.

Ekeh, P. P. 1975. Colonialism and the Two Publics in Africa: A Theoretical Statement. *Comparative Studies in Society and History*, 17(1): 91–112.

Elster, J. 1983. *Sour Grapes: Studies in the Subversion of Rationality*. Cambridge: Cambridge University Press.

Fafchamps, M. 1992. Solidarity Networks in Preindustrial Societies: Rational Peasants with a Moral Economy. *Economic Development and Cultural Change*, 41(1): 147–174.

Fafunwa, A. B. and Aisiku, J. U. 1982. *Education in Africa: A Comparative Survey*. London: George Allen & Unwin.

Fisher, I. 1906. *The Nature of Capital and Income*. London: The Macmillan Company:

Fitzsimons, P. 2015. Human Capital Theory and Education. In *Encyclopaedia of Educational Philosophy and Theory*. Edited by M. A. Peters, 1–4. Singapore: Springer Science Business Media.

Freidman, M. 1962. *Capitalism and Freedom*. Chicago: University of Chicago Press.

Frimer, J. A., Walker, L. J., Dunlop, W. L., Lee, B. H. and Riches, A. 2011. The Integration of Agency and Communion in Moral Personality: Evidence of Enlightened Self-Interest. *Journal of Personality and Social Psychology*, 101(1): m149.

Fukuyama, F. 1992. *The End of History and the Last Man*. London: Hamish Hamilton.

Goleman, D. 2006. *Working with Emotional Intelligence*. New York: Bantam, Dell.

Goleman, D. 1996. *Emotional Intelligence: Why It Matters More than IQ.* New edn. New York, NY: Bloomsbury Publishing plc.

Gyekye, K. 1996. *The Unexamined Life: Philosophy and the African Experience.* Accra: Sankofa.

Gyimah-Brempong, K. 2002. Corruption, Economic Growth, and Income Inequality in Africa. *Economics of Governance,* 3(3): 183–209.

Gylfason, T. 2001. Natural Resources, Education, and Economic Development. *European Economic Review,* 45(4): 847–859.

Haan, H. C. 2006a. Training for Work in the Informal Micro-Enterprise Sector: Fresh Evidence from Sub-Saharan Africa. Dordrecht, Netherlands: Springer.

Haan, H. C. 2006b. *Training for Work in the Informal Micro-Enterprise Sector: Fresh Evidence from Sub-Sahara Africa.* Vol. 3. New York, NY: Springer Science & Business Media.

Hall, P. A. and Soskice, D. 2003. Varieties of Capitalism and Institutional Complementarities. In *Institutional Conflicts and Complementarities.* Edited by R. Franzese, P. Mooslechner and M. Schiirz, 43–76. Cambridge: Springer US.

Haan, H. C. 2006. *Training for Work in the Informal Micro-Enterprise Sector: Fresh Evidence from Sub-Sahara Africa.* Vol. III. New York, NY: Springer Science & Business Media.

Hodge, D. R. and Derezotes, D. S. 2008. Postmodernism and Spirituality: Some Pedagogical Implications for Teaching Content on Spirituality. *Journal of Social Work Education,* 44(1): 103–124.

Hope, K. R. 1997. *African Political Economy: Contemporary Issues in Development.* London: M. E. Sharpe.

ILO. 2012. *Start and Improve Your Business – Global Tracer Study 2011.* Geneva.

ILO. 2014. *Start and Improve Your Business: Implementation Guide.* Available at www.ilo.org/wcmsp5/groups/public/–ed_emp/–emp_ent/–ifp_seed/documents/publication/wcms_315262.pdf. Accessed October 2016.

Jansen, J. D. 1998. Curriculum Reform in South Africa: A Critical Analysis of Outcomes-Based Education. *Cambridge Journal of Education,* 28(3): 321–331.

July, R. W. 2004. *The Origins of Modern African Thought: Its Development in West Africa During the Nineteenth and Twentieth Centuries.* Trenton, NJ: Africa World Press.

Kamoche, K. 2011. Contemporary Developments in the Management of Human Resources in Africa. *Journal of World Business,* 46(1): 1–4.

Kamoche, K. and Harvey, M. 2006. Knowledge Diffusion in the African Context: An Institutional Theory Perspective. *Thunderbird International Business Review,* 48: 157–181.

King, K. and McGrath, S. 2002. *Globalisation, Enterprise and Knowledge: Education, Training and Development in Africa.* Oxford, UK: Symposium Books Ltd.

Kraus, J. 2002. Capital, Power and Business Associations in the African Political Economy: A Tale of Two Countries, Ghana and Nigeria. *Journal of Modern African Studies*, 40(3): 395–436.

Lumpkin, G. T. and Dess, G. G. 1996. Clarifying the Entrepreneurial Orientation Construct and Linking It to Performance. *Academy of Management Review*, 21 (1): 135–172.

Lundvall, B. Å. and Foray, D. 1996. The Knowledge-Based Economy. In *Employment and Growth in the Knowledge-Based Economy.* Edited by B. A. Lundvall and D. Foray, 115–121. Paris: OECD.

Lutz, D. W. 2009. African Ubuntu Philosophy and Global Management. *Journal of Business Ethics*, 84: 313–328.

Makhudu, N. 1993. Cultivating a Climate of Co-operation through Ubuntu. *Enterprise Magazine*, 48: 40–42.

Mamman, A., Kanu, A. M., Alharbi, A. and Baydoun, N. 2015. *Small and Medium-Sized Enterprises (SMEs) and Poverty Reduction in Africa: Strategic Management Perspective.* Newcastle, UK: Cambridge Scholars Publishing.

Mamman, A. and Zakaria, H. 2016. Spirituality and Ubuntu as Foundation for Building African Institutions, Organizations and Leaders. *Journal of Management, Spirituality and Religion*, 13(3): 246–265.

Mamman, A., Zakaria, H. and Agbebi, M. 2017 in press. Training Entrepreneurs and Policy Makers for Poverty Reduction in Africa: Spirituality in Business Perspective. Edited by J. N. Bowale, F. Hossain, A. Ghalib, C. J. Rees and A. Mamman, *Development Management: Theory and Practice.* Abingdon, Oxford: Routledge: 101–115.

Mangaliso, M. P. 2001, Building Competitive Advantage from Ubuntu: Management Lessons from South Africa. *Academy of Management Executive*, 15(3): 23–33.

Marshall, A. 1948. *Principles of Economics.* 8th edn. New York: Macmillan.

Massari, L. 2011. Teaching Emotional Intelligence. *Leadership*, 40(5): 8–12.

Mayer, J. D. and Cobb, C. D. 2000. Educational Policy on Emotional Intelligence: Does It Make Sense? *Educational Psychology Review*, 12(2): 163–183.

Mazrui, A. A. 1978. *Political Values and the Educated Class in Africa.* Berkeley, CA: University of California Press.

Mbaku, J. M. 2004. *Institutions and Development in Africa.* Trenton, NJ: Africa World Press Inc.

Mbigi, L. 1997. Ubuntu: *The African Dream in Management, Knowledge Resources*. Johannesburg: Randburg.

Mbigi, L. 2002. The Spirit of African Leadership: A Comparative African Perspective. *Journal of Convergence*, 3(4): 18–23.

Mbigi, L. and Maree, J. 2005. *Ubuntu: The Spirit of African Transformation Management*. Knowres, Randburg: South Africa.

Mbiti, J. S. 1991. *African Religions and Philosophy*. 2nd edn. Portsmouth: NH: Heinemann.

McGrath, S. 2011. Where to Now for Vocational Education and Training in Africa? *International Journal of Training Research*, 9(1–2): 35–48.

McGrew, A. 2000. Sustainable Globalisation? The Global Politics of Development and Exclusion in the New World Order. In *Poverty and Development into the 21st Century*. Edited by T. Allen and A. Thomas, 345–364. New York: Oxford University Press Inc.

Metz, T. 2007. Toward an African Moral Theory. *Journal of Political Philosophy*, 15 (3): 331–334.

Mill, J. S. 1926. *Principles of Political Economy, with Some of Their Applications to Social Philosophy*. Edited by W. J. Ashley. New York: Longmans, Green and Company.

Mincer, J. 1958. Investment in Human Capital and Personal Income Distribution. *Journal of Political Economy*, 66(4): 281–302.

Minnis, J. R. 2006. Nonformal Education and Informal Economies in Sub-Saharan Africa: Finding the Right Match. *Adult Education Quarterly*, 56(2): 119–133.

Mitchell, M. and Hall, J. 2007. Teaching Spirituality to Student Midwives: A Creative Approach. *Nurse Education in Practice*, 7(6): 416–424.

Mungazi, D. A. 1982. *The Underdevelopment of African Education*. Washington, DC: University Press of America.

Mungazi, D. A. 1996. *The Mind of Black Africa*. London: Praeger.

Newenham-Kahindi, A., Kamoche, K., Chizema, A. and Mellahi, K. 2013. *Effective People Management in Africa*. Houndmills, Basingstoke: Palgrave Macmillan.

Nkondo, G. M. 2007. *Ubuntu* as Public Policy in South Africa: A Conceptual Framework. *International Journal of African Renaissance Studies*, 2: 88–100.

Noorbakhsh, F., Paloni, A. and Youssef, A. 2001. Human Capital Development and FDI in Developing Countries: New Empirical Evidence. *World Development*, 29(9): 1593–1610.

Nussbaum, B. 2003. African Culture and *Ubuntu*: Reflections of a South African in America. *Perspectives*, 17(1): 1–12.

Nyberg, A. J., Moliterno, T. P., Hale, D. and Lepak, D. P. 2014. Resource-Based Perspectives on Unit-Level Human Capital: A Review and Integration. *Journal of Management*, 40(1): 316–346.

Nziramasanga, T. 1999. *Report of the Presidential Commission of Inquiry into Education and Training*. Harare: CDU.

Obanya, P. 1999. *The Dilemma of Education in Africa*. Paris: UNESCO Regional Office.

Ohmae, K. 2000. The End of the Nation State. In *Globalization: The Reader*. Edited by John Beynon and David Dunkerley, 238–241. London: Athlone Press.

Oketch, M. O. 2007. To Vocationalise or Not to Vocationalise? Perspectives on Current Trends and Issues in Technical and Vocational Education and Training (TVET) in Africa. *International Journal of Educational Development*, 27(2): 220–234.

Omolewa, M. 2007. Traditional African Modes of Education: Their Relevance in the Modern World. *International Review of Education*, 53(5): 593–612.

Parsons, T. 1971. *The System of Modern Societies*. Englewood Cliffs, NJ: Prentice-Hall.

Persson, T. and Tabellini, G. 1994. Is Inequality Harmful for Growth? *The American Economic Review*, 84: 600–621.

Ployhart, R. E. and Moliterno, T. P. 2011. Emergence of the Human Capital Resource: A Multilevel Model. *Academy of Management Review*, 36(1): 127–150.

Ployhart, R. E., Weekley, J. A. and Ramsey, J. 2009. The Consequences of Human Resource Stocks and Flows: A Longitudinal Examination of Unit Service Orientation and Unit Effectiveness. *Academy of Management Journal*, 52(5): 996–1015.

Pritchett, L. 1996. Where Has All the Education Gone? World Bank Policy Research Working Paper No. 1581. Washington, DC.

Rwomire, A. 1998. Education and Development: African Perspectives. In *Education and Development in Africa*. Edited by J. Nwomonoh, 3–23. San Francisco: International Scholars Publications.

Salehyan, I., Hendrix, C. S., Hamner, J., Case, C., Linebarger, C., Stull, E. and Williams, J. 2012. Social Conflict in Africa: A New Database. *International Interactions*, 38(4): 503–511.

Scherer, M. 1997. Perspectives: Heart Start. *Educational Leader*, 54: 5.

Sibanda, P. 2014. The Dimensions of Huntu/Ubuntu (Humanism in the African Sense): The Zimbabwean Conception. *IOSR Journal of Engineering*, 4(1): 26–29.

Smith, A. 1952. An Inquiry into the Nature and Causes of Wealth of Nations. In *Great Books of Western World*. Vol. 10. Edited by R. M. Hutchins and M. J. Adler. New York: Encyclopedia Britannica.

Zohar, D. 2005. Spiritually Intelligent Leadership. *Leader to Leader*, 38: 45–51.

Zohar, D. and Marshall, I. 1994. *Quantum Society: Mind, Physics and a New Social Vision*. New York, NY: William Morris and Company.

Zohar, D. and Marshall, I. 2000. *SQ: Spiritual Intelligence, the Ultimate Intelligence*. New York, NY: Bloomsbury Press.

6 Africapitalism and Corporate Branding

Olutayo Otubanjo

INTRODUCTION

The role of business in sustainable development, which is at the heart of the Africapitalism agenda, is often expressed as Corporate Social Responsibility (CSR). In emerging markets and more importantly in Africa, CSR has in recent times generated immense interest (Chetty et al., 2015; Idemudia, 2014). A number of articles which address this subject in the African context (see Amaeshi et al., 2016; Raimi et al., 2015) provide evidence in this regard. The rationale for the rise in interest in CSR, particularly in Africa, can be traced to numerous scandalous events involving national and multinational organisations. Some of these scandals include the Shell Ogoni crisis (Pegg, 2015), which led to the execution of Ken Saro Wiwa; Pfizer's testing of 'Trovan', an experimental antibiotic that was tested in the northern part of Nigeria leading to the death of eleven children (Rogers, 2009); the collapse of numerous financial institutions in Nigeria triggered by poor governance structures (Nworji et al., 2011) as well as prevailing institutional corruption which continues to cripple the effectiveness of public and private-sector organisations. Other reasons include a better understanding, by multinational and national business organisations, of the impact of business on the environment, buoyed by change in the social attitude of these organisations towards the philosophy of sustainability, which has spawned a measure of media awareness and concern for ecological issues. Arguably, there is now a small but growing concern and belief among African business organisations about activities that threaten environmental sustainability, much of which manifest in positive attitudes against anti-sustainability activities in the media. The interest in CSR in Africa has led to the commitment of vast financial, human and material resources to good causes. For instance, Etisalat Nigeria devoted over US$500 million, between 2007 and 2012, to the training of business managers across various sectors (CSR Watch International Nigeria, 2012). In Ghana, it was reported that Gold Fields, the largest gold producer in Ghana, committed funds in excess of US$1 million yearly to social investment in education, health and income enhancement within its community of operation (Forstater, 2010). Similarly in South Africa, The Eskom Development Foundation, a CSR initiative of Eskom, a power-generation company, has delivered primary mobile health care to thousands of people living in rural communities with little access to health care facilities (Bizcommunity, 2016).

Just as CSR has attracted interest in Africa and emerging markets, so has corporate branding (Otubanjo et al., 2010, 2015). The swell in the volume of articles contributing to this subject from an African point of view (see Sandada and Finch, 2015; Ade-Johnson et al., 2015; Adiele and Opara, 2014; Mburu et al., 2013) provides evidence to substantiate this viewpoint. This can be explained by a number of factors including increased desire for differentiation in the aftermath of a numerous consolidation exercises (Yang, Davis and Robertson, 2012) in Africa; the redefinition of public-sector organisations from a marketing perspective (see Kaplan and Haenlein, 2009); the reorientation of organisations towards customer service (Skålén and Strandvik, 2005; Wilson, Zeithaml, Bitner and Gremler, 2012); the increased recognition of the value of marketing communications (Hill, 2015); the intensity of the coverage of corporate scandals in the press and electronic media (Bernile, Sulaeman and Wang, 2015); a better understanding of the role of branding as a tool that helps to weather-proof organisations from economic recession (Wilson, 2015); the increased value placed on corporate brand image development in the aftermath of privatisation and commercialisation exercises (see Herstein, Mitki and Jaffe, 2008); the strategy-induced factor of the influence of market globalisation on corporate branding

(Torelli, 2013); the impact of stiffer competition for markets and talents (Pillai, 2012); and the increased desire for transformation and change (Conroy, 2007). Interest in corporate branding in Africa equally suggests that huge financial resources have been committed to the development of this concept, especially among corporations head-quartered in this continent. For instance, in the aftermath of the recapitalisation exercise in the Nigerian banking sector, GT Bank was estimated to have spent about US$5 in its rebranding exercise over an eighteen-month period (Maklan, Knox and Michel, 2009). Nigeria's financial sector devoted the sum of N5.8 billion (US $18.4 million) to corporate communications, of which a significant proportion of this was for corporate branding (Financial Nigeria, 2016).

Put together, the rise in interest in CSR and corporate branding is also driven by a common desire to create positive corporate image or reputation, achieve corporate differentiation and establish market recognition. Essentially, these unifying benefits ultimately created the rationale behind the integration of both concepts into a cohesive discipline – CSR branding.

CSR branding has been defined as a phenomenon reflective of how organisations integrate shared corporate and societal values into their core competencies to address issues in societies (McCormick, 2012; Polonsky and Jevons, 2006). It is a strategy for seeking credibility (Uhrich, Koenigstorfer and Groeppel-Klein, 2014); improving finan-cial performance (Lai et al., 2010; Johnson, 2003; Miles and Covin, 2000); connecting with consumers (Porter and Kramer, 2002); raising the level of product quality (Montillaud-Joyel and Otto, 2004) as well as increasing the level of employee commitment (Dawkins and Lewis 2003; Maio 2003) to organisations. CSR branding is conceived today as being essential for developing brand values and personality (Lindgreen et al., 2012; Kitchen, 2003) as well as differentiating products and services within highly competitive markets (Johnson, 2003).

Contributions to this field of study have led to the development of a variety of conceptual models (Polonsky and Jevons, 2006, 2009;

Brüggenwirth, 2006; Vallaster, Lindgreen and Maon, 2012) and other practitioner initiatives such as 'Microsoft 4 Afrika' initiative (Knutsen, 2013). These models give insight into how CSR brands evolve. Consequently, this chapter builds on existing models by offering another model that further takes into account the unique challenges that businesses in African countries face.

The paper proposes the 'Africapitalism' brand as an approach to 'CSR branding', which is geared towards addressing Africa's socio-economic challenges. Put another way, this approach gives insight into how corporate brands domiciled in Africa can be built on the spine of Africapitalism (Elumelu, 2012), a philosophy that emphasises the private sector's commitment to economic transformation of Africa (Amaeshi and Idemudia, 2015).

This chapter is divided into five sections. It begins with the review of literature concerning the meaning and benefits of CSR and CSR branding and underscores the challenges of adapting and implementing CSR branding models in Africa. The chapter continues with an examination of what Amaeshi and Idemudia's (2015) pillars of Africapitalism mean for corporate branding and presents the Africapitalism brand framework in the following section. The chapter ends with a summary of finding together with their implications for theory and practice.

REVIEW OF LITERATURE

CSR and CSR Branding: Meaning and Benefits

Crane, Matten and Spence (2013) observed that over a thousand articles and reports have been contributed by academics, corporations, the media, NGOs and successive government towards the subject of CSR, leading to similarities and divergences in viewpoints on the meaning of the subject. Dahlsrud (2008) tried to make sense of these definitions by theorising the meaning of the concept of CSR along five conceptual dimensions: namely, (i) voluntary, (ii) stakeholder, (iii) societal, (iv) environment and (v) economic. While the voluntary nature of the concept underscores actions undertaken by business organisations that extend beyond the framework of legal obligations prescribed by law, the stakeholder dimension exemplifies how business organisations interact with employees, suppliers, customers and communities. The societal dimension of CSR promotes the integration of societal concerns with business operations, and the environmental dimension lays emphasis on the inculcation of environmental concerns in the operations of business organisations. The economic dimension champions organisational contribution to economic development and the preservation of profitability. Importantly, the variety of ways in which this concept has been defined underscores the confusion that permeates it (Crane, Matten and Spence, 2013; Lindgreen and Swaen, 2010). Nevertheless, these viewpoints help us to understand the concept of CSR.

The pursuit of CSR holds a variety of benefits for business organisations that engage in it. For instance, Du, Bhattacharya and Sen (2007) argued that by engaging in CSR, business organisations can foster loyalty across markets and turn consumers into brand ambassadors. Rahim et al. (2011) suggest that business organisations that engage in CSR activities enjoy a measure of visibility – thus enhancing the promotion of their public image (Dartey-Baah and Amponsah-Tawiah, 2011) and corporate reputation which is critical for value creation (Amaeshi and Adi, 2007). The support given to the practice of CSR heightens the profile of an organisation in the marketplace and impacts positively on consumer awareness and brand recognition (Sheikh and Beise-Zee, 2011). Ramasamy and Yeung (2009) believe that CSR increases consumer patronage in emerging markets and that it makes business organisations become more prominent and better perceived. More importantly, when viewed as a dynamic resource within Barney's (1991) resource-based view concept, CSR provides a framework for decision-making on how best to deploy resources (Taghian, 2008) whenever business organisations are responding to the demand of sustainability and environmental protection.

In practice, the benefits of CSR within the corporate marketing space manifest through the integration of 'shared values' of the organisation and the society to ensure that business gains are made and social needs are met (McCormick, 2012; Polonsky and Jevons, 2006). The result of this integration which is seen as 'business gain' is reflective of business value.

This view of CSR brand is strengthened in the work of Girod and Michael (2003), where it was argued that a CSR brand evolves through voluntary activities aimed at showing support to publics and the environment. Girod and Michael (2003) presented the business value aspect of the definition by arguing further that when a CSR brand activity is undertaken, consumers give such brands preference over generic brands. CSR branding is a viable means through which a brand can maximize its investments (Girod and Michael, 2003). This exemplifies the business value position. Similarly, Blumenthal and Bergstrom (2003) offered a business value perspective by contending that CSR investments are necessities that must be leveraged. Kotler's (1997) definition of CSR brand, which advocates the integration of the activities of organisations with the social well-being of people in societies as a way of differentiating products from those of competitors equally exemplifies this view.

Lindgreen, Xu, Maon and Wilcock (2012), making reference to Kotler (1997), presented a two-part definition which positioned CSR brand as both a societal and business value phenomenon. For Lindgreen et al. (2012), a CSR brand is defined as 'being a stakeholder-based, strategically integrated orientation toward ecological and social well-being; at the heart of CSR brands lies a socially responsible dimension intended to differentiate a firm's products or services from those of competitors'. This presents a societal angle to the definition given its focus on the social well-being of all people. More importantly, it creates a pathway for developing shared values within societies. Lindgreen et al. (2012) argued further that at the heart of CSR brands lies a socially responsible dimension intended to differentiate a firm's products or services from those of its competitors. This part represents the business value part as it brings into prominence the notion of differentiation, which is the benefit that business organisations obtain by pursuing CSR branding activities. Du, Bhattacharya and Sen (2007) put forward a societal view devoid of business value by avowing that a CSR brand evolves when firms 'go beyond just engaging in CSR to position themselves wholly in terms of CSR, becoming known as the socially responsible brand [i.e., the CSR brand] in a category'. Suprawan (2011), on the other hand, articulated a business value. He observed that CSR brand evolves from the process of gaining reputational benefits and performance when CSR is incorporated as an integral component of the corporate brand, provided that the brand is perceived as authentic and truly representative of the organisation's actual identity.

A few models and frameworks have been put forward in the literature to explicate how business organisations operating across a variety of industries become responsible in the marketplace. These include the Polonski and Jevons (2006, 2009) complexity issue model, the Brüggenwirth (2006) brand positioning grid, the Vallaster, Lindgreen and Maon (2012) strategic CSR brand framework and the Lindgreen et al.'s (2012) four CSR brand model. These are summarised in Table 6.1.

Business organisations that undertake CSR branding benefit from a variety of opportunities. These include the creation of trust and market credibility among customers (Uhrich, Koenigstorfer and Groeppel-Klein, 2014); improved financial performance (Lai et al., 2010; Johnson, 2003; Miles and Covin, 2000); better and stronger relations with consumers (Porter and Kramer, 2002) and other stakeholders; rise in the level of perceived service cum product quality (Montillaud-Joyel and Otto, 2004); increased employee commitment to the organisation (Dawkins and Lewis, 2003; Maio, 2003); stronger brand values and personality (Lindgreen et al., 2012; Kitchen, 2003) and better and more effective brand differentiation across markets (Johnson, 2003).

TABLE 6.1 *Summary of CSR branding models*

Model	Core elements	Managerial applications/ strengths	Weaknesses
Polonski and Jevons (2006, 2009) complexity issue model	(i) Issues to include in a CSR policy; (2) scope of CSR issues; (3) standards to measure performance; (4) the determination of when performance is in fact responsible	The four components of issue complexity help brand managers to integrate CSR into branding. Poor understanding of these issues may lead to exaggerated claims, which may damage a firm's reputation. The model highlights the complexities of stakeholder expectations, which are often not given enough attention in literature. The model gives insight into how the varieties of issue complexity enhances the integration of CSR into corporate brands.	Model does not capture the demand for organisational and deep commitment to the economic development of the country in which it operates.
Brüggenwirth (2006) brand positioning grid	(i) Defining the importance of CSR in brand positioning; (ii)	Model is used for monitoring, evaluating, repositioning	Model is focused mostly on self-promotion of the firm

TABLE 6.1 (*cont.*)

Model	Core elements	Managerial applications/ strengths	Weaknesses
	exploring CSR opportunities to support the brand positioning; (iii) developing campaigns to express the CSR of a brand	brands and analyzsing competitors. It is used to establish a scope for communicating CSR and offers insight into ways of creating a distinct brand. The grid helps to define the right CSR activity to undertake; it helps in decisions concerning how explicitly or implicitly CSR should be expressed and what the relationship with other brand values should be; it helps organisations to differentiate.	and does not accommodate the welfare and social well-being of stakeholders.
	(i) CSR entrepreneurs; (ii) Quietly	Framework can be applied to develop appropriate CSR	The four elements of strategic CSR framework do

TABLE 6.1 (*cont.*)

Model	Core elements	Managerial applications/ strengths	Weaknesses
Vallaster, Lindgreen, and Maon (2012) strategic approach to CSR framework	Conscientious; (iii) CSR Performers; (iv) vocal CSR converts	brand management programmes that reduce tension between organisations and stakeholders. The model adds value to the extant literature not only corporate social responsibility, but also – via its theoretical lenses – ethical identity and corporate branding. The model gives insight into the variety of approaches. The four elements of the strategic CSR framework can help organisations to act in the right way as new CSR issues and challenges evolve.	not recognise that wealth generated by business organisations often end up in the hands of a few at the expense of the community. As such it does not promote equitable distribution of wealth and financial profitability.

Source: Developed by author.

The Challenge of Adapting and Implementing CSR Branding Models in Africa

CSR branding models are often designed by business organisations to ride on well-articulated corporate strategies, which unfortunately are susceptible to unexpected changes in volatile and unpredictable business environments. Consequently, whenever a corporate strategy changes, the CSR branding initiatives change as well. As such, it may be safe to argue that the CSR branding activities by firms build largely on the philanthropic activities of these firms, which is a dominant framing of CSR (Amaeshi et al., 2006; Visser, 2008) and are designed to alleviate the impact of their activities on host communities (Amaeshi et al., 2006). Although these philanthropic activities in the short run are perceived by host communities as helpful, they are often ineffective and unsustainable in addressing the economic realities of these communities (Amaeshi et al., 2006; Idemudia, 2014) in the long run.

From the foregoing, the pursuit of CSR branding initiatives in Africa, especially by firms that follow existing CSR models, appears to lack a strategic, long-term and sustainable approach to the economic development of host communities. In order to effect a change, an Africa-centric philosophy which takes full consideration of the economic challenges of Africans is helpful. Such a pro-African philosophy, which Elumelu (2012) calls Africapitalism, has been fully enumerated in Amaeshi and Idemudia's (2015) seminal thesis on the subject.

Africapitalism is a management concept that seeks to entrench pro-development values into business operations across the continent. It seeks to engage private organisations as major actors in the socio-economic development of the continent and aims to address ills caused by weak institutions. Arguably, Africapitalism serves as a response to the capitalist philosophy, which largely dominates today's world. It takes a cue from the dominant understanding of capitalism in the West and seeks to create a customised approach to conducting business activities and processes within Africa and

beyond. Africapitalism seeks to promote the good of both organisations and the communities in which they operate. This implies that
a win-win outcome will be achieved through the adoption of this
management idea. Africapitalism is therefore a concept which is
aimed at transforming the status quo in business-society relationships
from a development perspective. Generally speaking, the concept
seeks to change the perspective adopted by firms in conducting business in Africa. For Amaeshi and Idemudia (2015), the Africapitalism
philosophy promotes the involvement of Africans in the development
of their continent and therefore encourages economic patriotism.
Africapitalism seeks to modify how business is currently conducted
by proposing a practice that encourages among other things the need
for Africans to do business with Africans in Africa. Africapitalism is
rooted in the values of Ubuntu (Kayuni and Tambulasi, 2012) which
seeks communal good.

TABLE 6.2 *Summary of the pillars of Africapitalism*

Pillars of Africapitalism	Highlights
Sense of progress and prosperity	Business organisations must create or support access to education, good quality health systems, social capital, democratic institutions, etc., all of which make life worth living (Brundtland, 1994).
Sense of parity	Financial profitability may end up in the hands of a few at the expense of the community. Therefore all stakeholders including customer and suppliers must enjoy social wealth & profits equitably.
Sense of peace and harmony	Liberal capitalism often results in socio-environmental imbalance. Therefore business organisations must balance the impact of consumption and production on the environment.
Sense of place and belongingness	This is the expression of patriotism to one's country; and the display of pride in it. It is about giving preference to its needs and interests over other countries.

Source: Developed by author.

In order to apply this management paradigm to understanding corporate branding in Africa, I follow Amaeshi and Idemudia's (2015) seminal text on Africapitalism, published in the *Africa Journal of Management*. In it, Amaeshi and Idemudia (2015) presented Africapitalism along the lines of four pillars, summarised in Table 6.2.

WHAT CAN THE PILLARS OF AFRICAPITALISM MEAN FOR CORPORATE BRANDING?

The sense of progress and prosperity arguably evolves through a combined effort of social wealth and financial profitability. It extends beyond the idea of materialism into the domain of psycho-social human well-being (Amaeshi et al., 2006). As such, Africapitalism promotes progressive conditions such as access to decent education, good quality health systems, social capital, democratic institutions, sustainability, etc., all of which make life worth living (Brundtland, 1994). The sense of progress and prosperity pillar manifests in corporate branding through corporate advocacy advertising, which is defined as a tool that is used in influencing political, economic or social action in favour of a campaign sponsor, cause or society (Lee, Haley and Yang, 2013). Access Bank Plc, one of Nigeria's leading financial institutions, has, in part, built its corporate brand by publishing a variety of corporate advocacy advertisements that capture its sensitivity to the sense of progress and prosperity. For instance, Figure 6.1 demonstrates Access Bank's concern for the conservation of animals and the environment. This campaign, which is reflective of Access's concern for the planet Earth, imbues it with a green corporate brand identity and image.

The sense of parity promotes the equitable distribution of social wealth and financial profits among stakeholders. Beyond that, it can also be interpreted to include creating opportunities for self and others in the marketplace. It is another way of making 'the cake' larger for all. Therefore, rather than committing huge resources to the development of corporate brand for self-benefit only, major business organisations may commit the same resources to the joint development of their

FIGURE 6.1: Access Bank's environmental protection campaign
Source: www.facebook.com/AccessBankPlc/photos/a.1477449085812752
.1073741828.1471004623123865/2102138510010470/?type=3&theater.

corporate brands and those of suppliers through a 'corporate co-branding' exercise. Corporate co-branding is a system of partnership between a major corporate brand and other corporate, product or service brands to establish a corporate co-branded identity (Tsiotsou, Alexandris and Bettina Cornwell, 2014) that all actors that pursue this exercise jointly can benefit from. Corporate co-branding is a form of strategic alliance that enables parties that have purposely decided to promote their brands jointly to grow as well as reinforce their corporate brand values collaboratively without diminishing their corporate brand equity (McDonald et al., 2001; Motion et al., 2003). The case of Oando Oil Marketing Ltd and Big Treat Confectionaries Plc provides an example of corporate co-branding. Oando is one of Nigeria's leading oil retailers while Big Treat is a bakery and confectionary company. Big Treat benefited from the social wealth already created by Oando by delivering its confectionery across fifty-eight of Oando's 500 service stations. Additionally, this enabled Big Treat to expand its distribution across Nigeria and gain greater market visibility. This also made Oando service stations a one-stop shop for consumables (Oando, 2008). Importantly, this co-branding exercise extends brand visibility and brand reach, brings down the cost of marketing and communications and enhances credibility for both organisations.

The sense of peace and harmony calls on business organisations to reverse the ills of capitalism by developing a strong desire to balance the impacts of consumption and production on the ecology, environment, society and economy. This position is similar to the concept of corporate green branding or corporate green brand identity, which is defined by a specific set of attributes and benefits related to activities undertaken by business organisations to reduce the environmental impact of the corporate brand on the society (Hartmann, Apaolaza Ibáñez and Forcada Sainz, 2005). Corporate green brands are becoming more attractive to consumers, and commitment to corporate green branding is becoming an important business practice that is likely to become central to all competitive activities. Consequently, there is a growing demand for the protection of the environment through the delivery of green products (Iannuzzi, 2011). Shoprite, one of Africa's largest retail store brands, pursues the sense of peace and harmony philosophy or what is here considered as green branding by promoting a sustainable consumption policy coded around the reduction, reuse and recycle of grocery bags. In Figure 6.2, the 'ShopRite customers are eco-superstars!' advertising campaign gives graphic details of its green branding policy.

Essentially, the ShopRite policy provides customers the opportunity to make a choice to carry groceries in paper, plastic or reusable

FIGURE 6.2: Sustainability campaign
Source: www.shoprite.com/the-environment/.

'canvas' as a way of reducing not only the volume of bags trashed and sent to the landfills but also the resources needed to create new bags. ShopRite also makes the recycling of plastic bags easy by providing recycling bins at the front of every store (Shoprite, 2016).

The 'reduce, reuse, recycle' policy gives ShopRite a powerful voice on issues relating to sustainability; and provides a platform to further engage customers and other stakeholders, thus making the ShopRite brand strategically visible. More importantly, the 'reduce, reuse, recycle' policy associates and personifies the ShopRite brand with environmental conservation and contributes remarkably to corporate image building and differentiation. This is achieved through corporate communications involving new and traditional media of corporate communications including the Internet, newspaper, TV and radio advertisements.

The sense of place and belongingness challenges globalised capitalism, which gives greater priority to place; it promotes greatly the value of sense of place and rootedness and champions, by no small means, the restoration of the link between place and economics on one hand and the connection between place and self-identity on the other. The sense of place and belongingness manifests as an expression of patriotism, which Amaeshi and Idemudia (2015), quoting Clift and Woll (2012: 314), say is attributable to 'an intrinsic moral value to the defence of the homeland, even if it does not specify its boundaries'. Stating further and making reference to Audi (2009: 367–368), Amaeshi and Idemudia (2015) contend that the sense of place and belongingness 'entails a significant degree of loyalty to one's country and an associated disposition to take pride in it, to be subject to emotions closely connected with one's perception of its well-being, and to give some degree of preference to its needs and interests over the needs and interests of other countries'. The principle of loyalty, discussed under this pillar, can learn a few things from the practice of corporate brand loyalty (Brown, 1952), which is defined as the purchase of a favourite brand time after time (Brown, 1952). More recently, Lam and Shankar (2014) quoting Oliver (1999: 34) defined brand loyalty as 'a deeply held commitment to rebuy or repatronise a preferred product/service consistently in the future, thereby causing repetitive same-brand or same brand-set purchasing, despite situational influences and marketing efforts having the potential to cause switching behaviour'. Following this viewpoint, corporate brand loyalty could be defined as positive impressions held in the minds of customers; that are capable of influencing repeated purchase of an organisation's service over a long period of time even in the face of escalating competitive pressures. Brand loyalty to Africa, in the context of this pillar, manifests when organisations exhibit total devotion and commitment to the use of the best human and material resources available within an organisation's country or region of operation. The case of Andela, a technology talent-recruitment firm, breathes life into this concept. On its website, Andela prioritises African talents for African organisations. This strategy is to give Africans a chance and the opportunity in a very crowded and competitive economic landscape. The policy states: we 'select the top 1% of tech talent from the largest pool of untapped talent in the world – the African continent. Dubbed 'the start-up that's harder to get into than Harvard' by CNN, we sift through tens of thousands of applicants so you don't have to'. In Figure 6.3, a webpage on Andela's website gives details of this position. This position personifies Andela by creating an association between it and Africapitalism. It imbues Andela with an economic patriotism personality through *new and traditional media of corporate communications including the Internet, newspaper, TV, radio advertisements*. More importantly, it instils Andela with

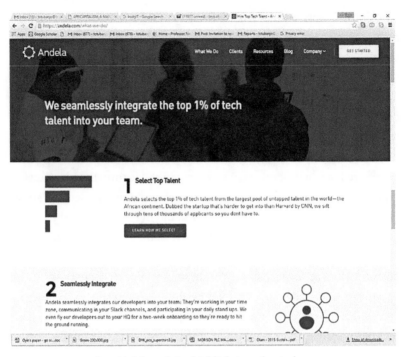

FIGURE 6.3: Andela website highlighting what it does
Source: https://andela.com/what-we-do/.

a personality that is only attributable to it – thus differentiating and giving it a competitive advantage over its competitors.

The dominant corporate branding concepts emerging from the discussion above are summarised in Table 6.3.

The relationship between the concepts of 'corporate advocacy advertising', 'corporate co-branding', 'corporate green brand' and 'corporate brand loyalty' draws from Table 6.2 and can be further articulated as a brand framework as illustrated in Figure 6.4.

THE AFRICAPITALISM BRAND FRAMEWORK

The pursuit of this framework (Figure 6.4) begins when managers make conscious effort at introducing a part or all of Amaeshi and Idemudia's (2015) pillars of Africapitalism into activities in departments across the

TABLE 6.3 *Summary of concepts emerging from the discussions*

Concepts	Highlights
Corporate advocacy advertising	This is a corporate branding tool that is generally deployed to influence political, economic or social action in favour of a sponsor, cause or society (Lee, Haley and Yang, 2013).
Corporate co-branding	This is a form of strategic alliance that enables parties that have purposely decided to promote their brands jointly to grow as well as reinforce their corporate brand values collaboratively without diminishing their corporate brand equity (McDonald et al., 2001; Motion et al., 2003).
Corporate green brand identity	This is a set of green activities undertaken by and attributable to a company to reduce environmental impact of the corporate brand on the society (Hartmann, Apaolaza Ibáñez and Forcada Sainz, 2005).
Corporate brand loyalty	Lam and Shankar (2014) quoting Oliver (1999, p. 34) defines brand loyalty as 'a deeply held commitment to rebuy or repatronise a preferred product/service consistently in the future, thereby causing repetitive same-brand or same-brand-set purchasing, despite situational influences and marketing efforts having the potential to cause switching behaviour'. Corporate brand loyalty therefore is the positive feeling about an organization, thus influencing customer dedication to repeated patronage of the organization's service over a long period of time even in the face of escalating competitive pressures.

Source: Developed by the author.

organization. These may include finance, production and logistics, marketing and sales, corporate communications, human capital management and corporate communications. The 'implication codes' for pursuing these pillars come in different brand management

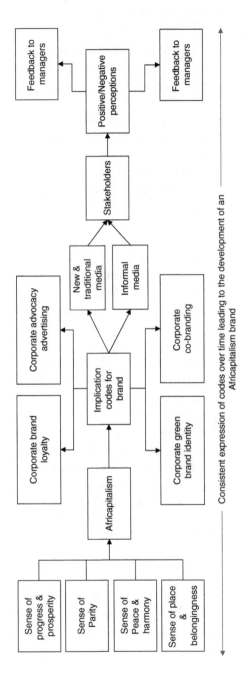

FIGURE 6.4: The Africapitalism brand development framework.
Source: Developed by the author.

ramifications. First is the pursuit of corporate advocacy advertising. This brings the 'sense of progress and prosperity' to life. Second is corporate co-branding with stakeholders such as suppliers as a way of supporting supplier growth plans. This speaks to the 'sense of parity'. Third is corporate green branding identity, which brings the 'sense of peace and harmony' to life. Fourth is corporate brand loyalty to the use of African resources. This signifies or represents the 'sense of place and belongingness'. Essentially, these activities are conveyed to a variety of stakeholders through a combination of new, traditional media and informal media of corporate communications. Informal media here refers to unplanned actions, behaviour, gestures, facial representations. These messages are interpreted by stakeholders who develop either positive or negative perceptions leading to positive or negative feed-back. The consistent expression of these pillars through corporate communications media leads eventually to the development of an Africapitalism brand.

This framework, if set in motion, can serve as a policy guideline and a system of principles for achieving rational outcomes. Moreover, this framework can function as a frame of reference for decision-making especially when addressing Africapitalism brand issues. In addition, this framework can fill possible information gaps that may evolve in the course of building the Africapitalism brand. The proposed framework explains the nature of the relationship that binds the concepts of 'corporate advocacy advertising', 'corporate co-branding', 'corporate green brand' and 'corporate brand loyalty' and provides a basis for understanding these concepts. The Africapitalism brand framework may in future support the formulation of propositions and hypothesis, which could be verified and tested to generate valuable theoretical insights.

SUMMARY AND CONCLUSION

CSR branding models are focused on complex CSR branding issues (Polonski and Jevons, 2006, 2009); positioning and repositioning of organisations (Brüggenwirth, 2006); and CSR branding strategy

(Vallaster, Lindgreen and Maon, 2012). This chapter builds on these studies by offering a framework that could further aid academic and practitioner discussions about CSR branding especially in Africa. This objective was accomplished through an examination of the implications of Africapitalism theory for corporate branding, firmly supported by an analysis of how these implications evolve into an Africapitalism brand.

Two important findings emerged from this chapter. First is an analysis of the implications of Africapitalism theory for corporate branding, achieved through an examination of the four pillars of Africapitalism within the context of four corporate branding concepts, namely 'corporate advocacy advertising', 'corporate co-branding', 'corporate green brand' and 'corporate brand loyalty'. Second is the development of the Africapitalism brand framework. The framework describes the aforementioned pillars and how these are translated into a variety of corporate branding concepts, which are in turn communicated formally and informally through the new and traditional media of corporate communications.

This chapter provides a different approach for African business organisations that wish to engage in CSR branding. More importantly, it also helps to achieve corporate differentiation, market recognition and positive image and reputation.

The implication of these contributions for practitioners is that they introduce brand managers to the unique nature of CSR branding in Africa and how it differs from existing CSR branding models. The success of a CSR branding exercise in Africa will be dependent on the ability of managers to apply and link the four pillars of Africapitalism documented in Amaeshi and Idemudia (2015) to the concepts of 'corporate advocacy advertising', 'corporate co-branding', 'corporate green brand' and 'corporate brand loyalty'. Essentially, what this means is that brand managers must ensure that sense of progress and prosperity, which focuses on the promotion of the psycho-social well-being of members of the community in which such a corporation operates, is entrenched into the company mission and policy. While managing their brands, sense of parity, which lays emphasis on the need for equality in the distribution of resources, should be put into consideration. Likewise, sense of peace and harmony, which calls on firms to promote the pursuit of business operations that promote the good of the community, should be looked into by brand managers. Similarly, brand managers need to focus on the sense of place and belonging, which hinges on 'patriotism' and calls on business organisations in Africa to be 'Africacentric'. Developing such an African-conscious attitude in decision making will have a ripple effect on the development of a brand and its reputation.

With regard to the theoretical implications, this chapter offers a different approach to the branding of 'doing good' in Africa, sets a new research direction and gives a new political economy perspective to the understanding of this discipline from an African point of view. It also helps to chart a new academic discipline and research within the framework of corporate branding and corporate-level marketing in general. Put another way, it brings to fore a framework that African researchers and academic can build on.

On a final note, this chapter is conceptual and therefore is limited by lack of empirical data that could have strengthened or refuted the arguments under the proposed framework. However, the absence of data provides opportunity to conduct further research in this area.

REFERENCES

Ade-Johnson, C. S. and Ajayi, J. O. 2014. Application of Social Media to Organisation Branding in Nigeria. *Journal of Mass Communication & Journalism*, 4(10): pp 1–4.

Adiele, K. C. and Opara, B. C. 2014. Analysis of Corporate Identity on Customer Patronage of Banks in Nigeria. *International Review of Management and Business Research*, 3(4): 1809.

Amaeshi, K. M. and Adi, B. 2007. Reconstructing the Corporate Social Responsibility Construct in Utlish. *Business Ethics: A European Review*, 16 (1): 3–18.

Amaeshi, K. M., Adi, A. B. C., Ogbechie, C. and Amao, O. O. 2006. Corporate Social Responsibility in Nigeria: Western Mimicry or Indigenous Influences? Available at SSRN 896500.

Amaeshi, K. and Idemudia, U. 2015. Africapitalism: A Management Idea for Business in Africa? *Africa Journal of Management*, 1(2): 210–223.

Audi, R. 2009. Nationalism, Patriotism, and Cosmopolitanism in an Age of Globalization. *The Journal of Ethics*, 13(4): 365–381.

Barney, J. B. 2000. Firm Resources and Sustained Competitive Advantage. *Advances in Strategic Management*, 17(1): 203–227.

Bernile, G., Sulaeman, J. and Wang, Q. 2015. Institutional Trading during a Wave of Corporate Scandals': Perfect Payday'? *Journal of Corporate Finance*, 34: 191–209.

Besharat, A. and Langan, R. 2014. Towards the Formation of Consensus in the Domain of Co-branding: Current Findings and Future Priorities. *Journal of Brand Management*, 21(2): 112–132.

Birkigt, K. K. and Stadler, M. M. 1986. Corporate Identity, Grundlagen, Functionen und Beispielen, Moderne Industrie, Landsberg an Lech. In *Principles of Corporate Communication*. Edited by C. B. M. van Riel. Harlow, UK: Pearson Education, 1995.

Biz Community. 2016. Eskom Foundation Steps Up Mobile Health Services. Available at www.bizcommunity.com/Article/196/157/149117.html. Accessed 17 October 2016.

Blumenthal, D. and Bergstrom, A. 2003. Brand Councils That Care: Towards the Convergence of Branding and Corporate Social Responsibility. *Journal of Brand Management*, 10(4): 327–341.

Brüggenwirth, B. 2006. The CSR Brand Positioning Grid. In *Management Models for Corporate Social Responsibility*. Edited by J. Jonker and M. de Witte, 140–146. Berlin, Heidelberg: Springer.

BudgIT. 2016. Simplifying the Nigerian Budget [Online]. Available at http://your budgit.com/. Accessed 28 August 2016.

Chetty, S., Naidoo, R. and Seetharam, Y. 2015. The Impact of Corporate Social Responsibility on Firms' Financial Performance in South Africa. *Contemporary Economics*, 9(2): 193–214.

Clift, B. and Woll, C. 2012. Economic Patriotism: Reinventing Control over Open Markets. *Journal of European Public Policy*, 19(3): 307–323.

Conroy, M. E. 2007. *Branded!: How the 'Certification Revolution' Is Transforming Global Corporations*. Gabriola Island, BC: New Society Publishers.

Crane, A., Matten, D. and Spence, L. J. 2013. Corporate Social Responsibility in a Global Context. In *Corporate Social Responsibility: Readings and Cases in a Global Context*, Vol. 2. Edited by A. Crane, D. Matten, and L. J. Spence, 3–26. Milton Park, Abingdon, UK: Routledge.

CSR Watch International Nigeria. 2012. Etisalat Leads the Way in CSR Education. Available at https://csrwatchinternationalnigeria.wordpress.com/2012/12/09/e tisalat-leads-the-way-in-csr-education/. Accessed 17 October 2016.

Dahlsrud, A. 2008. How Corporate Social Responsibility Is Defined: An Analysis of 37 Definitions. *Corporate Social Responsibility and Environmental Management*, 15(1): 1–13.

Dartey-Baah, K. and Amponsah-Tawiah, K. 2011. Exploring the Limits of Western Corporate Social Responsibility Theories in Africa. *International Journal of Business and Social Science*, 2(18): 126–137.

Dawkins, J. and Lewis, S. 2003. CSR in Stakeholder Expectations and Their Implications for Company Strategy. *Journal of Business Ethics*, 44(2–3): 185–193.

Du, S., Bhattacharya, C. B. and Sen, S. 2007. Reaping Relational Rewards from Corporate Social Responsibility: The Role of Competitive Positioning. *International Journal of Research in Marketing*, 24(3): 224–241.

Eco, U. 1972. Introduction to a Semiotics of Iconic Signs. *Versus*, 2(1).

Elumelu, T. O. 2012. Africapitalism: The Path to Economic Prosperity and Social Wealth: Rebuilding and Rebranding Africa as a Land of Investment, Innovation and Entrepreneurship. Available at www.heirsholdings.com/wp-content/uploa ds/2013/04/Africapitalism-Path-to-Economic-Prosperity-and-Social-Wealth.pdf. Accessed 29 October 2015.

Financial Nigeria. 2016. Nigeria's Advertising Spend Reaches N97.9 Billion. Available at www.financialnigeria.com/nigeria-s-advertising-spend-reaches-n97-9 -billion-sustainable-photovideo-details-495.html. Accessed 17 October 2016.

Forstater, M., Zadek, S., Guang, Y., Yu, K., Hong, C. X. and George, M. 2010. Corporate Responsibility in African Development: Insights from an Emerging Dialogue. *Corporate Social Responsibility Initiative*, Working Paper 60.

Girod, S. and Michael, B. 2013. Branding in European Retailing: A Corporate Social Responsibility Perspective, 1–6. Available at http://ejournal.narotama.ac.id/files/ BRANDING%2520CSR%2520PERSPECTIVE.pdf. Accessed 8 December 2015.

Hall, S. 1973. Encoding/Decoding. In *Culture, Media, Language*. Edited by S. Hall, D. Hobson, A. Lowe and P. Willis, 117–127. London: Hutchinson.

Helg, Å. 2007. Corporate Social Responsibility from a Nigerian Perspective. *Masters Thesis*. Götesborgs University. Available at https://gupea.ub.gu.se/bit stream/2077/4713/1/07-23.pdf. Accessed 27 January 2018.

Herstein, R., Mitki, Y. and Jaffe, E. D. 2008. Communicating a New Corporate Image during Privatization: The Case of El Al Airlines. *Corporate Communications: An International Journal*, 13(4): 380–393.

Hill, B. 2015. The Importance of Marketing and Communication. Houston: Demand Media.

Idemudia, U. 2014. Corporate Social Responsibility and Development in Africa: Issues and Possibilities. *Geography Compass*, 8(7): 421–435.

Johnson, H. H. 2003. Does It Pay to Be Good? Social Responsibility and Financial Performance. *Business Horizons*, 46(6): 34–40.

Kaplan, A. M. and Haenlein, M. 2009. The Increasing Importance of Public Marketing: Explanations, Applications and Limits of Marketing within Public Administration. *European Management Journal*, 27(3): 197–212.

Kayuni, H. M. and Tambulasi, R. I. 2012. Ubuntu and Corporate Social Responsibility: The Case of Selected Malawian Organizations. *African Journal of Economic and Management Studies*, 3(1): 64–76.

Kitchen, P. J. and Schultz, D. E. 2003. Integrated Corporate and Product Brand Communication (1). *Journal of Competitiveness Studies*, 11(1): 66.

Knutsen, E. 2013. Microsoft's 4 Afrika Initiative Is Good Business. *Forbes*.

Kotler, P. and Armstrong, G. 2010. *Principles of Marketing*. Pearson Education. Upper Saddle River, NJ: Prentice Hall.

Lai, C. S., Chiu, C. J., Yang, C. F. and Pai, D. C. 2010. The Effects of Corporate Social Responsibility on Brand Performance: The Mediating Effect of Industrial Brand Equity and Corporate Reputation. *Journal of Business Ethics*, 95(3): 457–469.

Lee, Y. J., Haley, E. and Yang, K. 2013. The Mediating Role of Attitude towards Values Advocacy Ads in Evaluating Issue Support Behaviour and Purchase Intention. *International Journal of Advertising*, 32(2): 233–253.

Lindgreen, A. and Swaen, V. 2010. Social Responsibility. *International Journal of Management Reviews*, 12(1): 1–7.

Lindgreen, A., Xu, Y., Maon, F. and Wilcock, J. 2012. Corporate Social Responsibility Brand Leadership: A Multiple Case Study. *European Journal of Marketing*, 46(7/8): 965–993.

Maio, E. 2003. Managing Brand in the New Stakeholder Environment. *Journal of Business Ethics*, 44(2–3): 235–246.

Maklan, S., Knox, S. and Michel, S. 2009. The Guaranty Trust Bank of Nigeria: From Niche Positioning to Mass-Market Branding. *Thunderbird International Business Review*, 51(4): 385–401.

Maon, F., Lindgreen, A. and Swaen, V. 2009. Designing and Implementing Corporate Social Responsibility: An Integrative Framework Grounded in Theory and Practice. *Journal of Business Ethics*, 87(1): 71–89.

Mburu, P., Matenge, T., Amanze, D. and Makgosa, R. 2013. Corporate Branding in Botswana: A Content Analysis of Visual Brand Elements. *Journal of Business Theory and Practice*, 1(2): 262.

McDonald, M. H. B., de Chernatony, L. and Harris, F. 2001. Corporate Marketing and Service Brands – Moving beyond the Fast-Moving Consumer Goods Model. *European Journal of Marketing*, 35(3/4): 335–352.

Miles, M. P. and Covin, J. G. 2000. Environmental Marketing: A Source of Reputational, Competitive, and Financial Advantage. *Journal of Business Ethics*, 23(3): 299–311.

Mohamed, B. E. B. 2015. Impact of Corporate Brand on Repurchase Intention, the Mediating Role of Relationship Quality. Doctoral dissertation, Sudan University of Science & Technology.

Montfort, N. and Wardrip-Fruin, N. (eds.). 2003. *The New Media Reader.* Cambridge, MA: MIT Press.

Montillaud-Joyel, S. and Otto, M. 2004. Why Should Companies Care about Environment and Social Responsibility? The Answer Is Simple: More and More Consumers Are Asking for It.

Motion, J., Leitch, S. and Brodie, R. J. 2003 Equity in Corporate Co-branding: The Case of Adidas and the All Blacks. *European Journal of Marketing*, 37(7/8): 1080–1094.

Nigeria's Advertising Spend Reaches N97.9 Billion. Available at www.financialnigeria .com/nigeria-s-advertising-spend-reaches-n97-9-billion-sustainable-photovideo-det ails-495.html. Accessed 25 October 2016.

Nworji, I. D., Adebayo, O. and David, A. O. 2011. Corporate Governance and Bank Failure in Nigeria: Issues, Challenges and Opportunities. *Research Journal of Finance and Accounting*, 2(2): 27–44.

Oando. 2008. Oando Marketing Signs Partnership with Big Treat. Available at www .oandoplc.com/media/press-release/oando-marketing-signs-partnership-with-big -treat. Accessed 25 October 2016.

Okhakume, B. 2013. Bank-Brands: Brand Building and Re-branding. *The Nation.* Available at http://thenationonlineng.net/bank-brands-brand-building-re -branding. Accessed 17 October 2016.

Oliver, R. L. 1999. Whence Consumer Loyalty? *Journal of Marketing*, 63: 33–44.

Otubanjo, O., Amujo, O. C. and Alleyne, L. B. 2015. Competence Branding: A Strategic Differentiation Approach for Business Organizations. *Journal of Euromarketing*, 24(2–3): 149–169.

Otubanjo, O., Amujo, O. C. and Cornelius, N. 2010. The Informal Corporate Identity Communication Process. *Corporate Reputation Review*, 13(3): 157–171.

Pegg, S. 2015. Introduction: On the 20th Anniversary of the Death of Ken Saro-Wiwa. *The Extractive Industries and Society*, 2(4): 607–614.

Pillai, A. 2012. Corporate Branding Literature: A Research Paradigm Review. *Journal of Brand Management*, 19(4): 331–343.

Polonsky, M. J. and Jevons, C. 2006. Understanding Issue Complexity when Building a Socially Responsible Brand. *European Business Review*, 18(5): 340–349.

Polonsky, M. and Jevons, C. 2009. Global Branding and Strategic CSR: An Overview of Three Types of Complexity. *International Marketing Review*, 26(3): 327–347.

Popoli, P. 2011. Linking CSR Strategy and Brand Image: Different Approaches in Local and Global Markets. *Marketing Theory*, 11(4): 419–433.

Porter, M. E. and Kramer, M. R. 2002. The Competitive Advantage of Corporate Philanthropy. *Harvard Business Review*, 80(12): 56–68.

Punch Newspapers. 2016. 2016 Budget: 10 Provisions Nigerians Are Unhappy with. Available at http://punchng.com/10-provisions-nigerians-are-not-cool-with-in -the-2016-budget-proposal/. Accessed 10 August 2007.

Rahim, R. A., Jalaludin, F. W. and Tajuddin, K. 2011. The Importance of Corporate Social Responsibility on Consumer Behaviour in Malaysia. *Asian Academy of Management Journal*, 16(1): 119–139.

Raimi, L., Akhuemonkhan, I. and Ogunjirin, O. D. 2015. Corporate Social Responsibility and Entrepreneurship (CSRE): Antidotes to Poverty, Insecurity and Underdevelopment in Nigeria. *Social Responsibility Journal*, 11 (1): 56–81.

Ramasamy, B. and Yeung, M. 2009. Chinese Consumers' Perception of Corporate Social Responsibility (CSR). *Journal of Business Ethics*, 88(1): 119–132.

Rogers, S. 2009. Profits Before People: 7 of the World's Most Irresponsible Companies. Available at http://eco-chick.com/ 192009/05/3845/profits-before -people/. Accessed 27 January 2018.

Sandada, M. and Finch, H. 2015. The Impact of Corporate Branding Dimensions on Firm Performance: Evidence from the Zimbabwean Petroleum Industry. *Acta Universitatis Danubius. Œconomica*, 11(6).

Schmidt, K. 1995. *The Quest for Identity: Corporate Identity. Strategies, Methods and Examples*. London: Cassell.

Sheikh, S. U. R., and Beise-Zee, R. 2011. Corporate Social Responsibility or Cause-Related Marketing? The Role of Cause Specificity of CSR. *Journal of Consumer Marketing*, 28(1): 27–39.

Shoprite. 2016. Environmental Sustainability. Available at http://www.shoprite .com/the-environment. Accessed 1 September 2016.

Singh, J. J., Iglesias, O. and Batista-Foguet, J. M. 2012. Does Having an Ethical Brand Matter? The Influence of Consumer Perceived Ethicality on Trust, Affect and Loyalty. *Journal of Business Ethics*, 111(4): 541–549.

Skålén, P. and Strandvik, T. 2005. From Prescription to Description: A Critique and Reorientation of Service Culture. *Managing Service Quality: An International Journal*, 15(3): 230–244.

Suprawan, L. 2011. Corporate Social Responsibility Branding: The Role of Organisational Identity and Its Impact on Performance. Doctoral dissertation, Curtin University, School of Marketing.

Taghian, M. 2008, January. Corporate Social Responsibility: A Resource-Based View of the Firm. In *ANZMAC 2008: Australian and New Zealand Marketing Academy Conference 2008: Marketing: Shifting the Focus from Mainstream to Offbeat*, 1–7. Promaco Conventions.

Theng So, J., Grant Parsons, A., and Yap, S. F. 2013. Corporate Branding, Emotional Attachment and Brand Loyalty: The Case of Luxury Fashion Branding. *Journal of Fashion Marketing and Management: An International Journal*, 17(4): 403–423.

Torelli, C. 2013. *Globalization, Culture, and Branding: How to Leverage Cultural Equity for Building Iconic Brands in the Era of Globalization*. New York, NY: Springer.

Tsiotsou, R. H., Alexandris, K. and Bettina Cornwell, T. 2014. Using Evaluative Conditioning to Explain Corporate Co-branding in the Context of Sport Sponsorship. *International Journal of Advertising*, 33(2): 295–327.

Uhrich, S., Koenigstorfer, J. and Groeppel-Klein, A. 2014. Leveraging Sponsorship with Corporate Social Responsibility. *Journal of Business Research*, 67(9): 2023–2029.

United Nations. 2016. Sustainable Development Goals: 17 Goals to Transform the World. Available at http://www.un.org/sustainabledevelopment/sustainable-consumption-production/. Accessed 29 August 2016.

Vallaster, C., Lindgreen, A. and Maon, F. 2012. Strategically Leveraging Corporate Social Responsibility. *California Management Review*, 54(3): 34–60.

Wang, C. H. 2014. How Relational Capital Mediates the Effect of Corporate Reputation on Competitive Advantage: Evidence from Taiwan High-Tech Industry. *Technological Forecasting and Social Change*, 82: 167–176.

Wilson, J. 2015. Making Sense of Branding-and How to Make an Enjoyable Brand. *Huffington Post*, 85–89. Available at www.slideshare.net/JonathanAJWilson/26themarketeersoct2015enjoyable-brandingpp8589. Accessed 27 January 2018.

Wilson, A., Zeithaml, V. A., Bitner, M. J. and Gremler, D. D. 2012. *Services Marketing: Integrating Customer Focus across the Firm*. McGraw Hill.

Yang, D., Davis, D. A. and Robertson, K. R. 2012. Integrated Branding with Mergers and Acquisitions. *Journal of Brand Management*, 19(5): 438–456.

Yang, A. and Veil, S. R. 2015. Nationalism versus Animal Rights: A Semantic Network Analysis of Value Advocacy in Corporate Crisis. *International Journal of Business Communication*, 54(4): pp.408–430.

Yu Xie, H. and Boggs, D. J. 2006. Corporate Branding versus Product Branding in Emerging Markets: A Conceptual Framework. *Marketing Intelligence & Planning*, 24(4): 347–364.

7   Who Is an Africapitalist? Reimagining Private-Sector Leadership in Africa

Adun Okupe and Kenneth Amaeshi

INTRODUCTION

Africa continues on its quest for development. Interventions (such as those offered by aid, NGOs and International Financial Institutions) which have been proffered in the past, have not yielded results promised. Africapitalism has now arrived as a possible intervention that can address the issues pertaining to the low level and low rate of development on the continent. The Africapitalism management philosophy introduced by Tony Elumelu in 2012 calls on the private sector to be an active participant in the sustainable development of Africa. This call to action is not unique, as the private sector has been recognised together with the state and civil society as important contributors to sustainable development (Igué, 2010; Amaeshi and Idemudia, 2015). What differentiates Africapitalism's remit, however, is its African-centric view, which highlights the role of context in the development narrative, a factor hitherto taken for granted in the literature on business in society (Amaeshi and Idemudia, 2015). Another differentiating factor is its attempt to contribute to the revision of what the role of business in the development of developing countries (Amaeshi and Idemudia, 2015) ought to be. The introduction of the concept, at this time, is also a timely one as African private-sector leaders, including entrepreneurs, continue to strive for how to create and provide innovative solutions to address local challenges on the continent.

It is within this premise of what the role of the private sector ought to be that we situate this chapter. Our focus is on private-sector leaders, including entrepreneurs. This is because the call for the private sector to be engaged in the sustainable development of Africa is inadvertently a call for leaders of private-sector organisations, as it is the leaders who are in the position to effect change. Taking our starting point from Amaeshi and Idemudia (2015)'s seminal article, which questions what Africapitalism can mean for management in Africa, we apply their four cardinal values of Africapitalism and explore leadership for sustainable development in Africa through these lenses. By so doing, we attempt to clarify analytically and practically, what Africapitalism can mean for private-sector leadership in Africa, or put in another way, the type of leadership required for African businesses and entrepreneurs – what it can mean to be an Africapitalist. We anchor our recommendations in the existing transformational and responsible business theories and conclude by suggesting some implications of Africapitalism for private-sector leadership in Africa.

AFRICA, SUSTAINABLE DEVELOPMENT AND LEADERSHIP

African countries are experiencing rapid change, driven in some part by the Africa rising narrative (August, 2013). The new scramble for Africa Rising (Carmody, 2011) is laden with economic self-interest, as capitalism seeks new lands to exploit. While this is not altogether unwelcome, Africa's weak bargaining position as a resource-rich supplier of raw materials to the Global North has not changed. These resources are exported from Africa in their raw or relatively untransformed state, and therefore at a lower price (since there was little to no value-addition on the continent), before being re-imported in their finished state, at higher price, back into the continent. This weaker trade position impacts on the level and rate of development of the continent (Kennedy, 1988). This is where Africapitalism tries to come in.

The Africapitalism management philosophy tries to refocus renewed attention on Africa by asserting that the private sector in Africa can contribute to the economic transformation of the continent through investments that generate both economic prosperity and social wealth for the continent (Elumelu, 2014). In this way, the African private sector can be engaged in investments that will contribute to sustainable development on the continent.

Africa's state of under-development marred by years of colonial rule, civil wars, poverty and poor leadership has yielded calls for multiple actors (the state, businesses and civil society) to play a part in the sustainable development of the continent. African countries are characterised by a weak institutional context, where governments, markets and civil society are not as robust as in the West. This also limits the extent to which the public sector can be relied upon to play a part in the sustainable development of Africa. This is the rationale for the call to other players, including businesses, to rise up as instruments of sustainable development.

Sustainable development refers to a process of change where human needs and environmental limits are placed above profit, presenting economic and social benefits to people, as well as the sustainable utilisation of resources. There is a widespread rise of interest in, and support for, the concept of sustainable development, marking an important shift in understanding the relationships of humanity with nature and between people. Achieved through a process of bringing together environmental and socio-economic questions, the definition of sustainable development was most famously expressed in the Brundtland Report as meeting the needs of the present without compromising the ability of future generations to meet their needs (World Commission on Environment and Development, 1987: 43; Springett, 2013).

Sustainable development means changes to the society which can be cultural, political and socio-economic. At its most basic, it refers to any change that society undertakes to move from one point to another, due to issues or challenges identified as inhibiting the quality of life in such a society. Maak and Pless (2009) argue that sustainable development (referred to as societal change) is important for the advancement of humanity, towards making the world a better place for others.

Sustainable development includes caring for the needs of others, but it goes beyond care, to include the active engagement in, and taking responsibility and being accountable for, ensuring that the needs of others are provided for. The meaning of sustainable development will differ from society to society, and at a more micro-level, from community to community (Gottlieb and Sanzgiri, 1996). To a large extent, the literature refers to social problems as those highlighted as developmental challenges in development literature: poverty, lack of access to clean drinking water, the need to develop human capabilities.

Sustainable development is important for African communities because of the need to improve the quality of life of inhabitants in African societies. The sustainable development of Africa will also impact positively on business organisations in several ways including the improvement of the state of security and safety in the environment, which will allow for businesses to continue their operations in a safe and harmonious society. Secondly, the transition from poverty will contribute towards converting the society's inhabitants to future consumers of businesses' products and services. Thirdly, alleviating health and mortality will contribute to a stronger and healthier workforce and a better society for businesses and their employees. There are several other effects of sustainable development on societies, but the above highlight the fact that tackling sustainable development has both economic and social benefits for businesses and society at large.

Introducing the role of the private sector into the sustainable development debate environment presents a few questions. What role can the private sector be expected to play? To what extent are business leaders aware of the social, political and environmental impacts of their decisions even as they seek to make economically viable decisions? How are they able to balance the contradictory demands of stakeholders, and to what extent are their leadership strategies applied to ensure the development of Africa (Horlings and Padt, 2013)? Providing the answers to all of these questions is beyond the remit of this chapter, but the questions do highlight the intricacies of what the involvement of the private sector in sustainable development in Africa can mean.

Sustainability research has not effectively tackled the role of private-sector leaders in the sustainable development of Africa. Yet, the private sector may be an important element of sustainable development in Africa, given the weak institutions present in the continent. Our chapter attempts to answer the question of what private-sector leadership for sustainable development can mean as a starting point to answering the other questions presented above. An exploration of private-sector leadership requires an examination of leadership literature, as we attempt to define who an Africapitalist is, a private-sector leader leading for sustainable development.

Leadership refers to the process of influencing others to achieve set goals (Yukl, 2010). Leadership is tasked with several roles including that of setting the vision and strategy for an organisation, inspiring and guiding followers towards working to achieve the set vision, and effective communication across various stakeholder levels (Sternberg and Hedlund, 2002). Leadership also includes the ability to manage moral complexity in a globalised business culture, the ability to define and sequence strategic business goals in a way that creates sustainable value, and the ability to address the competing value claims of diverse and vocal stakeholders (Thompson, 2010). In addition, several definitions of the different forms of leadership also discuss the characteristics of effective leaders, that is, those who are able to lead, inspire, motivate and adapt. These forms of leadership highlight the importance to effective leadership skills such as effective communication, the ability to work well with others in a collaborative work environment and the continuous development of the leader and his/her staff (Ruiz et al., 2011; Gottlieb and Sanzgiri, 1996; Knights and O'Leary, 1996; Burnes and By, 2012). Nonetheless, the understanding of leadership is constantly being examined and expanded, to take into consideration diverse contexts and experiences.

Leadership studies continue to evolve towards understanding leadership behaviour in various contexts, beyond the relationship of the leader with subordinates, to encompass other stakeholders of the organisation who may be within the organisation or outside of it (Crossan et al., 2008). The understanding of leadership is also expanding to include other levels, such as leadership of the industry in which the organisation operates, and the wider society at large, to include other people that the leader might be influencing, who are not his or her followers, such as community members, shareholders, competitors and public interest groups (Yukl, 2010). One reason for this expansion of the boundary of leadership is the need to include stakeholders who may be affected by the direct and indirect actions of an organisation, in the leadership equation. This expansion is relevant in the globalised world where the consequences of leadership behaviour may be far-reaching.

The purpose of leadership has been explored in various strands and is generally defined as an important component of organisation, to enable it to meet its goals (Yukl, 2010). Thus, the purpose of leadership is to work with others towards the achievement of set goals (Antonakis et al., 2004). To do this, the leader has responsibility for setting the direction and vision for the organisation, together with the creation of objectives by which the organisation sets about to achieve its goals. An organisation usually has objectives which are varied and, in some cases, competing (Yukl, 2010). Traditionally, a leader was said to be effective according to the extent s/he was able to ensure that the organisation met its objectives, where, in many cases, these objectives were profit and target related (Den Hartog and Dickson, 2004). However, just as the understanding of leadership is expanding, the evaluation of leadership behaviour is also being revised to take other aspects of leadership behaviour into account.

Leadership literature has focused on understanding leadership behaviour within the organisation, where the organisation is seen as the final boundary of the leadership equation (Amaeshi, 2014). This raises the questions of what goals are set, and to what ends within an organisation (Yukl, 2010). The traditional view of the firm views private-sector organisations as focused on profit-realisation and profit-maximisation alone, where goals of the organisation are set to meet this sole objective. This narrow focus has become increasingly problematic as multiple objectives are included into the role of organisations (Friedman, 1962; Scherer and Palazzo, 2011; Sassen, 1999; Stiglitz, 2002), as well as the recognition of the importance of expanding the boundary of leadership, to include the role that organisations can play in their society. The business in society literature discusses this to a large extent (see Scherer and Palazzo, 2011; Warhurst, 2005).

Leadership literature has hitherto focused on explaining the meaning of leadership, definitions of effective leadership and traits of effective leaders. However, the academic debate environment is plagued by its inability to draw definite conclusions without a firm understanding of what leadership is or ought to be. The research environment concerns itself with how best to govern and how best to lead, and most of the work in the leadership field has concentrated on North American institutions and organisations. Within such an archetypal backdrop, trying to understand what leadership can mean within the Africapitalism management philosophy can be seen as overly ambitious. That being said, scholars have called for more context-based research (House et al., 2004; Case, French and Simpson, 2011; Ladkin and Weber, 2011) into leadership practices that represent the leadership styles and practices of the Global South, to include Africa. Yet, much of the work on leadership in Africa remains of a political nature. Private-sector leadership has not yet received the attention it merits and needs to get, to move the conversation of what African private-sector leadership can mean in Africa and how leadership can contribute to the sustainable development of the continent.

This presents the opportunity for the Africapitalism management philosophy to define and encapsulate what private-sector leadership can mean and how private-sector leaders ought to lead, with a focus on sustainable development of the continent.

THE AFRICAPITALISM MANAGEMENT PHILOSOPHY

The Africapitalism management philosophy is a unique concept with 'transformational potential' (Amaeshi and Idemudia, 2015: 213) that seeks to amplify the relational nature of identity in Africa and harness it towards contributing to the betterment of society in Africa. In this way, Africapitalism places economic growth together with sustainable development as the focus of business, which is different from Western conceptions of the purpose of business. While there might be some contentions with Africapitalism seeing as it has 'capitalism' as a suffix, and is therefore laden with the criticisms of capitalism – resource extraction, accumulation by dispossession and inequality; the concept as 'an imaginative management idea' (Amaeshi and Idemudia, 2015: 211) contends that private-sector leaders can and ought to contribute to the development of Africa.

Amaeshi and Idemudia (2015) attempt to underpin the foundation for Africapitalism by presenting four cardinal values, which we represent below and relate these to private-sector leadership in Africa. The four cardinal values of Africapitalism are (1) sense of progress and prosperity, (2) sense of parity, (3) sense of peace and harmony and (4) sense of place and belongingness (ibid.: 216).

Sense of Progress and Prosperity

Africapitalism is focused on economic growth together with social wealth creation. Amaeshi and Idemudia (2015) argue that implicit within this definition is a sense of progress and prosperity. In this way, Africapitalism asserts that private-sector leaders have a role to play to generate progress and prosperity for their organisation, as well as a sense of progress and prosperity for society, where quality of life should be improved upon, as defined by the United Nations Millennium Development Goals and Sustainable Development Goals to include access to good health care, access to quality education, adequate infrastructural provision, stronger institutions, etc.

Sense of Parity

Parity refers to equitability, and the sense of parity argues for inclusivity where the benefits of economic growth are shared in an inclusive and equitable manner, taking into consideration the needs of stakeholders. In this way, Africapitalism calls on private-sector leaders to refocus on the purpose of business and essence of wealth, and to channel this wealth towards providing economic and social wealth for stakeholders.

Sense of Peace and Harmony

Amaeshi and Idemudia (2015) argue convincingly that Africapitalism by its very definition seeks to strive for balance, by coupling economic and social wealth creation. Although there will be tensions as to how this balance is achieved and understood, the Africapitalism management philosophy attempts to anchor, as its core, a focus on the common good, understanding that capitalism has resulted in growing inequality, which has resulted in struggles and at its extreme forms, bursts of anomie (Achcar, 2002). In this way, Africapitalism seeks for growth and development that benefit the society, and is therefore able to maintain peace and harmony. As such, the philosophy calls on private-sector leaders to constantly examine and reflect on how their business decisions can contribute to peace and harmony in their societies.

Sense of Place and Belongingness

Although presented as the fourth cardinal value, the sense of place and belongingness is at the very core of the Africapitalism management philosophy, as it seeks to position Africa as a homeland which should be engaged beyond the notion of providing lower input costs for materials. Rather, businesses ought to engage with the continent from a sense of economic patriotism in which Africans will play major roles towards the development of the continent. Amaeshi and Idemudia (2015) present a compelling example of how economic patriotism played significant roles in the reconstruction of Western Europe after World War II. This sense of place and belongingness, they argue, is an emotive tool that can catalyse the role of business in Africa's sustainable development.

The four cardinal values of Africapitalism are a useful foundational point with which to critically examine what private-sector leadership for sustainable development can mean for the Africapitalism management philosophy.

The four cardinal values of Africapitalism can also be typified as cardinal values of sustainable development, which should provide a sense of progress and prosperity, ensuring that the benefits of growth are equitably shared (sense of parity), ensuring that a sense of balance, peace and harmony is attained and maintained in communities, and focusing on improving the quality of life in African societies, sense of place and belongingness. In this way, the Africapitalism management philosophy has contributed to the understanding and narrative of sustainable development.

One way to understand leadership for societal change, also referred to as sustainable development, can be through viewing it as a spectrum, where on the one hand it can be understood to mean the leadership of the organisation towards achieving its vision, where the organisation's vision is already inclusive of societal change, in this case, it is the leadership of the organisation, together with the vision and strategy setting to incorporate a form of societal change in their core business activities. On the other hand, leadership for societal change can also refer to instances where a leader of an organisation attempts to lead the organisational field, that is the industry within which the organisation operates, towards change and in this way, modifies the industry's strategies to incorporate a focus on societal change. An example of this can be if an organisation changes its employment contracts with employees and becomes an ambassador for fair employment, thus precipitating other organisations in the industry to also change their employment contracts with their employees. In this way, the leaders of the change organisation have been exemplary and led their organisation towards societal change.

EXPLORING PRIVATE-SECTOR LEADERSHIP FOR SUSTAINABLE DEVELOPMENT THROUGH THE LENSES OF AFRICAPITALISM

In Africa, private-sector leaders do not currently see themselves, nor their organisations, as being able to contribute to sustainable development, beyond providing employment (and meeting consumers' needs). While employment is an important part of contributing to a society's economy, the private sector, especially in the face of supine public-sector leadership, can contribute to sustainable development. Individual private-sector leaders, where they attempt to contribute to sustainable development, currently do so in the form of private charitable deeds, some of which include commissioning of the building of schools and provision of utilities, mostly in rural areas. In some cases, these personal interventions are irregular, and infrequent, thus lowering their intended impact on the society. One reason for the irregularity is that the interventions may not be linked to the strategic objectives of their organisations. More needs to be done to raise awareness that the private sector can be seen as an instrument of development. There is a need to educate current private-sector leaders as well as to train future leaders on the variety of roles that the private sector can play in tackling some of Africa's developmental challenges. We will return to this later in the chapter, in our recommendations.

While it may appear that the Africapitalism philosophy is accepting of the seemingly inactive nature of the government, this is not so. The role of the state has traditionally been the provision of basic infrastructure such as electricity, roads, hospitals, schools and security, while the role of the private sector is to contribute to society by job creation and payment of tax revenues. This traditional divide of the state versus the private sector has contributed to the perceived division of responsibility between the state and the private sector. The Africapitalism management philosophy appreciates the current realities of many African societies, and proposes an alternative which raises the role and importance of business, an important player in society, towards addressing developmental challenges. The Africapitalism philosophy seeks to promote collaboration between the state and the private sector, in such a way as to promote social harmony between the two, and in this way the collaborations heralded by public-private partnerships can be advanced by Africapitalism.

There remain immense opportunities for government and private sector to work together to define what these priority areas for development are to be, and how interventions can be created to focus on these.

The current demographic of African societies is that of a young population and under-employment of skills. As such, there is a need for focus/priority areas to be determined, towards updating the educational curriculum and targeting it for vocational training that is able to equip young people with the skills they need to build better African societies. This becomes more relevant and pertinent when we combine this with the need for more value-addition on the continent, to contribute to economic growth. To do this, targeted knowledge and skills transfer will need to be undertaken for selected identified areas of the economy. Specific training in this regard will contribute to societal and economic change.

In our attempt to explain what private-sector leadership for sustainable development can mean for the Africapitalism management philosophy, we examined the key leadership theories for areas of congruence. We analysed the key components from what colleagues have written about leading for societal change, which lies at the intersection of leadership studies and business in society literature. In trying to answer the question of the type of leadership required for the achievement of the Africapitalism agenda, we propose that the philosophy requires leadership that is responsible, transformational and geared towards societal change. Our suggestion comes from our analysis where we examined several key constructs of leadership for relevance and applicability to the Africapitalism management philosophy. We anchor our discussion on the two key theories of transformational leadership and responsible leadership, which emerged from our analysis, because of their relevance to the concept of leadership for sustainable development.

Transformational Leadership

The transformational leadership theory introduced by Burns (1978) and extended by Bass (1985) postulates that leaders can inspire followers beyond a mere transactional form of leader-follower interaction. The transactional leadership theory emphasises that the relationship between a leader and his/her followers is based on exchanges (transactions). In this way, a leader and his/her followers' interactions are dependent on their self-interests. Followers that achieve the specified expected level of performance are rewarded materially or psychologically. The material reward is in form of financial compensation and psychological reward as positive feedback. Conversely, not accomplishing set objectives will be penalised (Bass, 1990; Bass and Stodgill, 1990).

The transformational theory of leadership seeks to move the relationship between leaders and followers, to a higher level where the followers transcend their self-interests and work together to enable the organisation achieve its potential (Bass, 1999, 2008; Storey, 2004). In other words, the leader guides followers to a higher level of commitment and involvement with the organisation beyond a transactional relationship that involves only financial reward for their work or penalties for poor behaviour. However, the transformational leadership theory focuses, as with many of the leadership theories, on the organisation as the final boundary in leadership.

We propose that the focus of transformational leadership can be expanded to go beyond the boundary of transforming the organisation alone. To the extent that transformational leadership is extended beyond the organisation, then a transformational leader can transform the organisation into one that actively pursues sustainable development. An area for further research will be to explore more deeply the linkages between transformational leadership and leading for sustainable development (Maak and Pless, 2009).

Leadership theories such as the transactional and transformational theories have been propagated as universal, because they comprise constructs that can be measured across contexts. However, the application of these theories and practical leadership behaviour may vary according to context. This context can be national culture, organisational or industry characteristics. Thus, it is important to integrate the context in which leadership exists into its study. So arises the question: how can African private-sector leaders be transformational leaders within their organisations and also be agents of societal transformation towards attaining sustainable development?

The transformational theory of leadership has focused on transforming followers. However, it has not considered how leaders can utilise their transformative capabilities to also contribute to societal transformation. We postulate the extension of the transformational leadership theory to incorporate multiple ways in which leadership can be truly transformational.

We argue that the requirement for leaders to expand beyond the boundary of the organisation, towards sustainable development, requires in addition to being transformational, the ability to be responsible.

Responsible Leadership

Responsibility is focused on the role of the leader to the organisation and the wider society at large. Responsible leadership is a construct focused on articulating how the responsibility of the organisation is dependent upon, and advanced by, the leader of the organisation. It advocates the importance of creating shared meaning of what change can mean, within and outside the organisation (Waldman and Gavin, 2008). Responsible leadership focuses on the individual leader, and assumes that this leader can be the source for responsible organisational behaviour. While this approach admits that shared meaning is created through dialogue with other followers, it assumes that the leader remains the embodiment of responsibility within an organisation. A responsible leader is one with a values-based and principles-driven relationship between the private-sector leaders and stakeholders who are connected through a shared meaning and purpose through which they seek to rise to higher levels of motivation and commitment for achieving long-lasting value creation and actualizing responsible change in their organisation and their society (Maak and Pless, 2009).

Responsible leadership takes into consideration the effects of an organisation's actions and inactions on the current and future well-being of society and nature (Rodriguez et al., 2002). In this light, the ultimate goal of a responsible leader of an organisation is to create value for shareholders and society as a whole. The responsible leadership construct explains this as leadership that strives to engage in behaviours for the right reasons while aiming to achieve a sustainable competitive advantage (Peterlin, Dimovski and Penger, 2013). In this way, responsible leadership is sustainable as it is premised on the goal of creating value for the stakeholders and the society (Harley et al., 2014; McCann and Sweet, 2014).

Leadership is argued to be morally neutral, given that the evaluation of effective leadership does not usually consider the means by which the end was achieved. Rather, effective leadership evaluates behaviour as to how effective the leader was in getting others to work towards achieving his/her objectives. However, Gini (1997) argues that leadership has a moral dimension. The moral element of leadership in this regards refers to the exercise of power, which can be social, economic and/or political. 'Moral' in this sense is subjective with meanings varying according to the culture or context. That said, private-sector leaders are in positions of power, and with such power comes responsibility. Leaders are in a position to propose policies and also have the power with which to implement them by providing the required infrastructure and financial resources. We argue that responsibilities come along with the power and privilege private-sector leaders enjoy, and the exercise of this power comes with a moral element as the leader needs to manage the responsibility of the organisation within the multiple moral complexities experienced in a globalised world with the multiplicity of interests of various stakeholders, and including, the responsibility to lead for sustainable development (Thompson, 2004, 2010).

Moral in this sense is neither good nor bad, but rather incorporates philosophical and ideological viewpoints of the leader which guide the manner in which leadership is enacted. Interested readers can read the Global Moral Compass (see Thompson, 2004 and 2010), which has been introduced as a tool for private-sector leaders to manage moral complexity. The Global Moral Compass can help to clarify moral values and contribute towards the building of moral values solidarity in a team, organisation or community, and can also contribute to leading responsibly (Thompson, 2004; Gini, 1997).

Leaders have responsibility for the consequences of their actions on society, and by extension, according to Maak and Pless (2009), they have responsibility for non-action. However, within this call to lead for sustainable development, leaders are not able to solve all societal problems, as that is not the focus of their organisations. Rather, we consider that private-sector leaders have some level of agency towards contributing to sustainable development (Wang et al., 2014) by being responsible and transformational, in this sense, able to set goals and objectives for their organisations which will impact on sustainable development, as well as transform the environment in which they operate through how they lead their organisations.

Who Is an Africapitalist: Following our brief presentations of the two key leadership constructs, we present our typology together with a discussion of characteristics that can contribute towards defining who an Africapitalist is. Seeing as the Africapitalism management philosophy calls on the private sector to be agents of economic and societal wealth creation, by extension an Africapitalist is a private-sector leader who is focused on leading for economic and societal wealth creation.

An Africapitalist is therefore a private-sector leader who exhibits characteristics of both transformational and responsible leadership. Africapitalists will need to be responsible and transformational leaders who are able to understand and appreciate the need for sustainable development in the society and as such create ways for their organisations to be actively engaged in contributing towards sustainable development. In this way, the leader recognises that the organisation is not the boundary for assessing effective leadership behaviour, but rather, an effective leader is one who has a holistic and germane view of the wider effects of leadership decisions of organisations on society, and takes concerted action towards decisions that will benefit the society.

Table 7.1 presents the key characteristics of transformational and responsible leadership. We integrate and describe these characteristics in brief detail, which we present below:

Effective Communicator: An initiative for leadership for sustainable development needs to start with dialogue between the organization and the community, to understand clearly what the needs of the community are, where the priority areas lie, and how the issue is to be dealt with. A leader must take into consideration the effects of his/her actions not only on different groups of stakeholders, each with varying and sometimes competing interests, but also on future groups of stakeholders. This is very challenging. Worthy, but challenging.

TABLE 7.1 *Summary of the key characteristics of transformational and responsible leadership*

Key characteristics	
Transformational Leadership	Responsible Leadership
Get followers to transcend their objectives and align with the group's objectives (Gardner, 1990; DeChurch et al., 2010)	Trustworthiness (Maak and Pless, 2006)
Charisma with which to communicate in a clear and compelling way with followers (Bass, 1985; Burns, 1978)	Focus on the long-term effects of decisions on the organisation and the wider society (Waldman and Gavin, 2008)
Adaptability (Storey, 2004; Horner, 1997)	Work with other leaders in the society to actualise societal change (Maak and Pless, 2009)
Ability to challenge and change systems (Horner, 1997; Kroeck et al., 2004; Storey, 2004)	Create platforms for collective action in society (Stahl and de Luque, 2014; Waldman and Gavin, 2008)

Stakeholder meetings – and there will be several, for the various stakeholders – will ensure that both sides, the organisation and the community, have a clear understanding of what the needs are, and will have been contributors to how the needs are to be met. For the organisation, it ensures the community has buy-in for the cause, and therefore can provide their support as required; and for the community, it means that the priority areas are the ones being met, as opposed to the organisation taking part in proffering solutions that may not be the most pressing issues, or may not work to resolve the needs of the community.

The dialogue and collaboration between the organisation and the community will ensure sustainable development priority areas are shared. This dialogue needs to be clear, and the message must be adapted and tailored to the respective stakeholders, first, to educate others as to the importance of sustainable development, and second to propagate the message as to how the organisation is seeking to alleviate societal issues. These communication drives should be through both action and the use of words (Herrick and Pratt, 2012; Epstein et al., 2012).

Trustworthy: An Africapitalist needs to be able to provide a compelling rationale to a diverse group of stakeholders about the requirement for the organisation to be an instrument of sustainable development. To do this, the leader needs to have a proven track record that demonstrates trustworthiness in order to inspire people (within and outside of the organisation) about the need to lead for sustainable development.

The local community needs to trust the leadership of the organisation to do what it says it is going to do, for their benefit. Only when there is trust among the stakeholders and any collaborating parties will there be sustainable social interventions that will lead to sustainable development. The ability to gain trust is important to leadership. Stakeholders, including shareholders, need to trust that the overall goals of the organisation are in line with those communicated, and that the leader will be consistent in working towards the attainment of the best results for the organisation and its stakeholders (Ruiz et al., 2011). Moreover, trust can help with the integration process of leadership for sustainable development.

Trust can be achieved by leaders allowing for open and shared discussions about what the objectives of the organisation should entail, and this dialogue, in which people are able to share their viewpoints, provides a space for deeper interrogation and debate and engagement with what morals the organisation should have and how these should affect the objectives of the organisation. However, this focus remains within the organisation. We argue that integration should also include discussions with stakeholders outside of the organisation in order to achieve better coherence and alignment across the various stakeholder groups in the society (Thompson, 2004; Safty, 2003).

Adaptable: Africapitalists will need to be adaptable, to be able to communicate openly and effectively with diverse groups of people and to tailor their messages accordingly. The leader will also need to be able to swiftly and adeptly respond to the changing requirements of the dynamic environment in which s/he will operate; as well as the changing needs of stakeholders in their societies. In this way, the Africapitalists, who are leaders or future leaders, will see leadership through the lens of changing society, for the better (Brown and Trevino, 2006; Brown, 2006).

Ability to Form a Strong Network with Other Leaders: It is important for private-sector leaders to have a network with other leaders with whom they are able to work together to drive and actualise change. This network is able to provide the encouragement, support(s) and confirmation of the need and importance for sustainable development. A strong network of leaders, representing various organisations and working together towards leading their organisations and communities towards tackling societal issues, provides concerted focus which can increase the impact of the cause.

Ability to Create Platforms for Collective Action: Sustainable development is not the sole responsibility of the government, NGOs or private-sector organisations. To actualise this sustainable development and to make it sustainable, it is important for people to be able to work together to collaborate and create platforms for collective action, which are tasked with defined objectives and focus (Igué, 2010). Organisations can work together to create platforms for collective action, separate from their organisations. Sustainable development work has been attempted by some private-sector organisations and NGOs in a bid to try to solve the developmental challenges in African societies. In many cases, these have been fragmented, and in some cases, there have been overlap. The resultant effect is one that is less than the sum of its parts. To achieve a more effective approach to tackling sustainable development, we argue for concerted effort towards bridging the boundaries between the NGOs, the government and the private sector, together with the community, to ensure that efforts are able to achieve the best results, as opposed to a dispersed and fragmented approach to sustainable development. This introduces civil society into the development agenda.

The Africapitalist philosophy is currently silent on the role of civil society, yet civil society can be a useful intersection between the public and the private, championing societal issues, and working with stakeholders to ensure sustainable solutions are provided for sustainable development. The major advantage that these platforms have is that they are able to provide concerted interventions, over a period of time, and in this way, are sustainable. Moreover, because their primary remit is to provide specific interventions for sustainable development, they are able to focus, direct and target resources towards this area, and by so doing, are able to be effective and efficient (Bernard et al., 1998; Kincsei, 2009; Gottlieb and Sanzgiri, 1996).

Africapitalists can work to create and support platforms for collective action that can be focused on tackling developmental challenges and in this way also strengthen civil society, to introduce more change agents into the development equation for Africa.

The Ability to Focus on the Current and Long-Term Requirements of Society: The requirement to meet current and future societal needs presents the importance of continuity and sustainability, the setting of sustainable goals that go beyond the leader and the current organisation, taking the future into account. In this way, leadership for sustainable development has to be a wider-than-individual level focus, and in that sense, be sustainable itself, so that when the leader is no longer in the position of leadership, the focus on sustainable development continues in the organisation (Hyatt et al., 2010; Peterlin et al., 2013).

In this way, the Africapitalist will need to be conversant with succession planning and, by so doing, empower others to be Africapitalists themselves.

SUGGESTIONS FOR FUTURE RESEARCH AND
IMPLICATIONS FOR AFRICAPITALISM

This chapter has sought to explore the type of leadership required for the achievement of the Africapitalism agenda. We have analysed the extent to which private-sector leadership can be a major player in the economic and social development agenda for African countries. We provide below some suggestions for future research and their implications for Africapitalism.

Businesses operate in environments designed and regulated by the public sector. The relationship between the public and the private sectors and their combined roles in sustainable development is an area for future research, particularly as it relates to achieving the Africapitalism agenda. The public sector remains relevant to the sustainable development discourse in Africa given that the sector sets the policies that govern the extent to which businesses can thrive, and thus, any sustainable development objective is paramount to work with and influence the policies that can create, encourage and enhance the ability for economic and social wealth creation in Africa.

We acknowledge that in dynamic and complex organisations and societies, leadership is faced with complexity and ambiguity, making leading for sustainable development a challenging task. However, should sustainable development be viewed as part of the goals and objectives of an organisation, then sustainable development will not be seen as a separate and additional component of leadership, but rather as an important part of the roles and responsibilities of an effective leader. This is where the future of leadership lies.

Africapitalism as a management philosophy provides a unique space to situate the argument for more business involvement in development; however, more work needs to be done to create awareness about Africapitalism, what the role of business can and should be and how private-sector leaders can collaborate in a concerted way to actualise development. The focus on societal change recognises the importance of followers and alters the dynamics of the relationship from followers as subordinates towards the leader and followers as collaborators and co-creators of positive change in the society (Bennis, 2007). This is an important observation to make, given that both parties are stakeholders of the organisation as employees but are also members of the community within which the organisation operates.

Africapitalists are able to adapt to this change and remain confident and effective leaders who are able to learn from several people. Further research may be done to define the type of followership needed for sustainable development in various contexts in Africa. We also suggest that research be done to integrate effective leadership and leading for sustainable development, in order to explore how the boundary for effective leadership behaviour may be expanded beyond the organisation.

Our chapter has detailed the importance of collaboration towards achieving sustainable development. It has also highlighted the need for a holistic view to leadership for sustainable development, one that is able to appreciate and understand how various actors and stakeholders can play a part towards achieving the Africapitalism agenda. In defining and outlining the characteristics of an Africapitalist, we realise the role that leadership education can play in furthering this objective. Business schools and other training providers for business managers and future leaders have a role to play in incorporating in their curriculum the importance of leadership for sustainable development. Together with this, policy makers can work together with private-sector leaders to brainstorm and discuss how to create a more conducive business environment for businesses to thrive.

We have explored the meaning of an Africapitalist from the point of view of a private-sector leader, but this is not to say that leaders outside the private sector, for example leaders of public-sector organisations, civil society or employees within an organisation cannot be Africapitalists. Being an Africapitalist refers to an overarching objective to succeed as well as contribute to sustainable development in one's community. To this end, we all can be and should be Africapitalists. It will be useful for further research to explore and articulate what being an Africapitalist can mean as a follower, as well as for other stakeholders in the community.

CONCLUSION

Africapitalism has the potential to be a vehicle to convey ideas that emerge from the social dynamics of African communities, their social needs and their requirements of leadership. This chapter has probably raised more questions than it has answered. It is our hope that the questions will become conversation starters for further interrogation in academia and in practice, of how private-sector leadership as a construct can become focused on sustainable development, of how it can bring that closer to home, of what the purpose of leadership should be and of how leadership, political and business, can contribute towards sustainable development in Africa.

Our chapter also discussed the role of trust as an important component in achieving leadership for sustainable development. Leaders need to ensure their followers and other stakeholders trust that they are doing the best for the organisation and the society.

The Africapitalism management philosophy is still at its early stages, and some may argue that it does not present anything new. That argument is well considered. However, we can agree that the key messages of the philosophy, private-sector leadership for sustainable development in Africa, needs to be propagated among current leaders, and future leaders, providing Africa with leaders that are motivated and equipped to lead for sustainable development in Africa. In this way, the Africapitalism management philosophy becomes a useful vehicle to convey these messages.

Finally, the Africapitalism management philosophy needs to ensure that it is not simply repackaging Western management ideals and philosophies. Rather its definitions and interpretations of development, together with proposed solutions and changes to society, need to be congruent with the environment to which they are to be applied, requiring an informed understanding of the social dynamics at play in such African societies.

REFERENCES

Achcar, G. 2002. *The Clash of Barbarisms: September 11 and the Making of the New World Disorder.* Monthly Review Press. The University of Michigan.

Amaeshi, K. and Idemudia, U. 2015. Africapitalism: A Management Idea for Business in Africa? *Africa Journal of Management*, 2(1): 210–223.

Antonakis, J., Cianciolo, A. and Sternberg, R. 2004. *The Nature of Leadership.* Thousand Oaks, CA: Sage Publications, Inc.

August, O. 2013. Africa Rising: A Hopeful Continent. *The Economist.* Available at www.economist.com/news/special-report/21572377-african-lives-have-already-gre atly-improved-over-past-decade-says-oliver-august2. Accessed 4 December 2014.

Bass, B. 1985. *Leadership and Performance beyond Expectations.* New York, NY: Free Press.

Bass, B. 1990. From Transactional to Transformational Leadership: Learning to Share the Vision. *Organizational Dynamics*, 18(3): 19–31.

Bass, B. M. and Steidlmeier, P. 1999. Ethics, Character, and Authentic Transformational Leadership Behavior. *The Leadership Quarterly*, 10(2): 181–217.

Bass, B. M. 2008. The Bass Handbook of Leadership. *Theory, Research and Managerial Applications.* 4th edn. New York, NY: Free Press.

Bass, B. M. and Stogdill R. M. 1990. *Bass and Stogdill's Handbook of Leadership: Theory, Research, and Managerial Applications.* 3rd edn. New York, NY: Free Press.

Bennis, W. 2007. The Challenges of Leadership in the Modern World: Introduction to the Special Issue. *American Psychologist*, 62(1): 2.

Bernard, A., Helmich, H. and Lehning, P. B. 1998. Civil Society and International Development, North-South Centre of the Council of Europe, Development Centre of the Organization for Economic Co-operation and Development, France.

Brown, M. and Trevino, L. 2006. Ethical Leadership: A Review and Future Directions. *The Leadership Quarterly*, 17(6): 595–616.

Brown, M. T. 2006. Corporate Integrity and Public Interest: A Relational Approach to Business Ethics and Leadership. *Journal of Business Ethics*, 66(1): 11–18.

Burnes, B. and By, R. T. 2012. Leadership and Change: The Case for Greater Ethical Clarity. *Journal of Business Ethics*, 108(2): 239–252.

Burns, J. 1978. Leadership. New York, NY: Harper and Row.

Carmody, P. 2011. *The New Scramble for Africa*. Cambridge: Polity.

Case, P., French, R. and Simpson, P. 2011. Philosophy of Leadership. In *The Sage Handbook of Leadership*. Edited by A. Bryman, D. Collinson, K. Grint, B. Jackson and M. Uhl-Brien, 242–254.Thousand Oaks, CA: Sage Publications.

Crossan, M. and Mazutis, D. 2008. Transcendent Leadership. *Business Horizons*, 51 (2): 131–139.

DeChurch, L., Hiller, N., Murase, T., Doty, D. and Salas, E. 2010. Leadership across Levels: Levels of Leaders and Their Levels of Impact. *The Leadership Quarterly*, 21: 1069–1085.

Den Hartog, D. N. and Dickson, M. W. 2004. Leadership and Culture. In *The Nature of Leadership*. Edited by J. E. Antonakis, A. T. Cianciolo and R. J. Sternberg, 249–278. Thousand Oaks, CA: Sage Publications, Inc.

Elumelu, T. O. 2012. The Path to Economic Prosperity and Social Wealth. Available at www.heirsholdings.com/wp-content/uploads/2013/04/Africapitalism-Path -to-Economic-Prosperity-and-Social-Wealth. Accessed 16 January 2015.

Elumelu, T. 2014. Africapitalism. Available at www.tonyelumelu.com/africapital ism. Accessed 10 September 2014.

Epstein, M. J., Buhovac, A. R. and Yuthas, K. 2012. Implementing Sustainability: The Role of Leadership and Organizational Culture. *Strategic Finance*, 91(10): 41.

Friedman, M. 1962. Capitalism and Freedom. Chicago, IL: University of Chicago Press.

Gardner, J. 1990. On Leadership. New York: Free Press.

Gini, A. 1997. Moral Leadership: An Overview. *Journal of Business Ethics*, 16(3): 323–330.

Gottlieb, J. Z. and Sanzgiri, J. 1996. Towards an Ethical Dimension of Decision Making in Organizations. *Journal of Business Ethics*, 15(12): 1275–1285.

Harley, C., Metcalf, L. and Irwin, J. 2014. An Exploratory Study in Community Perspectives of Sustainability Leadership in the Murray Darling Basin. *Journal of Business Ethics*, 124(3): 413–433.

Herrick, C. and Pratt, J. 2012. Sustainability in the Water Sector: Enabling Lasting Change through Leadership and Cultural Transformation. *Nature and Culture*, 7 (3): 285–313.

Horlings, I. and Padt, F. 2013. Leadership for Sustainable Regional Development in Rural Areas: Bridging Personal and Institutional Aspects. *Sustainable Development*, 21(6): 413–424.

Horner, M. 1997. Leadership Theory: Past, Present and Future. *Team Performance Management*, 3(4): 270–287.

House, R. J., Hanges, P. J., Javidan, M., Dorfman, P. W. and Gupta, V. (eds.). 2004. *Culture, Leadership, and Organizations: The GLOBE Study of 62 Societies.* Thousand Oaks, CA: Sage Publications.

Hyatt, L., Schmieder-Ramirez, J. and Madjidi, F. 2010. Sustainable Leaders – Responsible Action: 'A Call for Courage During a Crisis of Confidence'. SAM *Advanced Management Journal,* 75(1): 17.

Igué, J. O. 2010. A New Generation of Leaders in Africa: What Issues Do They Face? *International Development Policy | Revue internationale de politique de développement,* 1: 115–133.

Kennedy, P. T. 1988. *African Capitalism: The Struggle for Ascendency.* Cambridge: Cambridge University Press.

Kincsei, É. 2009. 'Abszurd dolog nem növekedni' (It Is Absurd Not to Extend), Index.hu. Available at http://index.hu/gazdasag/magyar/2009/06/20/abszurd_do log_nem_novekedni/?rnd=411. Accessed June 2009.

Knights, D. and O'Leary, M. 2006. Leadership, Ethics and Responsibility to the Other. *Journal of Business Ethics,* 67(2): 125–137.

Kroeck, K. G., Lowe, K. B. and Brown, K. W. 2004. The Assessment of Leadership. In *The Nature of Leadership.* Edited by J. Antonakis, A. Cianciolo and R. Sternberg, 71–98. Thousand Oaks, CA: Sage Publications.

Ladkin, A. and Weber, K. 2011. Leadership Issues and Challenges in the Tourism Industry: A Hong Kong Perspective. *Asia Pacific Journal of Tourism Research,* 16 (3): 273–288.

Maak, T. and Pless, N. M. 2006. Responsible Leadership in a Stakeholder Society – A Relational Perspective. *Journal of Business Ethics,* 66(1): 99–115.

Maak, T. and Pless, N. M. 2009. Business Leaders as Citizens of the World: Advancing Humanism on a Global Scale. *Journal of Business Ethics,* 88(3): 537–550.

McCann, J. and Sweet, M. 2014. The Perceptions of Ethical and Sustainable Leadership. *Journal of Business Ethics,* 121(3): 373–383.

Peterlin, J., Dimovski, V. and Penger, S. 2013. Creation of Sustainable Leadership Development: Conceptual Model Validation. *Managing Global Transitions,* 11 (2): 201–216.

Rodriguez, M. A., Ricart, J. E. and Sanchez, P. 2002. Sustainable Development and Sustainability of Competitive Advantage: A Dynamic and Sustainable View of the Firm. *Sustainable Development and Competitive Advantage,* 11(3): 135–146.

Ruiz, P., Ruiz, C. and Martínez, R. 2011. Improving the 'Leader–Follower' Relationship: Top Manager or Supervisor? The Ethical Leadership Trickle-Down Effect on Follower Job Response. *Journal of Business Ethics,* 99(4): 587–608.

Safty, A. 2003. Moral Leadership: Beyond Management and Governance. *Harvard International Review*, 25(3): 84–85.

Sassen, S. 1999. Globalization and Its Discontents: Essays on the New Mobility of People and Money. New York, NY: New Press.

Scherer, A. G. and Palazzo, G. 2011. The New Political Role of Business in a Globalized World: A Review of a New Perspective on CSR and Its Implications for the Firm, Governance, and Democracy. *Journal of Management Studies*, 48(4): 899–931.

Springett, D. 2013. Editorial: Critical Perspectives on Sustainable Development. *Sustainable Development*, 21(2): 73–82.

Stahl, G. K. and de Luque, M. S. 2014. Antecedents of Responsible Leader Behavior: A Research Synthesis, Conceptual Framework, and Agenda for Future Research. *The Academy of Management Perspectives*, 28(3): 235–254.

Stampini, M., Leung, R., Diarra, S. and Pla, L. 2013. How Large Is the Private Sector in Africa? Evidence from National Accounts and Labor Markets. *South African Journal of Economics*, 81(1): 140–165.

Sternberg, R. J. and Hedlund, J. 2002. Practical Intelligence, g, and Work Psychology. *Human Performance*. 15(1–2): 143–160.

Stigliz, J. E. 2002. Globalization and Its Discontents. New York, NY: W.W. Norton.

Storey, J. 2004. Leadership in Organizations: Current Issues and Key Trends. London: Routledge.

Thompson, L. J. 2004. Moral Leadership in a Postmodern World. *Journal of Leadership and Organizational Studies*, 11(1): 27–37.

Thompson, L. J. 2010. The Global Moral Compass for Business Leaders. *Journal of Business Ethics*, 93(1): 15–32.

Waldman, D. A. and Galvin, B. M. 2008. Alternative Perspectives of Responsible Leadership. *Organizational Dynamics*, 13(3): 26–40.

Wang, X., Van Wart, M. and Lebredo, N. 2014. Sustainability Leadership in a Local Government Context: The Administrator's Role in the Process. *Public Performance and Management Review*, 37(3): 339–364.

Warhurst, A. 2005. Future Roles of Business in Society: The Expanding Boundaries of Corporate Responsibility and a Compelling Case for Partnership. *Futures*, 37 (2): 151–168.

World Commission on Environment and Development. 1987. *Our Common Future*. Oxford: Oxford University Press.

Yukl, G. 2010. *Leadership in Organizations*. 7th edn. New York, NY: Pearson Prentice Hall.

8 Social Entrepreneurship and Africapitalism: Exploring the Connections

Diane Holt and David Littlewood

INTRODUCTION

Increasingly, business is being called upon to help address a wide range of sustainable development challenges, such as the acute and complex social and environmental problems facing the African continent. Across Africa these various challenges offer significant 'opportunity' spaces for the formation of new businesses, products and services, and we are seeing the emergence of varying social, environmental and 'hybrid' enterprises that have at the heart of their business model the goal to address these challenges through an income-generating approach (Haigh et al., 2015; Holt and Littlewood, 2015). Concurrently, in recent times we have witnessed the emergence of the notion of Africapitalism, which posits that the private sector can be at the heart of, and generate, both economic prosperity and social wealth in Africa (Amaeshi and Idemundia, 2015).

The potential of social entrepreneurship as a mechanism for addressing social and environmental challenges is increasingly recognised by Africa's policy makers. For example, the South African Government's 2010 Decent Work Country Programme identifies a key role for the country's emerging social economy, including cooperative enterprises and social businesses, with this reaffirmed in the New Growth Path Framework (2011), which identifies growth in the social economy – comprising a myriad of organisation types including co-operatives, NGOs, social businesses and stokvels (informal savings schemes) – as a significant source of new jobs. Similarly, the African

Leadership Institute, established by Archbishop Desmond Tutu and underpinned by the African philosophy of Ubuntu and notions of reciprocity (see Mangaliso 2001; West 2014), also advocates social enterprise and wider ethical business as forces for positive societal change and black economic empowerment (Littlewood and Holt, 2015) and particularly for promoting transformative change. It is argued that such enterprises (Doherty et al., 2014) can target unmet social needs and bridge institutional voids neglected by the state (e.g., Mair et al., 2012). In this chapter, we examine these specialised mission-driven organisations that are emerging in the social economy in Africa, and specifically we consider such organisations in the light of the emerging framing of the Africapitalism concept (see Amaeshi and Idemudia, 2015).

From early criticisms of universalism implicit in US-centric management research by Boyacigiller and Adler (1991), to the recent paper by Zoogah et al. (2015) calling for more Africa-focused management research, and particularly around institutional influences, many acknowledge the need for further scholarship on business and management in Africa. Indeed Walsh (2015) recently stated, 'Many of the world's organisation and management scholars know little about business practice in Africa.' The idea of an African style of management is discussed by Mangaliso (2001) in his exploration of philosophical concept of Ubuntu. This is a term from the Nguni group of languages, which Lutz (2009) defines as 'humanness, or being human' and introduced through the words of Archbishop Desmond Tutu:

> Ubuntu is very difficult to render into a Western language. It speaks of the very essence of being human. When we want to give high praise to someone we say, 'he or she has Ubuntu.' This means they are generous, hospitable, friendly, caring and compassionate. They share what they have. It also means my humanity is caught up, is inextricably bound up, in theirs.
>
> *(cited in Lutz, 2009: 314)*

The philosophy of Ubuntu is one that is foundational to the idea of Africapitalism (Lutz, 2009; Amaeshi and Idemudia, 2015). In their exploration of Africapitalism, Amaeshi and Idemudia (2015) point to the idea that the private sector has a key role to play in the socio-economic development of Africa drawing on calls from Elumelu (2012) that African businesses have an obligation to step up and meet this responsibility. This idea of business playing a key role in addressing these sustainable development problems clearly resonates with the ideas of social entrepreneurship. Although Amaeshi is at pains to stress that all African business have a part to play in Africapitalism (Young, 2014), including through what he describes as inclusive capitalism, responsible capitalism, sustainable capitalism and progressive capitalism, as well as social entrepreneurship.

Thus we see firstly that there are acute, complex and intractable social and environmental problems to be addressed in Africa. Secondly, we see arguments that businesses may have a role to play in addressing these problems, particularly those firms driven by a mission, like social enterprises. Yet it is also suggested that management practice on the African continent is influenced by a specific 'African-centric' context. Thus, the concept of Africapitalism has emerged as a way to both rethink the role of business within society and in the achieving of development goals and addressing Africa's challenges, and as recognising the potential for special characteristics of management unique to an African context.

We begin this chapter by setting the scene, considering the nature of social entrepreneurship (and to some extent hybrid firms) in an African context. Next we discuss in greater detail the ideas of Africapitalism and consider its intersection with social entrepreneurship and specifically with African social entrepreneurship. We illustrate our discussion drawing on our research with a range of mission-based enterprises including social, environmental and hybrid firms (and support agencies or NGOs) across eastern and southern Africa in our 'Trickle Out Africa' research project.[1]

MISSION-DRIVEN FIRMS

The study of social entrepreneurship and other forms of mission-driven firms such as hybrid organisations remains embryonic and contested, particularly around the boundary conditions that delineate such firms. Most agree that such firms combine an enterprise-based income-generation model and place the achievement of their social or environmental goals at the heart of their activities and investments (Dacin et al., 2011). However beyond that, heated debate tends to emerge when considering how much profit can be taken or how assets are (or are not) locked in (Rivera-Santos et al., 2015; Holt and Littlewood, 2015). The significance of context and environmental characteristics is receiving increasing attention within social entrepreneurship scholarship, much akin to calls within Africapitalism debates. Indeed Amaeshi and Idemudia (2015) note that prior discussions of the role of business in society often take context for granted, and only really consider how historical institutional contexts may influence 'why' a firm has behaved in a particular manner.

The impact of the context in which a social enterprise is based is discussed by a number of authors, including Bacq and Janssen (2011) and Littlewood and Holt (2015). In developing countries, it is arguably this context that shapes the kinds of institutional voids (Mair et al., 2012) or 'gaps' (Kolk, 2014) that provide business opportunities (Santos, 2012) for both mainstream commercial business and those that sit more within non-profit, social or hybrid enterprise spaces. Suggestions from Julian and Ofori-Dankwa (2013) of an institutional difference hypothesis between developed and developing countries touches on the influence of different institutional contexts on Corporate Social Responsibility (CSR). In Rivera-Santos et al. (2015), this debate goes further to suggest differences not just between devel-

---

[1]   Essex Business School, Trickle Out Africa Project, www.trickleout.net.

oping and developed countries in terms of social entrepreneurship but across Africa, between different African nations, and indeed perhaps even between differing regions or groups. This can be illustrated with reference to places like South Africa with its specific institutional environment, including the promotion of the Broad Based Black Economic Empowerment (BBBEE) agenda which has led to closer business relationships between social enterprises and larger commercial firms (Littlewood and Holt, 2015) in a manner different to other African nations who have not legislated for transformation.

This raises an interesting query with regard to Africapitalism: if social entrepreneurship varies across the African continent, then perhaps there are multiple variants of Africapitalism? Does Africapitalism 'look' the same in Nigeria versus say South Africa, or Burundi or indeed one of the African Small Island States like the Seychelles?

THE PRINCIPLES OF AFRICAPITALISM

The idea of Africapitalism was developed by the Nigerian economist, business person and philanthropist Tony O. Elumelu, in part informed by his activities as the chairperson of Heirs Holdings, the United Bank for Africa, and Transcorp. In light of our prior comments, we should note that he draws on his particular Nigerian heritage in his discussions of Africapitalism – this is a factor that needs to be revisited in the theoretical explorations being called for by Amaeshi and Idemudia (2015) of the positioning of the Africapitalism concept. These formative experiences appear to have shaped his belief in private-sector investment as a way to create catalytic and sustainable change in communities in a manner he argues that charity and aid relief cannot.

We can explore the positioning of the Africapitalism concept by considering how it is presented by his Tony Elumelu Foundation,[2] which he founded in 2010. They suggest:

---

[2]   Tony Elumelu Foundation, http://tonyelumelufoundation.org/faqs/africapitalism-faqs/, accessed 10 March 2016.

- That, through Africapitalism, the private sector can solve Africa's development challenges more effectively and with greater sustainability than either the philanthropic or public sector
- That Africapitalism is an economic activity that is value-adding and that can have a social impact that creates wealth value within Africa by Africans for the long term
- That it will lead to transformation of Africa in a profitable and sustainable manner
- That the chief responsibility of African governments within an Africapitalism perspective should be to create an enabling environment in which the private sector can engage in wealth-generating economic activity
- That there is a different role for philanthropy in African as either a form of relief or charity to address issues such as natural disasters or providing funding to allow risk-taking with new business initiatives and programmes not possible when considered purely through a return-on-investment approach

Edwards (2013) in her review of Africapitalism for the *Guardian* discusses how this idea draws on notions of shared value (see for instance Porter and Kramer, 2011) and what she describes as the double bottom line; the doing well by doing good mantra that has emerged in the multinational business environment over the last decade. She suggests that 'doing well and doing good are in fact co-dependent' in Eleumelu's concept and that this re-imagines CSR by focusing on aspects such as the health of their 'local' communities in order to secure future profits and custom for the business. This is much like the *people, planet, profits* mantra of the triple bottom line and the win-win perspective of corporate sustainability (after Elkington, 1997), though we would argue that in Eleumelu's perspective it is more of a profit for people and planet approach.

Amaeshi and Idemudia (2015) explore the foundational ideas underpinning the Africapitalism notion in the founding issue of the *African Academy of Management Journal*. They suggest that the notion differs from other sustainability-related concepts such as CSR, shared value and the many other proliferations around the idea that business can solve wicked sustainable development problems, due to the four cardinal values that are embedded within Africapitalism. They suggest that these values are ideas of sense of progress and prosperity, sense of parity, sense of peace and harmony and sense of place and belongingness. We now consider these cardinal values in our exploration of the intersection between Africapitalism as a concept and the various social, environmental and hybrid firms we have observed in our fieldwork across sub-Saharan Africa.

CONSIDERING MISSION-DRIVEN FIRMS THROUGH THE LENS OF AFRICAPITALISM

In this section, we consider how Africapitalism speaks to the emerging narratives on firms associated with delivering a social and/or environmental mission; namely those commonly described as social enterprises (which includes those that have a specific environmental mission) and the recent discussions of hybrid firms (Haigh et al., 2015). All these mission-based firms seek to address one or more specific issues facing society, from macro-level issues like climate change to highly localised issues such as access to clean water in a specific locale or offering employment to specific marginalised groups. Each will 'sacrifice' profit (or reinvest surplus) in order to achieve these goals, which are at the heart of their business model or the distribution of 'benefits' from their income streams. All have an element of trading, though they may draw on other sources of funding.

This leads to our first discussion point in terms of the intersection of Africapitalism with these mission-driven firms. The positioning of Africapitalism seems to suggest that African enterprises have a specific role to play in development that cannot be achieved by aid and philanthropic efforts, as if these are somehow part of separate entities. However, many of our case examples are types of social enterprises that we might think of as hybrids (see Holt and Littlewood, 2015) or they are social enterprises that sit much closer to the charitable/non-profit end of the spectrum. But they still trade. They are still enterprises. They still demonstrate characteristics and operational practices that are found in 'traditional' businesses. So, as such they can be a composite and amalgamation of elements from across these organisational forms, suggesting that Africapitalism has a hybrid form that incorporates the charitable and philanthropic dimensions as integral parts of its genetic structure or business model.

This then leads to our next point – the role of profit. As we discuss earlier, we suggest that Africapitalism as currently framed is about profits for people and planet. This perhaps suggests that profit is to be maximised in order to generate maximum impact. But this is fundamentally against the principles seen in the various social, and indeed hybrid, entrepreneurship discourses. These narratives are about 'tempered' profit-taking if profit is taken at all – where the social mission takes primacy. In some of the 'pure' social enterprise narratives, it is suggested no profit distribution can occur and that all surpluses should be reinvested into the social mission and assets locked in to protect this. On the surface this seems to suggest a fundamental disconnect between a social entrepreneurship agenda and Africapitalism. However, as we explore in our study of hybrid social enterprises in Holt and Littlewood (2015) there are social enterprise variants that 'take' profit. What distinguishes them, though, from commercial firms is a limitation on profit maximisation and where solving the social/environmental mission is the primary reason for generating income, rather than the social issue as the opportunity being exploited in order to ensure dividends for shareholders. Whilst Africapitalism makes some reference to benefits to stakeholders, how this plays out in practice remains opaque. Other hybrid firms include community-based organisations where the income generated is invested into the local community. These again are not a particular African concept but the designation of who the 'community' consists of may be influenced by normative values that are particularly African, such as a particular tribal identity.

Therefore, we face a dilemma when considering the role of profit in the discussion of such mission-based firms in Africa, as we do in the wider conversions happening around social enterprises (Rivera Santos et al., 2015). If we really want the best and brightest entrepreneurs to come up with the most innovative solutions to the myriad of social, economic and environmental problems facing Africa, then we have to realise that their altruism has to be balanced alongside a need to generate an income. A particular characteristic often stressed about African nations is the role of the extended family – not just immediate siblings but also through tribal bonds and extended family networks. This means that individuals do not have to provide just for themselves but are likely to have a need to provide for this wider family also. They have an obligation to be successful in order to repay the help they have most likely received and as part of an obligation they will feel towards their extended families. So perhaps the difference we see between the western construct of social enterprises as non-profits and the more hybridised form of social enterprises we have experienced in Africa is *because* of the influence of Africapitalism dimensions on the organisational forms that emerge.

Our third macro-level consideration of the Africapitalism concept and our African social enterprises was introduced earlier – the influence of context. The Africapitalism concept recognises a difference between capitalism in say the West and capitalism in Africa linked to the four cardinal values we discuss in more depth below. However, little is mentioned of potential differences in Africapitalism across the African continent.

If, as discussed in Rivera-Santos et al. (2015) and Littlewood and Holt (2015), differences emerge in social entrepreneurship in differing institutional regimes with varied regulatory, normative and cognitive dimensions, then this must surely be influential in Africapitalism. Africa is not one institutionally homogenous space – it has varied cultural, colonial, economic and social influences. Even across one Africa nation we see differences – for instance across Kenya where long-standing tribal differences have erupted into violence on a number of occasions. Some tribal groups, like the Kikuyu, are often described as more entrepreneurial than others. In West Africa, the Akans of Ghana are matrilineal, with property passed down the maternal line at death, and new families locate close to the bride's relatives not the groom's. The Maasai, however, are a strongly patriarchal tribe with male elders speaking for the tribe. Amine and Staub (2009) explore women entrepreneurs in sub-Saharan Africa, noting institutional differences between groups in terms of regulatory dimensions (e.g., access to capital, microcredit, inheritance laws, and property ownership), normative dimensions (e.g., community norms, beliefs systems, ethnicity, cultural factors and social role) and cognitive dimensions (e.g., level of education, training and technological literacy). Thus institutional logics – as 'the socially constructed, historical patterns of material practices, assumptions, values, beliefs, and rules by which individuals produce and reproduce their material subsistence, organise time and space, and provide meaning to their social reality' (Thornton and Ocasio, 1999: 804) – are clearly part of the framing of Africapitalism. But we need to explore if these institutional logics differ across Africa or even within one African nation.

We now turn to the four cardinal values suggested by Amaeshi and Idemudia (2015) as the foundational ideals of Africapitalism.

SENSE OF PROGRESS AND PROSPERITY

In their exploration, Amaeshi and Idemudia refer to the idea of progress and prosperity, which goes beyond social wealth and financial prosperity to incorporate what they describe as 'psycho-social' human well-being. They draw on the Bundtland (1994) discussion of prosperity as more than just an absence of poverty. This core value of progress and prosperity can be clearly linked to the ideas of multidimensional poverty alleviation (after Alkire and Foster, 2011) that have been adopted by development agencies including the World Bank. It speaks to Sen's (2001) exploration of capabilities through his 'Development as Freedom' classic text. Even just offering access to secure employment – for example Tribal Textiles in Zambia or Khayelitsha Cookies in South Africa (Holt and Littlewood, 2013b) – can lead to other impacts that are linked to this income security such as investing in education.

However, the Africapitalism concept also recognises environmental sustainability and especially aspects such as carrying capacity and sustainable resources. Many of the environmentally focussed mission-driven organisations we have seen in our fieldwork speak to this same narrative. The solar lights being used across Africa as rental/ sales models also seek to help reduce air pollution by reducing kerosene consumption, and have substitution effects when savings from the lamps are invested in school fees and food security. In our hybrid environmental business models, you see profit-making and the enterprise dimension taking primacy but not at the expense of failing to achieve a social/environmental mission (Holt and Littlewood, 2015; Littlewood and Holt, 2013a). Organisations such as Cookswell are focused on environmental sustainability through a seed-to-ash cycle and energy-efficient cookstoves, recognising the continued reliance on charcoal in Africa that is very unlikely to ever fully disappear (Littlewood and Holt, 2013a). Their business model (see also Holt and Littlewood, 2015) speaks to this narrative on sustainable natural resource use but also recognises that savings incurred through reduced charcoal costs can be reinvested in other well-being activities. They promote the reforestation and wise use agenda through advocacy but also through providing seeds in the products they sell to allow individuals to self-plant. So here we see organisations 'sacrificing' profit in order to generate these additional well-being dimensions not just as an add-on but as a fundamental component of their business models. We see Cookswell as a hybrid firm that seeks to address an environmental mission with associated social benefits yet with limited profit-taking. This is a firm that is specifically focused on the characteristics of the African environment – the dominance of charcoal – yet is now beginning to export its ovens to Europe where they are bought as luxury camping and home items for the barbeque market.

In some social enterprises, the mission is the key focus of their activities, and they operate much more like non-profits: for instance, the BookBus and its focus on literacy within African schools (Holt and Littlewood, 2013a). They do not address all of the aspects covered in the Millennium (and now Sustainable) Development Goals but seek to improve literacy that will then hopefully have a ripple-out impact in the future on these other aspects.

We can argue that secure employment leads then to investments in these other well-being dimensions not just the domain of these mission-driven organisations. Indeed any firm can generate such impacts. The difference between our social/environmental/hybrid mission-based enterprises is the primacy of the mission over profit beyond that of CSR dimensions. These aspects, which we consider fundamental to progress and prosperity, such as empowerment, food security, illiteracy and many others, are the reason our mission-driven enterprises were formed, and their activities directly focus on addressing one or more of these, taking primacy over the generation of profit.

SENSE OF PARITY

This value within Africapitalism is about the creation of wealth for all – with financial and social wealth created for all stakeholders, not just shareholders. In the 'pure' social enterprise narratives then, the assets of the social enterprise are locked in to be reimbursed to the 'community', though we argue elsewhere that this narrow view of social enterprises is not a feasible one on the African continent. We would debate whether all traditional forms of business in Africa can ever truly seek parity and the inclusivity agenda that this value suggests.

However, many of the African mission-driven firms from across the spectrum from profit-taking to non-profit do 'share' some aspect of their wealth creation. But not everyone receives the 'same' wealth – even in our mission-based firms. They may receive 'literacy' but do not necessarily receive other forms of capital. The achievement of providing literacy then leads potentially to this other wealth for beneficiaries. This idea of parity is one that highlights the issues facing socially driven firms – they cannot fix all problems: (i) they can only address the one specific aspect they focus on such as access to clean water or lighting (e.g., Solar Sisters) and (ii) it is inevitable that not everyone benefits in the same manner as they often focus on a specific marginalised group. In our discussion of hybrid African firms, we also note the trade-offs that occur and the possibility of negative impacts (Holt and Littlewood, 2015), where, for instance, positive social impacts might have a negative environmental impact. So even within our sample there is not parity between social and environmental dimensions, and certainly only specific beneficiary groups will gain. Mumwa Crafts focuses on farmers in Western Zambia (Littlewood and Holt, 2013b) but not those in urban communities. The Book Bus selects specific schools in Zambia and Malawi. In Africapitalism, there is a mention of the idea of local communities – what is local? The idea of benefiting stakeholders as part of Africapitalism does resonate with the mission-driven firm's agenda. But in both cases the decision on who the stakeholders are is determined by the nature and size of the business in question, whether it is a traditional African commercial firm, a non-profit social enterprise or a hybrid firm.

SENSE OF PEACE AND HARMONY

Here Amaeshi and Idemudia (2015) recognise that capitalism often leads to creative destruction and the emergence of new forms of business, leading to potentially massive financial returns when this is successful and more problems if it fails. They suggest that Africapitalism should seek balance in consumption and production akin to the sustainability movement. Here we see more parallels with our mission-based organisations whose primary focus is on environmental dimensions. Solar lights have the potential to be disruptive technology that also generates environmental benefits. Similarly Cookswell's focus on sustainable charcoal seeks this balance and harmony – to be disruptive but also leading to a new 'steady-state'. However, perhaps this cardinal value of Africapitalism speaks most clearly to the idea of hybrid firms in the African context which seek to maximise positive social/environmental benefits and reduce the negative ones but that recognise the two cannot be mutually exclusive

(Haigh et al., 2015; Holt and Littlewood, 2015). There is a balance struck by each firm in the relative positioning of the social and environmental benefits they seek to achieve for stakeholders and the relative importance of economic benefits (to the firm and its shareholders).

SENSE OF PLACE AND BELONGING

This cardinal value speaks to the normative influences of culture such as Ubuntu and the importance of the extended African family and thus associated obligations that we have discussed earlier in this chapter. Africapitalism is arguably by its very nature about being African – African business in Africa by Africans to benefit Africans. That does not mean it cannot operate elsewhere – perhaps we will see elements of Africapitalism in the diaspora in places such as the USA and in Europe especially where those from different parts of Africa might set up business in a regional cluster or tend to live in a diaspora community.

Our work on social enterprises in Africa also suggests that the institutional logics of Africa have a key role to play in the nature and mission of various types of socially focused firms. Here in Africapitalism the sense of place may be about being in a particular part of Africa – perhaps even as wide as being 'African'. But perhaps this sense of the wider classification of being African only really plays out when an individual is outside of the continent. Where as a group they identify with the larger continent when feeling an outsider? Certainly in those parts of Africa suffering from tribal violence individuals are more likely to describe themselves as belonging to a particular tribe. In South Africa there have been recent clashes between those from different African countries clashing with those from South Africa. Here would someone describe themselves as African or South African? So the sense of place is also geographically constrained – much like the idea of what 'local' is and therefore who your stakeholders are in the context of your firm.

Arguably also the sense of space, that idea of understanding the specific nature of the environment in which a firm is based, and thus the opportunities that might exist, is common across all businesses that draw on a regional framing. But Africapitalism suggests that there is a stronger, more unifying force where patriotism to their specific African nation and perhaps the wider continent shapes what firms seek to achieve. In part, this is perhaps due to the sheer scale of the problems the continent faces and the lack of seemingly viable alternatives, especially in the absence of strong state institutions and state support.

Certainly within African social and hybrid firms, the idea of a responsibility to a community – be that local, or national, or even the African continent, shines through in the discussions we have had. That sense of place and belonging is particularly acute in those regional enterprises like Ecofinder Kenya who focus on enterprise-based initiatives to support the lakeside community of Kisumu. Indeed Mumwa Crafts clearly identifies with the specific regional challenges of Western Zambia (Littlewood and Holt, 2013b). Tribal textiles, for instance, set up in South Luangwa in Zambia rather than the more accessible location in the capital Lusaka specifically because it wanted to offer employment in a region where few businesses were located beyond safari firms. Thus they feel a loyalty to this region and remain there even though it 'costs' more in transport and lack of passing trade. They have a sense of self associated with this region that is then part of the story they tell in their marketing literature and part of what they leveraged to gain their international contracts.

Yet whilst Africapitalism talks about enterprises set up by African for Africans we also see some of the African mission-driven enterprises set up by expatriates where they can sometimes bring with them skills and access to resources that an indigenous group might currently lack. When we look at the most successful African firms, many of these are headed by individuals educated outside of Africa, who bring back with them additional capabilities that have been inculcated elsewhere – albeit with an African twist.

Yet the dominance of the expatriate within many mission-driven social enterprises (especially the non-profit kind) is a challenge to the development of the social economy in some parts of Africa. When they leave, as they often do, this can lead to the failure of the enterprise. Perhaps their sense of the place (and thus that of their organisation) is not African? The ones suffering from this, the least in our experience, are those where succession planning is built into the operation of the enterprise by those who have seen themselves merely as custodians of an enterprise that belongs to a community. That is not to say we did not see lots of examples of mission-driven firms led by Africans. Mumwa Crafts is a very good example where previous craft-based projects by expatriates had failed. They believe that they have succeeded where others from outside could not because of, not despite of, their local identity.

So this idea of sense and place and belonging is arguably shaped by three things regardless of the type of business in question: (i) the opportunities that the business model exploits or the social need being addressed; (ii) the loyalty given to a specific community (with the scale dependent on the scale of the business); and (iii) the nature of the stakeholders this organisation then identifies.

FINAL THOUGHTS

So does Africapitalism have a place in the consideration of mission-driven firms such as social enterprises, cooperatives, trading NGOs, charities with a business model, Fairtrade, green businesses like solar and organics or the more encompassing term 'hybrids'? Basically does it have a place within firms where profit-making takes a backseat to the social mission the business is focused on?

We think there is much to draw on within the Africapitalism framing that resonates with all of these non-traditional types of business models. Certainly, there is emerging evidence of an African 'difference', but also perhaps a 'within-Africa' variability. So at an umbrella, macrolevel we have an African identity, but this is nested within a specific regional, national or tribal African identity that shapes the nature of the businesses created, how they operate, the stakeholders they see, the opportunities they exploit or the social problems they address and the barriers that they face.

The idea of obligation and responsibility is strong within our mission-driven firms, but also we see this across the more commercial organisations within Africa. We must not forget that those running these commercial firms are as much aware of the social problems facing the continent as those running social enterprises. They just take a different path in the type of business created.

However, we do see a role for philanthropic and aid-based organisations in our types of firms. Having an enterprise arm of such organisations makes them more sustainable in the longer term – especially in the era of austerity and diminished funding. There is also a role for governments; but only those that are institutionally strong, fair and transparent. Many of the social enterprises we see emerge to address the voids left by weak states and lack of state provision.

It is tempting to see market-based mechanisms and a win-win scenario of private firms solving the challenging problems we face as a society. This was the premise behind the green business movement from the early 1990s in the UK and USA – where the utopian ideal of the free market regulating environmental excesses and providing innovative solutions to environmental challenges was supposed to transform society in a sustainable and profitable manner. Much like Africapitalism, this same mantra is still in force today and indeed is here to stay. However, the UK also has one of the fastest-growing social enterprise sectors in the world – and still faces many of the environmental problems the free market was supposed to fix. There is no one solution to the wicked sustainable development problems we face, so commercial 'traditional' firms cannot solve these with only market-based solutions.

So what is our answer to the question we posed? Africapitalism is an embryonic concept which is in flux and perhaps transition. It is also something that may move beyond the scope and framing of its originator. There are elements of the Africapitalism premise being discussed in the literature that are very similar to those in the social and hybrid enterprise domains, the primary one being the need to take a specific African-centric approach and recognise how the specific institutional logics at play on the continent then shape organisational forms, function and management.

REFERENCES

Alkire, S. and Foster, J. 2011. Understandings and Misunderstandings of Multidimensional Poverty Measurement. *The Journal of Economic Inequality*, 9(2): 289–314.

Amaeshi, K. and Idemudia, U. 2015. Africapitalism: A Management Idea for Business in Africa? *Africa Journal of Management*, 1(2): 210–223.

Amine, L. S. and Staub, K. M. 2009. Women Entrepreneurs in Sub-Saharan Africa: An Institutional Theory Analysis from a Social Marketing Point of View. *Entrepreneurship and Regional Development*, 21(2): 183–211.

Bacq, S. and Janssen, F. 2011. The Multiple Faces of Social Entrepreneurship: A Review of Definitional Issues Based on Geographical and Thematic Criteria. *Entrepreneurship and Regional Development*, 23(5–6): 373–403.

Boyacigiller N. A. and Adler N. J. 1991. The Parochial Dinosaur: Organizational Science in a Global Context. *Academy of Management Review*, 16: 262–290.

Brundtland, G. H. 1994. What Is World Prosperity? *Business Strategy Review*, 5(2): 57–69.

Dacin, M. T., Dacin, P. A. and Tracey, P. T. 2011. Social Entrepreneurship: A Critique and Future Directions. *Organization Science*, 22(5): 1203–1213.

Doherty, B., Haugh, H. and Lyon, F. 2014. Social Enterprises as Hybrid Organizations: A Review and Research Agenda. *International Journal of Management Reviews*, 16(4): 417–436.

Edwards, R. 2013. Can Africapitalism Save the Continent? *The Guardian*, 12 July. Available at www.theguardian.com/world/2013/jul/12/africa-africapitalism -tony-elumelu. Accessed 28 January 2018.

Elkington, J. 1997. *Cannibals with Forks. The Triple Bottom Line of 21st Century*. Oxford, UK: Capstone Publishing.

Elumelu, T. O. 2012. The Path to Economic Prosperity and Social Wealth. Available at www.heirsholdings. com/wp-content/uploads/2013/04/Africapitalism-Path-to -Economic-Prosperity-and-Social-Wealth. pdf. Accessed 18 January 2015.

Haigh, N., Walker, J., Bacq, S., and Kickul, J. 2015. Hybrid Organizations: Origins, Strategies, Impacts, and Implications. *California Management Review*, 57 (3): 5–12.

Holt, D. and Littlewood, D. 2013a. The Book Bus 'Improving Children's Lives One Book at a Time'. The Trickle Out Africa Project Case Study Series No. 2. February, ISSN 2052–0026.

Holt, D. and Littlewood, D. 2013b. The Khayelitsha Cookie Company 'Creating Opportunity One Bite at a Time'. The Trickle Out Africa Project Case Study Series No. 4. May, ISSN 2052–0026.

Holt, D. and Littlewood, D. 2015. Identifying, Mapping, and Monitoring the Impact of Hybrid Firms. *California Management Review*, 57(3): 107–125.

Julian, S. D. and Ofori-Dankwa, J. C. 2013. Financial Resource Availability and Corporate Social Responsibility Expenditures in a Sub-Saharan Economy: The Institutional Difference Hypothesis. *Strategic Management Journal*, 34 (11): 1314–1330.

Kolk, A. 2014. Linking Subsistence Activities to Global Marketing Systems, the Role of Institutions. *Journal of Macromarketing*, 34(2): 182–194.

Littlewood, D. and Holt, D. 2013a. Cookswell Enterprises 'Save Money, Save Energy, Save Our Forests and Eat Well'. The Trickle Out Africa Project Case Study Series No. 1. February, ISSN 2052–0026.

Littlewood, D. and Holt, D. 2013b. The Mumwa Crafts Association Community 'Development through Craft Production'. The Trickle Out Africa Project Case Study Series No. 3. April, ISSN 2052–0026.

Littlewood, D. and Holt, D. 2015. Social Entrepreneurship in South Africa: Exploring the Influence of Environment. *Business and Society*, DOI: 10.1177/ 0007650315613293.

London, T., Anupindi, R. and Sheth, S. 2010. Creating Mutual Value: Lessons Learned from Ventures Serving Base of the Pyramid Producers. *Journal of Business Research*, 63(6): 582–594.

London, T. and Hart, S. L. 2010. *Next Generation Business Strategies for the Base of the Pyramid: New Approaches for Building Mutual Value*. Pearson Education India.

Lutz, D. W. 2009. African Ubuntu Philosophy and Global Management. *Journal of Business Ethics*, 84: 313–328.

Mair J., Martí I. and Ventresca M. 2012. Building Inclusive Markets in Rural Bangladesh: How Intermediaries Work Institutional Voids. *Academy of Management Journal*, 55(4): 819–850.

Mangaliso, M. P. 2001. Building Competitive Advantage from Ubuntu: Management Lessons from South Africa. *The Academy of Management Executive*, 15(3): 23–33.

Porter, M. E. and Kramer, M. R. 2011. The Big Idea: Creating Shared Value. *Harvard Business Review*, 89(1): 2.

Rivera-Santos, M., Holt, D., Littlewood, D. and Kolk, A. 2015. Social Entrepreneurship in Sub-Saharan Africa. *The Academy of Management Perspectives*, 29(1): 72–91.

Santos, F. 2012. A Positive Theory of Social Entrepreneurship. *Journal of Business Ethics*, 111(3): 335–351.

Sen, A. 2001. *Development as Freedom*. Oxford: Oxford University Press.

Thornton, P. H. and Ocasio, W. 2008. Institutional Logics. *The Sage Handbook of Organizational Institutionalism*, 840: 99–128.

Walsh, J. P. 2015. Organization and Management Scholarship in and for Africa ... and the World. *The Academy of Management Perspectives*, 29(1): 1–6.

West, A. 2014. Ubuntu and Business Ethics: Problems, Perspectives and Prospects. *Journal of Business Ethics*, 121(1): 47–61.

Young, H. 2014. 10 Thoughts on Africapitalism and Social Enterprise. Available at www.theguardian.com/global-development-professionals-network/2014/jun/23/africapitalism-economics-development-social-enterprise. Accessed 28 January 2018.

Zoogah, D. B., Peng, M. W. and Woldu, H. 2015. Institutions, Resources, and Organizational Effectiveness in Africa. *The Academy of Management Perspectives*, 29(1): 7–31.

9 Foreign Investors and Africapitalism: The Case for Chinese Foreign Direct Investment in Africa

Amon Chizema and Nceku Nyathi

INTRODUCTION

In general, there is a widespread rise of interest in, and support for, the concept of sustainable development, marking a potential and important shift in understanding relationships of humanity with nature and between people. Achieved through a process of bringing together environmental and socio-economic questions, the definition of sustainable development was most famously expressed in the Brundtland Report as meeting 'the needs of the present without compromising the ability of future generations to meet their needs' (World Commission on Environment and Development, 1987: 43). Implied in this definition is the idea that natural resources deriving from the environment are finite; thus their exploitation should be carefully managed and indeed a global concern, moving away from the perception that environmental problems are mainly local. Thus, the concept of sustainable development is the result of the growing awareness of the global links between mounting environmental problems, socio-economic issues to do with poverty and inequality and concerns about a healthy future for humanity. It therefore transcends geographical regions and industries.

For example, following the global financial crisis of 2008 and the growing recognition of the economic, developmental and environmental challenges facing individual countries and the international economy alike, the nature and role of the investment industry is becoming increasingly important (World Investment Report, 2013).

The emphasis has gone beyond the need to realise economic growth to how that growth should be achieved (Giamporcaro and Pretorius, 2012). Consequently, financial instruments, markets and direct investments have the potential to shape social, economic and environmental outcomes, ushering in a new form of market governance and consequent sustainable development (World Investment Report, 2014). This view is at the heart of the emerging field and practice of socially responsible investment (SRI). Put differently, sustainable development is achievable, in part, by engaging in responsible and sustainable investment.

SRI is referred to by a number of other names including 'ethical investing', 'green investing', 'targeted investing', 'values-based investing', 'sustainable investing' and just 'responsible investing' (Cranston, 2004). While there is no clear definition of the term, SRI can be broadly defined as an investment strategy that balances financial, social and environmental objectives (De Cleene and Sonnenberg, 2004). Such a view recognises the role of investors as socially responsible actors, typically integrating ethical as well as environmental, social and corporate governance (ESG) considerations into investment analysis and ownership practices. A key assumption in this observation is that socially responsible investors share the idea that the manner in which they invest matters, possibly moving away from the long-held view that investors maximise their value at the expense of other stakeholders or the environment (Domini, 2001).

The origins of SRI can be traced back to a period before the 1960s, when ethical investors driven by religious convictions avoided 'sin stocks' such as tobacco, alcohol or gambling (Lydenberg and Louche, 2006). This was followed by the 1960s when investment and shareholder activism emerged as a vehicle for social change in the United States, where the peace and green movements led to divestiture in certain industries to match ethical positions (Alinsky, 1971; Heese, 2005). In the early 1970s, US investors refused to invest in South African companies in order to protest against apartheid. Scholars argue that this act by US investors played a key role in bringing the concept of SRI into the international arena through dis-investment, shareholder activism practices and campaigns (Sparkes, 2006). This investment approach quickly spread to the United Kingdom from the 1980s, at first through the lens of the anti-apartheid struggle.

Dialogue and engagement with companies broadened in the 1990s to a wider range of social and environmental concerns (Sparkes, 2006). In continental Europe, by the year 2000 Switzerland, France, Belgium, Germany and the Netherlands had become the first to embrace SRI with a strong influence of the sustainable. It is estimated that the global size of the SRI market is about US$13.6 trillion (Global Sustainable Investment Alliance, 2013). In Africa the concept of sustainable investment or development is fairly new. While considerable steps have been taken by some countries (e.g., South Africa) to embrace sustainable development, most of the investments taking place across the continent still follow the old model. Consequently, there is considerable literature on sustainable and responsible investment on developed economies such as the United States, United Kingdom and Europe, but very little has been done on markets such as Africa.[1]

In recent years, Chinese foreign direct investment (FDI) into sub-Saharan Africa (SSA) has grown rapidly, a development that has generated debate around the motivation of China's engagement with the continent (Broadman, 2006) and more importantly about the implications for Africa's sustainable development (ADB, 2008; Goldstein, 2006). While Africa needs investment to accelerate economic growth, some scholars have questioned the suitability of China to do this given its poor record in good governance and human and labour rights (Bosshard, 2008), characteristics that are distinct from the involvement of the OECD (Gu, 2009). A different school of thought argues that since 2005 the private sector, rather than the government, is increasingly the engine of economic exchange between China and Africa (Berger, 2008; Wang, 2007). A better

---

[1]   Most of the limited literature at the moment is driven by professional bodies and multinational institutions.

understanding of the investment environment in the context of the Chinese government's involvement, as both the state and/or the private sector, is necessary in order to ascertain the implications of sustainable development in Africa through the lens of Africapitalism.

While sustainable investment can be through portfolio and direct investment, this chapter emphasises FDI[2] flows in particular. This emphasis is appropriate because of the distinctive potential contributions of FDI to sustainable development through various channels including technology transfer. Moreover, portfolio investments are not common in Africa due to the lack of developed stock markets in many countries across the continent. In addition, portfolio investments may not necessarily be suitable for Africa because they are volatile and incapable of generating employment opportunities (Onyeiwu and Shrestha, 2004).

We also acknowledge the importance of domestic investment in attaining sustainable development and the presence of multiple sources of foreign direct investment in Africa; however, we choose to focus on FDI from China for a number of reasons. First, the business landscape of Africa has changed dramatically following the arrival of Chinese investors. Second, the subject of Chinese investments in Africa is a subject of great controversy, covering social issues such as labour rights, economic issues including poor quality and low-priced products, and environmental issues. In short, Chinese investments raise important questions about sustainable development in Africa.

This chapter is important for at least two reasons. First, it aims to provide a full picture of what we know about sustainable development in the context of Chinese investors in Africa, a continent that is fast growing, is replete with natural resources and lags behind on all social development indicators. Understanding the current state of

---

[2]   **Foreign direct investment** (FDI) is a direct investment into production or business in a country (host) by an individual or company of another country (home), either by buying a company in the host country or by expanding operations of an existing business in that country. Foreign direct investment is in contrast to **portfolio investment**, which is a passive investment in the securities of another country such as stocks and bonds.

affairs provides a chance to detect the gaps in our knowledge and direct future research work. Second, at a time when so much hope has been placed on Africa as the rising continent, it is important to understand how the latest wave of investments is consistent with Africapitalism.

The chapter is structured as follows. The next section provides an account of investment in Africa, particularly foreign direct investment. While a broad discussion will be made for FDI inflows to Africa, emphasis will be placed on trade and investment between Africa and China. This is followed by a discussion of the contested benefits as well as the social impact of Chinese investments in, and trade with, Africa. Next is a section on the environmental impact of Chinese investments in Africa. We then provide suggestions for improving sustainable trade and investment between Africa and China. The penultimate section discusses areas for possible academic research. In the last section, we provide some concluding thoughts.

INVESTMENTS IN AFRICA

Due to their accumulation of unsustainable external debts in the 1980s, many African countries have increasingly adopted alternative strategies for mobilising development finance. For example, the New Partnership for African Development (NEPAD) is one such initiative, designed to move African countries away from debt and towards trade and investment. Of course, this is conditional on improved governance. The aim is to attract new inflows of FDI.

FDI can play an important role in Africa's sustainable development in a number of ways. First, it supplements domestic investments, which in Africa have continued to be at very low levels (Anyanwu, 2006). Second, FDI has the potential to directly create new employment opportunities or increase employment indirectly through increased linkages with domestic firms. Third, FDI enhances international trade, thus providing a vehicle for the integration of African countries into the global economy. Fourth, FDI allows the transfer of technological know-how, raising skills of the local workforce in the process (Dupasquier and Osakwe, 2003).

Previous studies show that the level of FDI in a country is determined by a favourable institutional environment characterised by effective institutions (North, 1990) that include the rule of law (Globerman and Shapiro, 1999), democracy, property rights, tax systems and economic freedom in mobilising both domestic and foreign capital (Collier and Gunning, 1999). In many African countries, these institutions are absent, or at least ineffective, a situation that has made foreign investors continue to avoid these countries (Anyanwu, 2006). Moreover, Africa has long been perceived as a risky continent in which to conduct business (Anyanwu, 2006). Foreign investors perceive Africa as a continent ravaged by poverty, ethnic and tribal violence, political uncertainties and lawlessness. As a result, Africa has received the least FDI in the world (Onyeiwu and Shrestha, 2004); however, there are indications this may be changing for a variety of reasons (Ibeh, Wilson and Chizema, 2012). Part of this is due to the increased demand in natural resources by emerging countries, in particular China, alongside improvements in political and economic governance in some African countries (e.g., Botswana) and sustained political stability in others (e.g., Rwanda).

With expectations for further sustained economic and population growth, investors' interest continues to grow not only in extractive industries but also in consumer market–oriented sectors that target the rising middle-class population (World Investment Report, 2013). Technology firms have also started to invest in innovation in Africa. For example, in November 2013, IBM opened its first African research laboratory, on the outskirts of Nairobi, with an investment of more than $10 million for the first two years (World Investment Report, 2014).

In 2014, FDI inflows to Africa remained stable at $54 billion, with decreases in North Africa being offset by rises in sub-Saharan Africa (World Investment Report, 2015). SSA saw an increase of 5 per cent over the previous year. These recent positive trends in FDI inflows to Africa seem to be largely driven by natural resources and market size (Asiedu, 2006). This perception is consistent with the data. Indeed, over the years, the three largest recipients of FDI have been Angola, Nigeria and South Africa. South Africa and Nigeria have large local markets, and the former contributes about 46 per cent of sub-Saharan Africa's GDP.

Nigeria and Angola are oil-producing countries, a product that accounts for over 90 per cent of their total exports. According to Asiedu (2006), this situation breeds three important observations. First, it suggests that FDI in the region is largely determined by an uncontrollable factor that needs proper management to achieve sustainable development before it expires. Second, natural resource–poor countries or small countries, by comparison, will attract very little FDI. Of course, among the small countries themselves, those that have better infrastructure, an educated labour force, macroeconomic stability, openness to FDI, an efficient legal system, less corruption and greater political stability are more likely to attract more foreign investments. Countries in SSA are small in terms of income: twenty-three out of forty-seven countries in the region have a GDP of less than US$3 billion. Third, FDIs in resource-rich countries are concentrated in natural resources, and investments in such industries do not normally generate positive spillovers, such as technological transfers and employment creation, that are often associated with FDI (Asiedu, 2004). Indeed, Asiedu (2004) finds that natural resource availability does not have a significant impact on employment by multinational corporations in SSA. While not the main focus of this chapter, these observations carry a lot of policy implications. Moreover, foreign investors search for natural resources, and the current trends of investment across the continent have introduced a new actor in African business – the Chinese investor. To understand the changing landscape in African capitalism, in the context of China's role in Africa, the next subsection will review the historical and economic ties of China and Africa, and the stages of entry of Chinese investments on the continent.

Enter the Dragon: Chinese Investments in Africa

Foreign investment into Africa is increasingly being made by developing-country multinational enterprises, such as firms from India

TABLE 9.1 *Growth stages of Chinese companies in Africa*

Stages	Main features
Stage One: 1949–1980s	Limited number of Chinese companies, mainly implementing the Chinese government's development aid projects.
Stage Two: 1980s to mid-1990s	Large national and provincial-level state-owned trading companies, closely associated with diplomatic agenda; few private companies.
Stage Three: Mid-1990s to 2000	Emergence of large state-owned enterprises (SOEs) mainly resource-seeking, strategic asset–seeking and infrastructure investments; increasing number of private companies start exploring African market.
Stage Four: 2000–2005	Expansion of large SOEs and private companies; emergence of clustering development strategy, e.g., trade zones; industry parks.
Stage Five: 2005–present	Acceleration of private companies in various sectors and continued expansion of SOEs; the development of clustering industry strategy.

Source: China-Africa Project Survey (Gu, 2009).

and, particularly, from China. For that reason, we suggest that the starting point to understand Chinese investments in Africa is to look at the growth stages of Chinese companies in Africa.

A number of scholars trace the entry of Chinese investments at different stages (Gu, 2009; Kaplinsky and Morris, 2009). For example, Gu (2009) discusses five growth stages of Chinese companies in Africa (see Table 9.1), while Kaplinsky and Morris (2009) consider three overlapping phases. According to Gu (2009), the first stage dates between 1949 and 1980 and relates to Chinese aid projects in Africa. At this stage, a few companies from China carried out the work. The second stage (1980s to mid-1990s) involved large state-owned enterprises (SOEs) and a few private companies. This was followed by the third stage (mid-1990 to 2000), with large national

and provincial SOEs as well as an increased number of private companies, seeking resources and strategic assets and engaging mainly in
infrastructure development.

The fourth stage (2000–2005) witnessed the expansion of SOEs'
operations and the emergence of trade zones and industrial parks.
The fifth stage (2005–present), the main focus of this chapter, is wit-
nessing the acceleration of private companies in various sectors and
continued expansion of SOEs' operations across the region.

From this information, it is clear that both the private sector and
the government, through SOEs, are investors in Africa. Given the size
of their combined investment and the remarkable speed of its growth
(Cai, 2006), it is imperative to understand the motives of both state
and private investors and their attitude to sustainable development in
Africa.

The Chinese state's involvement in Africa is a reflection of its
change in foreign policy and its intention to be an influential world
player. To achieve this, China has to continue growing its economy
while engaging in expanded diplomatic and trade relations with other
countries, especially developing ones. Africa provides both motives.
It is in need of financial resources, accessed through trade and investments. and it is replete with natural resources that China, in turn,
needs (Kaplinsky and Morris, 2009). Consequently, trade and investment, particularly in commodities, between Africa and China have
been growing over the years. According to Dollar (2016), the nature
and size of exports to China show the importance and dominance of
natural resources in trade and investment between African countries
and China. For example, while exports of fuel to China reached
$45 billion dollars in 2014, the value of manufactured goods and
food items was, by comparison, very small (Dollar, 2016).

SOEs typically invest in extractive and infrastructure projects,
while small private enterprises dominate investment in commerce
and manufacturing. While large SOEs continue to operate mostly in
infrastructure development, small and private Chinese firms are
increasingly getting involved in commerce and manufacturing

(Bosshard, 2008) and other industries such as construction (Mohan and Tan-Mullins, 2009). For example, Dobler (2006) notes that in Namibia, smaller private construction firms are competing with Namibian firms for contracts. In Tanzania, Baregu (2008) notes that out of 147 Chinese companies in the country only twenty-two had portfolios of more than $1 million, marking the majority out as private and medium enterprises (SMEs).

Chinese private-sector investment comprises a mixture of firms, estimated to be more than 2000 (Kaplinsky and Morris, 2009). Some are incorporated in China and have extended their operations from China to SSA. According to Gu (2009: 572), such firms have sought an 'escape from the pressure cooker of domestic competition and surplus production. China's private firms find some relief overseas in Africa's large markets and relatively less intense market competition from local firms. Others were started in SSA, in some cases by Chinese citizens who had previously been employed in large-scale SOE activity in Africa, and through legal or illegal means had stayed on to become autonomous entrepreneurs (Dobler, 2006). In other cases, building on family or community links, migrants have moved to SSA to join existing enterprises or to start new ones (Ho, 2008; Mohan and Kale, 2007).

The Chinese government does not directly interfere in the investment decisions of the enterprises it owns, but offers support and incentives in the form of finance and diplomatic support. While small enterprises finance their investments through family ties and informal capital markets, China ExIm Bank is a key source of finance for the Africa projects carried out by SOEs (Kaplinsky and Morris, 2009).

BENEFITS AND SOCIAL IMPACT OF CHINESE INVESTMENTS IN AFRICA

An important issue that follows a discussion of the motivation of Chinese investments in Africa is that of the benefits that accrue to the region. To what extent are these investments contributing to the development of Africa? Is this form of development sustainable?

Recent scholarship argues that Africa's sustainable development can be achieved through Africapitalism (for the conceptualisation of Africapitalism, see Amaeshi and Idemudia, 2015).

Amaeshi and Idemudia (2015) theorise that Ubuntu values underpin the type of capitalism that Africa needs.[3] Such values include respect for the dignity of others, group solidarity, participation, sharing, the spirit of harmony and interdependency (Makhudu, 1993; Mbigi, 2002). Without losing sight of these values, Africapitalism should be able to deliver social progress and economic prosperity in a manner that eradicates inequality, giving Africans a sense of belonging to and pride in the space they occupy and the ways they live and work. Thus, poor treatment of workers including unsuitable working conditions, low wages or disregard for the environment – indeed aspects that hinder social progress and economic parity – are all examples of what Africapitalism does not espouse. Equally, since Africapitalism is a function of the private sector, any behaviour that impinges on the growth of African businesses negates sustainable economic development in the African sense. Indeed, Africapitalism is rooted in the social, economic and governance model that believes that the private sector has a significant role to play in the development of Africa through long-term investments that create economic prosperity and social value.

The important question is, therefore, to what extent do Chinese investments (discussed above) respond to Africapitalism, i.e., to the form of sustainable development identifiable within the context of African values? Using the nascent theoretical lens of Africapitalism, we examine the social impact of Chinese investments. First impressions, drawn from China's recent economic history, may suggest that China, as a developing country, can arguably offer experiences and goods that are better suited to the needs of African societies than the advice and products from industrialised countries (Mohan and

---

[3]   Ubuntu is seen as humaneness, a pervasive spirit of caring and community, harmony and hospitality, respect and responsiveness that individuals and groups display for one another.

Tan-Mullins, 2009). As Bosshard (2008) states, China is arguably a world leader in renewable energy technologies, which are essential for rural electrification in Africa. Moreover, Chinese investment and consumer goods are usually more affordable than Western products.

However, selling cheap products has the effect of destroying local industries (Broadman, 2006). Indeed, due first to its large and cheap labour force and second to the acute poverty in vast parts of Africa, China offers low-price export goods such as textiles and clothing, electronic devices and machines which find a huge and soaring demand. The future of Africa lies in diversified economies, and not simply in commodity exports, and thus the threat to SSA manufacturing sectors may, in future, widen the economic gap between Africa and the rest of the world. Thus, while these cheap products may be welcome by many in Africa due to their current lack of wealth, the fact of the matter is that they will hurt Africa in the long run.

Moreover, unlike Western countries' and international financial institutions' approach, the Chinese nexus of aid, trade and investment does not include economic and governance conditionalities on particular public policies (Kaplinsky and Morris, 2009). For example, for several years the Zambian government repeatedly failed to attract funding from private Western investors, the World Bank and the European Investment Bank (EIB) for the Lower Kafue Gorge Project. After a government delegation visited China in October 2003, Zambia's electricity utility signed a Memorandum of Understanding with Sinohydro within a few weeks (Phiri, 2004). In a similar vein, before approaching the China ExIm Bank Ghana's government had failed to get the Bui Dam funded by the World Bank and the EIB. African governments have interpreted this approach of no conditionalities by China as one of friendliness and respect for the dignity of others, echoing Amaeshi and Idemudia's view of Africapitalism. However, this approach by China has often been criticised for supporting dictatorships and corrupt political regimes (Hodzi et al., 2012).

Other benefits, though not unique to Chinese investments, draw on the usual effects of FDI on host countries. Indeed, it has long been known that FDI brings positives to the host economies. For example, local people get employment, and local firms benefit from spillovers such as technological transfers. In the context of Chinese investments, the expectation should be that as Chinese enterprises relocate to Africa, they should provide opportunities for local enterprises to learn from Chinese experience, to access Chinese value chains and to gain enhanced value-added access to global value chains in the global economy. Potentially, too, Chinese investors provide an important source of additional investment capital that could contribute to poverty alleviation and generate a significant multiplier effect through the local economy.

However, although there is a large potential for Chinese investment to bring developmental benefits to Africa, the reality is that the actual development impacts on the host country depend upon several factors. Consistent with this observation, Kragelund (2007) points out that there are four factors that are of particular importance: (1) the investment motives of the investing firms; (2) the time horizon of the investment; (3) the extent of linkages to other firms in the economy; and (4) the capacity of the local firms to absorb spillovers and face competition.

In the context of Kragelund's (2007) views, the effect of Chinese investments in Africa continues to be a subject of great debate. For example, evidence from the interview survey of Chinese CEOs of private firms, carried out in 2008 in Ghana, Nigeria and Madagascar, clearly shows that private investment is market-driven (Guy, 2009). Moreover, as stated before, Chinese private investment in Africa reflects the intensive competition being experienced in the Chinese marketplace. This, according to Brautigam (2008), suggests that without a clear policy guide or regulations from the host country, the opportunities for technology and knowledge transfers are limited, especially with a shortage or lack of local business personnel with the requisite technical know-how and skills. Brautigam's observation receives support from Kaplinsky and Morris (2009: 551) who state that 'Whilst China has a strategy for Africa, Africa lacks a strategy for

China.' Of course, this view suffers from the weakness of treating Africa as a homogeneous society, as different countries are likely to follow different strategies.

According to the same survey by Gu (2009), there is no viable production and supply capacity in the host economies, suggesting that the Chinese firm cannot use local sourcing linkages. Where such local networks of specialised supplies exist, the high cost or poor quality of goods forces many Chinese firms to turn to their known suppliers back in China. Here, there is loss of business opportunities for local firms and inevitably higher prices for the consumer due to the higher costs of production caused by importing raw materials and possibly higher transaction costs. And without experience and with limited chances of linkages with Chinese firms, local African firms do not have the capacity or opportunities to absorb spillovers and compete, destroying local firms' ability to grow and export (Kaplinsky and Morris, 2008).

Mohan and Tan-Mullins (2009) state that Chinese firms in the construction and mining industries sometimes bring low-cost labour from China; however, the perception that they only employ Chinese labour is misleading. For example, in the ExIm-funded Bui Dam in Ghana, the agreement with Sinohydro ensures that jobs go to Ghanaians with about 700 Chinese expatriates working on the project compared with 3000 Ghanaians. Presumably, the 700 Chinese expatriates occupy managerial and supervisory roles, given the lack of requisite skills locally (Naidu, 2008). This situation, alongside poor conditions of workers, has been observed in the Democratic Republic of Congo (Mohan and Tan-Mullins, 2009), Angola (Curtis, 2008; Kaplinsky and Morris, 2009), South Africa and Mauritius (Wong, 2006) leading to labour disputes in the last two countries.

ENVIRONMENTAL IMPACT OF CHINESE INVESTMENTS IN AFRICA

Besides the socio-economic elements, a number of studies have addressed the impact of Chinese investment on the environment.

Indeed, Chinese investments have been subject to intense scrutiny, evoking strong criticism regarding alleged lack of corporate social responsibility ranging from failures over labour rights, as pointed out above, to environmental neglect (Chan-Fishel, 2007). Such negative practices have arguably found their way into African countries. Indeed, while African governments have found it easy to access funding and investments from China, as pointed out earlier, some high-profile examples have illustrated the risks created by Chinese investments for Africa's environment. For example, in Gabon, Sinopec explored for oil in Loango National Park until the country's national park service ordered exploration to stop in September 2006 (Centre for Chinese-Stellenbosch, 2007). Despite calls by the conservation groups that oil exploration threatened rare plants and animals, and that the environmental impact study had not been approved by the environment ministry, Sinopec had started work on their project. There are also fears that the Sinohydro Bui Dam in Ghana will flood about a quarter of Bui National Park. The Lower Kafue Gorge Dam in Zambia will put additional pressure on the ecologically important Kafue Flats and its national parks.

Scholars attribute the lack of social and environmental consideration by Chinese investors to the past and present of China's business environment that had little regard for the social element of business. Such scholars (e.g., Chan-Fishel, 2007) argue that China's spectacular economic growth came with a high environmental cost, with corporate social responsibility a lower priority for the government. This suggests that corporate social responsibility was not part of China's enterprise society (Gu, 2009). Consistent with path-dependence[4] arguments (Bebchuck and Roe, 1999), Chinese investors may still not consider social and environmental issues in their operations in Africa. However, with increasing international pressure on

---

[4]   **Path dependence** explains the continued use of a product or practice based on historical preference or use. Due to the previous commitment made, this continued use holds true even if newer, more efficient products or practices are available. Path dependency occurs because it is often easier or more cost effective to simply continue along an already set path than to create an entirely new one.

China to conform to global standards of corporate social responsibility (CSR), the Chinese government has of late come up with stricter regulations that emphasise sustainable and harmonious growth (Gu, 2009). As a result, thousands of Chinese firms failing to reach the new green standards have been closed down by the government, and some of these have relocated to countries, including some in Africa, where regulatory requirements are less stringent or less strictly enforced (Kaplinsky, 2008).

The question, of course, is why are the new pressures on Chinese firms to be responsible at home not being transferred to Africa? Answers to this question depend, in part, on the lack of good investing policies by African governments or on the weak implementation of such policies. Indeed, African countries lack state capacity. State capacity is broadly defined as the administrative and organisational ability of the state to identify, evaluate, formulate and implement policies (Guillen and Capron, 2015). There is need to improve state and institutional capacity that can deal with the demands and pressures of global business. The success or failure of Africapitalism as a variety of an economic or corporate governance model will depend on the strength of institutions that support business. This observation may suggest that the goals of many African states and those of the private sector, as seen in the lens of Africapitalism, may not be consistent. It must be abundantly clear that it is not principally the responsibility of Chinese businesses to ensure that value is delivered in the framework of Africapitalism, but this responsibility should be taken seriously by local institutions. Chinese businesses like any other businesses are guided by the notion of maximising their utility. As one Chinese ambassador said, 'China is not coming to babysit Africa. She is coming to engage in business.'

ACHIEVING SUSTAINABLE DEVELOPMENT—SUGGESTIONS FOR AFRICA

As indicated earlier, sustainable development should be achieved in a manner that satisfies current needs, however, without compromising the needs for future generations. This is summarised in the Haida[5] proverb 'We do not inherit the land from our ancestors; we borrow it from our children.' Investments in Africa should take this observation into consideration; however, the literature discussed above suggests otherwise. In the context of the increasing investments that are flowing to Africa, in particular, by both Chinese private and public investors, a number of steps should be taken to ensure the realisation of sustainable and harmonious development.

First, there is a concern that the lack of institutional regulatory frameworks and government and state capacity to monitor and encourage direct investment, in terms of local skills development and technology transfer, will limit the positive knock-on effect of Chinese activity in African economies. African governments need to put in place mechanisms that improve human capital and conditions that allow local firms (domestic investment) to learn from foreign investors. Indeed, sustainable economic development also needs increased human capital investment to generate the requisite skills in a competitive global environment.

Second, as discussed earlier, there are poor, or no, linkages between local firms and Chinese enterprises, and the later have been shown to source their supplies from China (Gu, 2009). This is worsened by the influx of Chinese workers and businessmen, indeed a potentially serious social issue in the context of a continent ravaged by high levels of unemployment (Centre for Chinese-Stellenbosch, 2007). There is, therefore, a strong need by African governments to come up with a clear strategy, policies and regulations that are effectively enforced to ensure that their countries achieve sustainable development.

Third, there is also a strong possibility that African governments, pressured by their citizens to provide employment and immediate needs, could focus on the social dimension, neglecting the environment. In an interview survey carried out in South Africa,

---

[5]   The Haida are an indigenous people of the Pacific Northwest Coast of North America.

Giamporcaro (2011) observes that there is a belief by both civil society and the market that the country needs to deal with more urgent social priorities, such as social transformation and infrastructure improvement, potentially blocking environmental concerns from reaching equal levels of importance. The tension between social development goals and environmental goals is, therefore, a potential major political obstacle at national level.

Fourth, as pointed out earlier, Chinese investors do not consider the state of governance as a condition to invest in Africa, possibly because of a shorter institutional distance[6] between China and Africa. While this may appear as a positive factor from the African governments' perspective, the opportunities that come with competition are lost, resulting in excessive supplier power (in this case Chinese investors), potentially leading to higher cost of capital and possible negative externalities. Indeed, with poor governance and political instability, Western investors stay away. There is, therefore, need to improve the legal, judicial, political and regulatory environment in order to encourage competitive private investment, both domestic and foreign (Anyanwu, 2006).

Fifth, the success of any local economy should be underpinned by the prevalence and active participation of local businesses. The British economy's success can be traced back to the Industrial Revolution in which local firms were born and subsequently nourished. The same can be said about the United States, Germany, Japan, South Korea and recently China. In the same vein, the success of African economies with an African character, i.e., Africapitalism resides in the birth of home-grown businesses. We argue here that Tony Elumelu's vision of Africapitalism is certainly grounded in the salience of local businesses. It is the same reason that his foundation, The Tony Elumelu Foundation, has embarked on a continent-wide strategy of starting local businesses. Locally born and bred businesses

---

[6]   **Institutional distance** is the difference in the regulative, cognitive and normative institutions between home country and host country institutions (Kostova and Roth, 2002).

have a natural understanding of their environment and the values and expectations of the various stakeholders in the business space. The number of African business success stories is growing (e.g., Dangote Group, MTN, Ecobank, etc.). We are not suggesting that foreign businesses should be discouraged. Quite the contrary, what we suggest is that governments and various other local institutions in Africa should help provide incentives that lead to the formation and growth of more local businesses. Business schools and researchers should adopt more relevant syllabi and teach business models that are consistent with what is on the ground. That way any investments that come to Africa would be shaped by what they find on the ground, i.e., capitalism of an African variety.

AREAS FOR FURTHER RESEARCH

Based on the foregoing review of the literature, a number of questions are worth pursuing. First, while we now know about who is investing in Africa, there is a dearth of studies about investors' attitudes towards sustainable development. Do the investors care only about maximising their value, or do they consider profit as only a part of a bigger picture that embraces society and the environment? To what extent is the institutional logic[7] of sustainable development similar or different between domestic, Western and Chinese investors? A useful approach would be to use interviews in order to gain a better understanding of investors' perception of sustainable development in the context of Africa. Such an understanding would help to guide investment policies and regulatory frameworks in African countries. Despite the importance of such insight, there are no studies that examine the link between investors' perceptions and sustainable development, at least in the context of Africa. Moreover, given that sustainable

---

[7]   An **institutional logic** is defined as 'the socially constructed, historical patterns of material practices, assumptions, values, beliefs, and rules' that create norms around 'the way a particular social world works' (Thornton and Ocasio, 1999: 804). Logics provide guiding principles for selecting and applying appropriate types or forms of practices to specific problems, justifying the changes taken or to be taken by actors to incorporate new practices (Lawrence and Suddaby, 2006).

development requires the commitment of multiple stakeholders, the approach proposed above could be extended to entrepreneurs, policy makers and civil society.

Extant studies in management and corporate governance emphasise the salience of the institutional environment in the adoption of practices (Chizema and Shinozawa, 2012). This suggests that differences in institutional contexts matter. Given, therefore, the heterogeneity of regional and national contexts, and Africa's unique history before and after colonialism, it is plausible that the Western concept of sustainable development may not be the same in Africa. There is need to gain a better understanding about the notion of sustainable development in the context of African countries. Such an approach will enable businesses to invest in projects that are deemed necessary by the stakeholders in Africa.

CONCLUSION

This chapter has examined the nature of the pattern of trade and investment in Africa, in particular FDI from and trade with China. While trade relations between African countries and China date back to the late 1940s, the current wave of trade and investment started in the early 2000s. Driven by China's huge demand for resources to sustain its fast-growing economy, exports from Africa have been mainly been about commodities. This demand for commodities explains the recent Africa rising narrative, with the continent experiencing an average growth rate of 5 per cent over the last fifteen years (World Economic Forum, 2015). Out of Africa's total fifty-four countries, twenty-six have achieved middle-income status, while the proportion of those living in extreme poverty has fallen from 51 per cent to 42 per cent in 2014 (African Development Bank, 2014).

Against this background, this chapter has examined the sustainability of Chinese investments in Africa, going beyond the impressive statistics, and seeking to understand whether and how development on the continent should continue to take place under the light of Africapitalism. A central tenet of Africapitalism is that sustainable development should be driven by the private sector, however, unlike in the past, driven by African values and way of life. Guided by this theoretical lens, the chapter discussed the various issues in the growing literature on China–Africa trade and investment relations, including threats to some local industries as a result of flooding cheap products from China, the lack of respect for labour and human rights and the environment. While there are plenty of positives that can be drawn from China's engagement with Africa, the success of this development cooperation depends on the elimination of institutional voids, i.e., the absence of market-supporting institutions, improving infrastructure, creation of mechanisms that allow technological and managerial spillover and enhancing state capacity in general. Moreover, the creation of a form of capitalism that has an African and indeed sustainable character cannot be left to chance. It has to be consciously shaped by instituting supporting mechanisms and practices that are consistent with the institutional environment. Apart from the state capacity to formulate and implement relevant supporting and guiding institutions, we also propose that the business space should be highly populated with successful local businesses that have the capacity to learn from foreign businesses and more importantly that have the capability to shape the local business landscape.

REFERENCES

African Development Bank. 2008. *African Development Report* 2007. Abidjan: African Development Bank.

African Development Bank. 2014. African Development Bank Group Strategy for Addressing Fragility and Building Resilience in Africa. Abidjan, Côte d'Ivoire: African Development Bank Group. Available at www.afdb.org/fileadmin/uploa ds/afdb/Documents/Policy Documents/Addressing_Fragility_and_Building_Res ilience_in_Africa-_The_AfDB_Group_Strategy_2014%25E2%2580%25932019 .pdf. Accessed 12 November 2015.

Alinsky, S. 1971. *Rules for Radicals: A Practical Primer for Realistic Radicals.* New York, NY: Random House.

Amaeshi, A. and Idemudia, U. 2015. Africapitalism: A Management Idea for Business in Africa? *Africa Journal of Management,* 1(2): 210–223.

Anyanwu, J. C. 2006. Promoting of Investment in Africa. *African Development Bank*. 42–71.

Asiedu, E. 2004. The Determinants of Employment of Affiliates of US Multinational Enterprises in Africa. *Development Policy Review*, 22(4): 371–379.

Asiedu, E. 2006. Foreign Direct Investment in Africa: The Role of Natural Resources, Market Size, Government Policy, Institutions and Political Instability. *United Nations University*, 63–77.

Baregu, M. 2008. The Three Faces of the Dragon: Tanzania-China Relations in Historical Perspective. In *Crouching Tiger, Hidden Dragon? Africa and China*. Edited by K. Ampiah and S. Naidu, 152–166. Scottville, KY: University of KwaZulu-Natal Press,

Bebchuk, L. A. and Roe, M. J. 1999. A Theory of Path Dependence in Corporate Ownership and Governance. *Stanford Law Review*, 52(1): 127–170.

Berger, A. 2008. China and the Global Governance of Foreign Direct Investment. Berlin: GDI German Development Institute Discussion Paper, 10.

Bosshard, P. 2008. China's Environmental Footprint in Africa. China in Africa Policy Briefing (SAIIA), 3: 1–12.

Brautigam, D. 2008. Chinese Business and African Development: 'Flying Geese' or 'Hidden Dragon'? In *China Returns to Africa: A Rising Power and a Continent Embrace*. Edited by C. Alden, D. Large and R. M. S. Soares de Oliveira, 51–68. London: Christopher Hurst.

Broadman, H. G. 2006. *Africa's Silk Road: China and India's New Economic Frontier*. Washington, DC: World Bank Publications.

Cai, C. 2006. Outward Foreign Direct Investment Protection and the Effectiveness of Chinese BIT Practice. *Journal of World Investment and Trade*, 7(5): 621–652.

Centre for Chinese studies (CCS). 2007. China's Engagement of Africa: Preliminary Scoping of African Case Studies, University of Stellenbosch, South Africa.

Collier, P. and Gunning, J. W. 1999. Explaining African Economic Performance. *Journal of Economic Literature*, 37: 64–111.

Cranston, S. 2004. Government Employee Pension Funds: Taking the High Ground. *Financial Mail*, November 27, 2009.

Curtis, D. 2008. Partner or Predator in the Heart of Africa? Chinese Engagement with the DRC. In *Crouching Tiger, Hidden Dragon? African and China*. Edited by K. Ampiah and S. Naidu, 86–107. Scottville, KY: University of KwaZulu-Natal Press.

De Cleene, S. and Sonnenberg, D. 2004. *Socially Responsible Investment in South Africa*. 2nd edn. Report Prepared for the African Institute of Corporate Citizenship. Johannesburg: AICC.

Dobler, G. 2006. South-South Business Relations in Practice: Chinese Merchants in Oshikango, Namibia. Available at www.ids.ac.uk/asiandrivers. Accessed 21 June 2014.

Dollar, D. 2016. *China's Engagement with Africa – From Natural Resources to Human Resources*. Washington, DC: John L. Thornton China Center at Brookings.

Domini, A. L. 2001. *Socially Responsible Investing: Making a Difference and Making Money*. Chicago, IL: Dearborn Trade Publishing.

Dupasquier, C. and Osakwe, P. N. 2003. Performance, Promotion and Prospects for Foreign Investment in Africa: National, Regional and International Responsibilities. Paper presented for the Eminent Persons Meeting on Promotion of Investment in Africa, Tokyo.

Giamporcaro, S. 2011. Sustainable and Responsible Investment in Emerging Markets: Integrating Environmental Risks in the South African Investment Industry. *Journal of Sustainable Finance and Investment*, 1: 121–137.

Giamporcaro, S. and Pretorius, L. 2012. Sustainable and Responsible Investment (SRI) in South Africa: A Limited Adoption of Environmental Criteria. *Investment Analysts Journal*, 75: 1–18.

Global Sustainable Investment Alliance. 2012. *Global Sustainable Investment Review*. Available at http://gsiareview2012.gsi-alliance.org/pubData/source/Global%2520Sustainable%2520Investement%2520Alliance.pdf. Accessed 28 January 2018.

Globerman, S. and Shapiro, D. 1999. The Impact of Government Policies on Foreign Direct Investment: The Canadian Experience. *Journal of International Business Studies*, 30(3): 513–532.

Goldstein, A., Pinaud, N., Reisen, H. and Chen X. 2006. *The Rise of China and India: What's in It for Africa?* Paris: OECD Development Center Studies.

Gu, J. 2009. China's Private Enterprises in Africa and the Implications for African Development. *European Journal of Development Research*, 21: 570–587.

Guillen, M. and Capron, L. 2015. State Capacity, Minority Shareholder Protections, and Stock Market Development. *Administrative Science Quarterly*, 20: 1–36.

Heese, K. 2005. The Development of Socially Responsible Investment in South Africa: Experience and Evolution of SRI in Global Markets. *Development Southern Africa*, 22(5): 729–739.

Ho, C. 2008. The 'Doing' and 'Undoing' of Community: Chinese Networks in Ghana. *China Aktuel*, 3: 45–76.

Hodzi, O., Hartwell, L. and De Jaeger, N. 2012. 'Unconditional Aid': Assessing the Impact of China's Development Assistance to Zimbabwe. *South African Journal of International Affairs*, 19(1): 79–103.

Ibeh, K., Wilson, J. and Chizema, A. 2012. The Internationalization of African Firms 1995–2011: Review and Implications. *Thunderbird International Business Review*, 54(4): 411–427.

Kaplinsky, R. 2008. What Does the Rise of China Do for Industrialization in SSA? *Review of African Political Economy*, 35(1): 7–22.

Kaplinsky, R. and Morris, M. 2008. Do the Asian Drivers Undermine Export-Oriented Industrialisation in SSA? *World Development*, 36(2): 254–273.

Kaplinsky, R. and Morris, M. 2009. Chinese FDI in Sub-Saharan Africa: Engaging with Large Dragons. *European Journal of Development Research*, 21: 551–569.

Kostova, T. and Roth, K. 2002. Adoption of an Organizational Practice by Subsidiaries of Multinational Corporations: Institutional and Relational Effects. *Academy of Management Journal*, 45: 215–233.

Kragelund, P. 2007. Chinese Drivers for African Development? The Effects of Chinese Investments in Zambia. In *Africa in China's Global Strategy*. Edited by M. Kitissou, 162–181. London: Adonis and Abbey.

Lawrence, T. B. and Suddaby, R. 2006. Institutions and Institutional Work. In *Handbook of Organization Studies*. Edited by R. Clegg, C. Hardy, T. B. Lawrence and W. R. Nord, 2nd edn, 215–254. London: Sage.

Lydenberg, S. and Louche, C. 2006. Socially Responsible Investment: Differences between Europe and the United States. In Vlerick Leuven Gent Management School Working Paper Series. RePec: vlg:vlgwps: 2006–22.

Makhudu, N. 1993 Cultivating a Climate of Co-operation through Ubuntu, *Enterprise Magazine*, 48: 40–42.

Mbigi, L. 2002. The Spirit of African Leadership: A Comparative African Perspective. *Journal of Convergence*, 3(4): 18–23.

Mohan, G. and Kale, D. 2007. The Invisible Hand of South-South Globalisation: A Comparative Analysis of Chinese Migrants in Africa. Report to the Rockefeller Foundation. Development Policy and Practice. Milton Keynes: Open University.

Mohan, G. and Tan-Mullins, M. 2009. Chinese Migrants in Africa as New Agents of Developments? An Analytical Framework. *European Journal of Development Research*, 21: 588–605.

Naidu, S. 2008. Balancing a Strategic Partnership? South Africa-China Relations. In *Crouching Tiger, Hidden Dragon? African and China*. Edited by K. Ampiah and S. Naidu, 167–191. Scottville, KY: University of KwaZulu-Natal Press.

North, D. 1990. *Institutions, Institutional Change and Economic Performance*. Cambridge: Cambridge University Press.

Onyeiwu, S. and Shrestha, H. 2004. Determinants of Foreign Direct Investment in Africa. *Journal of Developing Societies*, 20(1–2): 89–106.

Phiri, I. 2004. A New Era for Hydropower, Ministry of Energy and Water Development, Zambia, presentation in Porto, 18–21 October 2004.

Sparkes, R. 2006. A Historical Perspective on the Growth of Socially Responsible Investment. In *Responsible Investment*. Edited by R. Sullivan and C. Mackenzie, 39–55. Sheffield: Greenleaf Publishing.

Thornton, P. and Ocasio, W. 1999. Institutional Logics and the Historical Contingency of Power in Organizations: Executive Succession in the Higher Education Publishing Industry, 1958–1990. *American Journal of Sociology*, 105: 801–843.

Wang, J.-Y. 2007. What Drives China's Growing Role in Africa. Washington, DC: IMF. IMF Working Paper WP/07/211.

Wong, M. 2006. Chinese Workers in the Garment Industry in Africa: Implications of the Contract Labour Dispatch System on the International Labour Movement. *Labour, Capital and Society*, 39(1): 69–111.

World Commission on Environment and Development Report. 1987. *From One Earth to One World: An Overview*. Oxford: Oxford University Press.

World Economic Forum. 2015. The Africa Competitiveness Report 2015. African Development Bank, Organisation for Economic Co-operation and Development, World Bank Group, and World Economic Forum Report. Cologny: World Economic Forum. Available at http://www3.weforum.org/docs/WEF_AC R_2015/Africa_Competitiveness_Report_2015.pdf. Accessed 17 January 2016.

World Investment Report. 2013. Global Value Chains: Investment and Trade for Development. Geneva: UNCTAD.

World Investment Report. 2014. Investing in the SDGs: An Action Plan. Geneva: UNCTAD.

World Investment Report. 2015. Reforming International Investment Governance. Geneva: UNCTAD.

10 Good African Coffee: Adding Value and Driving Community Development in Uganda

Lyal White and Adrian Kitimbo

INTRODUCTION

The year was 2003 when Andrew Rugasira, a Ugandan entrepreneur, had a big idea. He would sell his events and management business and start a coffee company. But the company, which was later named Good African Coffee, would be no ordinary African coffee enterprise. Rugasira was bent on becoming the first African to capture the entire coffee value-adding chain and export a finished product directly to British supermarkets.

In so doing, he would transform Uganda's and even Africa's role in the coffee industry – from being merely exporters of green beans to becoming exporters of high-quality roasted and packaged coffee that could be bought straight off shelves in Europe. By empowering farmers in western Uganda through training in best farming practices, selling their coffee at a fair market price and giving back half of the company's profits to the farming communities, he would demonstrate that it is trade, not aid, that can truly catalyse the economic development of poor communities. Moreover, Rugasira's approach to entrepreneurship well encompasses the notion of Ubuntu, which underpins Africapitalism. It demonstrates that companies can achieve financial progress, while at the same time placing the social welfare of communities at the centre of their mission by pursing the fundamental tenets of Africapitalism, including fostering a sense of parity, a sense of progress and prosperity, a sense of peace and harmony and a sense of place and belongingness (Amaeshi and Idemudia, 2015).

UGANDA: BACKGROUND AND OVERVIEW

Located in East Africa, Uganda is a small, landlocked country with a population of around 41 million in 2016 (The World Bank, 2017a). With over 40 indigenous ethnic groups (New Vision, 2014), Uganda is one of the most ethnically diverse countries in the world. Uganda's official language is English, a remnant of British colonial rule. The country became fully independent in October 1962, but post-colonial Uganda has been punctuated with political instability. The violence perpetuated by the regimes of Milton Obote, Uganda's first non-European prime minister and that of former president Idi Amin, claimed more than 400,000 lives (Blas, 2014). Since President Yoweri Museveni's National Resistance Movement (NRM) captured power through a guerrilla struggle in 1986, relative stability was established in Uganda. However, peace did not return to the entire country, as the NRM's rule was challenged by the Lord's Resistance Army (LRA), a rebel movement led by Joseph Kony that ravaged northern Uganda for almost twenty years before it was driven out of the country in 2005.

Uganda is categorised as a Least Developed Country (LDC) with a Gross National Income (GNI) Per Capita of around $660 (The World Bank, 2017a). Agriculture is the most important sector of the economy and employs at least 70 per cent of the workforce. Coffee, which has a long history in Uganda, is one of its largest sources of foreign exchange.

The Ugandan government undertook liberal reforms in the late 1980s, embarking on pro-market policies, which resulted in economic growth averaging 7 per cent per year during the 1990s and early 2000s (The World Bank, 2017b). But growth slowed to around 5 per cent per year in late 2000s as Uganda felt the effects of the global economic downturn (The World Bank, 2017b).

While more recent public-sector investments, an increase in foreign direct investment (FDI), oil finds and an increase in agricultural production have made some observers bullish about Uganda's economy, its growth has not returned to the levels of the 1990s, and the economy was expected to expand by around 5.2 per cent in 2016 (IMF, 2016).

COFFEE: A KEY COMMODITY IN AFRICA AND UGANDA

There are many different species of coffee but only two, Arabica and Robusta, dominate the world coffee market. The more sought-after and refined Arabica represents between 70 and 80 per cent of global coffee production, while Robusta accounts for not more than 20 per cent (Kolb, 2016).

For many African countries coffee beans are a major export commodity. However, between 1963 and 2013, Africa's overall coffee production, as a share of world production, has dropped from 25 per cent to 14 per cent (ICO, 2014). This fall in production is due to a combination of factors, from a shift in demand from Europe which guaranteed demand in the early years of post-independence through regulated markets, to new competitors from Latin America and Asia (ICO, 2014). Regional conflicts as well as structural factors as a result of ageing coffee trees and low yields also contributed significantly to the decline in Africa's overall coffee production (ICO, 2014). For example, Côte d'Ivoire, which produced up to an annual average of 4 million bags prior to 1990, now manages only around 2 million bags (ICO, 2014). Angola has also lost its production dominance on the global stage. By the mid-1970s Angola produced over 200,000 tons of coffee; and in the year 2012–13 the country's production stood at not more than 33,000 bags (Brown, 2014).

However, there have been exceptions to this. Ethiopia and Uganda have both experienced growth in coffee production in the last few decades. With a 3.6 per cent increase in production since the 1990s, Ethiopia has demonstrated the strongest growth (ICO, 2014). In 2015, the country produced up to 6.7 million bags (ICO, 2017). Uganda, whose growth has been more moderate, increased its annual production from 2.8 million bags during the regulated market in the 1970s to 4.9 million bags in 2015 (ICO, 2017).

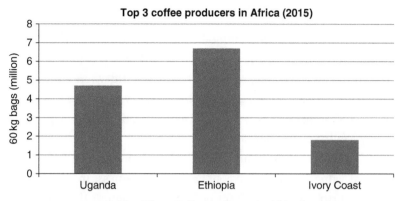

FIGURE 10.1: Top Three Coffee Producers in Africa (2015)
Source: International Coffee Organization.

Located at the equator, Uganda has the ideal climate for coffee production. Largely supported by small-scale farmers in eastern and central Uganda, the coffee industry supports over 3.5 million Ugandan families through various coffee-related activities.

Both Robusta and Arabica are grown in Uganda. Presently, Uganda is Africa's second-largest producer of coffee after Ethiopia (Figure 10.1), and the continent's biggest exporter of the commodity. Interestingly, the country only consumes 3 per cent of its crop, unlike Ethiopia with a traditional coffee culture that consumes almost half of its coffee production. In 2014–15 Uganda exported up to 3.5 million bags bringing in $450 million (Padmore, 2014), with Robusta coffee accounting for at least 70 per cent of this figure (Bariyo, 2014). This makes the country the fifth largest exporter of this variety in the world. Uganda's long history of coffee production, as well as the government's commitment to positioning Uganda as a major player in the global coffee industry through bodies such as the Uganda Coffee Development Authority (UCDA), has been pivotal in leading to the establishment of companies such as Good African Coffee.

BREAKING THE CYCLE: ENTREPRENEURIAL COFFEE

Like many other African commodities, the majority of coffee beans produced on the continent are not processed before being exported. Green beans are exported to other parts of the world where substantial value is then added. Ugandan coffee beans are typically sent to destinations including the USA, EU and Russia (Ojambo, 2014). Uganda is merely a cultivator of beans.

Coffee-producing countries like Uganda only earn a fraction of the total value of the massive global coffee business. In an industry that is worth more than $100 billion (Goldshein, 2011), producer countries such as Brazil, Vietnam and Uganda retain no more than $20–$25 billion collectively of the total (Rugasira, 2015). The biggest benefactors are those countries that have the capacity to process, market and sell coffee to consumers.

Andrew Rugasira wanted to reverse this trend. As a Ugandan entrepreneur, Rugasira sought to capture the entire value chain of coffee and sell directly to international markets by starting Good African Coffee. This required the integration of production, processing, marketing and selling quality coffee to attain business success. But Rugasira also wanted to use coffee trade as a vehicle to bring about economic improvement in the lives of coffee farmers in Western Uganda (Rugasira, 2013).

ANDREW RUGASIRA: BORN OF RESILIENCE
AND DYNAMISM

Rugasira was born in Uganda. He grew up during the brutal Idi Amin regime of the 1970s and his family was directly affected by some of the atrocities committed by the government at the time. In an interview with the *New York Times* (Bergner, 2012), he recalled a time when his father was imprisoned and exiled in Kenya for two and half years. At one point, Amin's soldiers were also responsible for looting his family's property. Andrew's persistence, as well as strength of spirit amidst the enormous hurdles he has encountered while building his coffee business, may have been forged as a child growing up in an uncertain and terrifying political climate.

Good African Coffee was not Rugasira's first stint at running a business. In his early years after university, he ran his father's chalk factory until it was driven out of business by cheap imports (Bergner, 2012). A true entrepreneur, the loss of his father's business did not stop him from exploring other business opportunities. He went on to start one of Uganda's leading events management companies at the time, VP Promotions. Rugasira has long nurtured his passion to use economics to bring about economic transformation in Uganda. Before he founded Good African Coffee, he obtained a degree in Law and Economics from the University of London. He also holds a Master's degree in African Studies from the University of Oxford.

The success of Rugasira's business model has won him and his company many accolades. He was nominated as a Young Global Leader by the World Economic Forum (WEF) in 2007 and was a member of Uganda's presidential investor roundtable, and his company has also previously been selected for the Legatum Pioneers for Prosperity Award.

GOOD AFRICAN COFFEE: A FLAVOUR FROM THE CONTINENT TO THE WORLD

> We started Good African with the vision to bring quality coffees
> to the global market by working with small scale farmers in Western
> Uganda.

Andrew Rugasira, IFAD, 2015.

Good African Coffee was founded in 2004. It is the first Ugandan company, under a sole proprietor, to cultivate, produce and process coffee for consumer markets. It was also the first African-owned coffee brand to be stocked in UK supermarkets including Waitrose, Sainsbury's and Tesco Plc (Kalinaki, 2011).

Moreover, the company increased its sales from $80,000 during its early years to $2 million in 2012 (Bergner, 2012). Coffee production in western Uganda, where the company has a network of over 14,000 farmers, has also dramatically gone up. In 2012, the SME purchased more than 430,000 kg of coffee from its farmers. This was a significant increase from the 7000 kg that was purchased when the company was in its infancy in the mid-2000s (Murphy, 2012).

A Challenging Start

In the early 2000s, Rugasira, along with a few colleagues, travelled to western Uganda (Kasese district) to assess the possibility of producing quality coffee in the region (Good African, 2013a). It took two years of feasibility studies before the company hit the ground running. During this period, Rugasira and his team gathered important information such as the average farm size that each farmer had, as well as yield capacity. This knowledge would allow them to later develop a comprehensive business model to build efficiency and overall competitiveness geared for international markets.

Good African Coffee's journey to building a recognised coffee brand has not been easy. They have had to confront enormous challenges. One of the first major hurdles Rugasira faced when starting the company was to convince as many local farmers as possible to embrace his business model. Given the small land sizes that each farmer had, it was vital to build a large network of farmers as this would build both scale as well as efficiency. But as an outsider, gaining the farmers' trust was essential and proved more difficult than expected. In addition, the area where Rugasira sought to produce coffee was very rural and had impoverished farmers. And since most of the farmers were ill-trained and had previously relied on archaic and inefficient agrarian methods of coffee production, Rugasira's other task was to persuade them to adopt new practices that would lead to the production of quality beans, higher yields and in the end, larger profits that would drive his social mission (Adams, 2005). By making a strong case through various meetings with the farmers and seeking the help of local leaders (Rugasira, 2013), Rugasira was eventually able to build a network of farmers willing to produce the quality of coffee that was required by the company.

A Quadruple Bottom-Line Business Approach

Good African Coffee uses a quadruple bottom-line business approach, which incorporates the farmers, the communities in which they live, shareholders and employees as the stakeholders. The company's vision is 'to be a leading African agribusiness producing quality products for the global market and using trade to bring about sustainable community development' (Good African, 2013b). A strong partnership with marginalised farmers is critical to the company's sustainable working model.

Good African Coffee is not unique in its model. Organisations that conduct commercial activities in order to drive their social mission have been around for a long time. These include Work Integration Social Enterprises (WISE), which focus on enhancing the employment prospects of people who have been out of work for a long time, microfinance organisations and others. They are often referred to in the literature as 'hybrid organisations' – combining multiple organisational forms (Battilana et al., 2015). Battilana and Lee (2014) define hybrid organisations as 'activities, structures, processes and meanings by which organizations make sense of and combine aspects of multiple organizational forms'. For these organisations, sustaining their operations, long-term, requires both engaging in business as well as advancement of their social mission.

In the case of Good African Coffee, it is a balance between producing high-quality coffee that can be sold all over the world and generating enough profit to empower farming communities through various initiatives. What makes this company different is that rather than only bolstering its farmers' coffee earnings, it is also heavily involved in multiple on-the-ground schemes aimed at transforming the economic fortunes of entire communities in western Uganda. Most other organisations that seek to help coffee producers in Africa use initiatives such as fair trade – a model whose goal is to improve the trading conditions for poor farmers by paying higher prices for their products. At the core of fair trade is the idea that it 'protects against exploitation in international trade and reconnects consumers with producers' (Rugasira, 2013). But Good African Coffee goes beyond just offering better prices; it also addresses the structural problems that keep African farmers poor. In so doing, it drives integrated, grass-roots development that reflects the tenets espoused by Africapitalism.

Promoting a Sense of Parity

Building an organisation that would enhance a sense of parity among the farmers has always been at the centre of Good African Coffee's mission. Rugasira recognised that in order for both the company and its farmers to succeed, growth must be equitably shared. This is especially significant in rural parts of western Uganda where the company operates. With high unemployment, endemic poverty and lack of opportunities, growth that is inclusive becomes all the more important. The company's commitment to shared value and prosperity is reflected in how it uses its coffee earnings. In addition to selling the farmers' produce at a fair market price, the organisation gives back 50 per cent of profits which go toward various community development initiatives (Rugasira, 2013). Moreover, it has established up to sixteen savings and credit cooperatives (Frontani, 2015), allowing farmers to pool their resources together to address critical needs, without having to resort to high-interest loans from banks.

Equipping Local Farmers: Producing Quality and Promoting a Sense of Progress and Prosperity

Producing high-quality coffee was always a strategic priority for Good African Coffee (Musiitwa, 2013). Without coffee that was of top quality, the company would never be able to enter its target markets in Europe or make the required profits to drive its social mission. But poor farming practices and a less-than-advanced agricultural sector threatened its objective to reliably produce beans of the highest standard with increasing volumes. If the company was to succeed, it needed to devise ways to achieve this goal.

Beyond making profits or material accumulation through quality coffee, it was also important for the organisation to improve the farmers' agricultural knowledge and skills. This would enhance their confidence, allow them to become self-sustaining and lessen the toll that poor and arduous farming methods were having on their productivity and health.

And so Rugasira set out to train local farmers in best farming practices. The company began by first organising farmers into groups of fifty. Each group chose its own leaders who were trained in best farming methods, and this knowledge was then passed on to the members of their group (Adams, 2005).

The farmers were encouraged to move away from old, inefficient practices such as 'dry processing' coffee beans and to embrace 'wet processing' – a better method of producing high-quality beans (FAO, 2005). Prior to the arrival of Rugasira and his team the only method the farmers were familiar with was the former (Bergner, 2012). They were also trained in crop rotation, how to terrace their fields and how to efficiently harvest their produce (MacNamara, 2007).

Good African Coffee did not stop with training and educating. The company purchased a number of pulping machines – equipment that is operated by a hand crank that frees the bean from its skin (MacNamara, 2007). These machines, which made the coffee production process faster and easier, were the first examples of coffee machinery the farmers had ever used, and a real, much-needed capital investment to enhance and innovate the coffee sector (Easterly and Reshef, 2010).

By equipping farmers with new skills, knowledge and modern tools, as well as increasing their financial gains, Rugasira ensured that the organisation would holistically enhance the farmers' progress and prosperity.

Creating a Sense of Peace and Harmony

From the outset, Rugasira set out to start an organisation that not only generated profit and empowered farmers, but also carefully balanced economic prosperity and environmental sustainability. This was done with awareness that the single-minded focus on coffee production, without concern for environmental protection, would eventually not only undermine Good African Coffee's mission, but also endanger the livelihoods of the very farmers it was trying to help.

The Rwenzori Mountains where the organisation produces coffee are considered one of the most beautiful alpine areas in Africa. They boast glaciers, waterfalls and lakes, and provide a habitat for many endangered species (UNESCO, 1994). The Rwenzori Mountains also include the third highest peak in Africa, Mount Margherita, after Kilimanjaro and Mount Kenya. It is also well known for its rich flora and fauna.

Good African Coffee has played a significant role in preserving the diverse ecology of the mountain region, which had increasingly come under threat from human activity. The company has managed to do this while successfully building a social enterprise that has benefited thousands of farmers. By signing on new farmers and training them in farming methods, the organisation has created opportunities for people who had previously engaged in poaching as their only means of earning an income. Equipping farmers with environmentally friendly farming methods has also reduced the erosion of mountain slopes by introducing terracing methods, and has curbed biodegradation that had been spurred by cutting down trees (Good African, 2013c).

VALUE-ADDITION: CORRECTING AN IMBALANCE AND CHAMPIONING PLACE AND BELONGINGNESS

> Instead of relying on exports of raw materials, the continent should add value to its commodities to promote sustained growth, jobs and economic transformation. Economic Commission for Africa (2013).

Good African Coffee was not built to be just another coffee-producing company, sending green beans to Europe. A major strategic objective was to establish an innovative African company which would control the entire coffee production and value-adding chain. For Rugasira, it is important that Africans break the cycle of merely producing products for export without first adding value. The present cycle, he argues, is costing producing countries billions of dollars, as they only retain a smaller share of the profits.

But the lack of capital (Gouillart, 2009) and absence of technology to process coffee after harvesting meant that Rugasira's dream of making a finished product in Uganda was still far off. For the first five years after the company started, it roasted and packaged its coffee in South Africa and the Republic of Ireland (Bergner, 2012). In 2009, however, the company was finally able to establish a roastary and packaging plant in Uganda's capital, Kampala. Built at a cost of US$1 million, the plant has a processing capacity of 3 million kilogrammes of coffee a year (Gossier, 2009). The capital needed to establish the factory was largely raised through loans and shareholders' capital (Global Data, 2009). By successfully setting up a coffee roasting and packaging plant in Kampala, the company marked the first time that a Ugandan-owned company was able to produce, roast and package coffee under a single owner. It was also an assertion of corporate patriotism, the notion that a company should embrace decisions that advance its country's economy, while strengthening its bottom line. In other words, adding value to coffee meant that Good African Coffee was not only correcting an imbalance when it comes to where African commodities are processed and packaged, but also enhancing Uganda's economy, thereby promoting a sense of place and belongingness which, within the context of Africapitalism, can be a form of corporate patriotism (Amaeshi and Idemudia, 2015). This is especially evident in the company's decision to establish a factory, which brought previously outsourced processing and packaging jobs, as well as tax revenue, back to the country which the farmers called home.

BREAKING INTO THE INTERNATIONAL MARKET

Uganda does not have a coffee-consuming culture like Ethiopia or the UK and the USA. So from the outset, Rugasira's competitive strategy was essentially orientated around international business, to build a brand that would penetrate markets beyond Africa.

Some key issues or features that characterised Good African Coffee's international expansion are discussed in the following sections.

South Africa and the Importance of Relationships and Networks

Good African Coffee's foray into the international market began in 2004 when for the very first time a Ugandan coffee brand was sold in South Africa. Through business relationships he had nurtured while running VR Promotions, Rugasira and his team managed to persuade Shoprite Checkers, a leading South African retailer, to sell his company's roasted and ground coffee beans. For many small African companies, entering foreign markets is often a tall order. Rugasira attributes the success in entering the South African market largely to the commercial relationships he had built with the supermarket: 'Our coffees could never have entered the South African market had it not been for my relationship with Shoprite Checkers. Social and commercial networks are so critical in building trading opportunities in any territory and it is one of the key determinants of market entry' (Sunday Monitor, 2013).

Beyond Africa: Resilience, Changing Perceptions and Marketing Strategies

After establishing its brand in South Africa, the company set its sights on Europe. The UK was a key market. But expanding beyond Africa would prove to be a daunting task. With limited capital and no business connections, entering the European market was a real test of Rugasira's resilience and commitment to achieving his objectives. It took fourteen visits to the UK before a retailer finally agreed to put Good African Coffee on its shelves (The Economist, 2010). Rugasira attributes the difficulty in penetrating the EU market not only to a lack of capital or business networks, but also to the skewed perception of Africa that UK retailers had (BBC, 2013). For many retailers, the idea of buying a finished product directly from a small African company was unheard of. During a speech at the International Fund for Agricultural Development (IFAD) he said: 'It took me 2.5 years to get a finished product on UK shelves. Why? Convincing a UK buyer that an African SME could bring a quality product to the British market. They had never before dealt with an SME bringing a finished product to the market. And so changing their mind-set was a huge challenge' (Rugasira, 2015).

Rugasira received his first break when, through a colleague, he was put in contact with a buyer at Waitrose, a major supermarket chain in the UK. After a series of meetings, they finally won Waitrose over (The Economist, 2010). Yet as much as Waitrose was a big win, it was not enough to keep Rugasira's company profitable. More capital and buyers were needed if the company was to grow and be sustainable in the long term. Since funds to market his product were not imme-diately available, Rugasira tried a number of things to bring attention to his coffee brand, including giving speeches and writing opinion editorials in the popular press such as the *Guardian*, an important UK print and online news outlet.

Good African Coffee's association with Waitrose as well as the speeches and articles he wrote did indeed raise the company's profile, and after another arduous process a larger UK chain, Sainsbury's, came on board (Musiitwa, 2013). Waitrose and Sainsbury's were the begin-ning of a journey that saw the company break into other UK retailers including Tesco and into the American market.

Good African Coffee's success in building a brand that pene-trated Western markets provides valuable lessons in resilience, alter-ing perceptions and innovative marketing approaches when faced with limited resources, and shows what is possible for other African companies with ambitions to sell their products beyond local markets.

Building a Global Brand

Part of the strategy behind successfully accessing the international market was to smartly brand Good African's Coffee and to clearly tell the story behind the company. To this end, Rugasira has tirelessly spread the message that drives his company. On a number of international and local platforms, he has regularly spoken of the need to disrupt the current status quo, in which African commodities are not processed at home into finished products, using local expertise and capital. He has also adamantly condemned the aid regime and has argued in favour of trade as the real driver of economic transformation in developing countries such as Uganda. Rugasira's eloquence when speaking about the philosophy that underpins his company has won him and his brand many supporters.

Beyond a marketing effort through speeches, Good African Coffee developed carefully designed, airtight packages that are difficult to miss on the shelves. The coffee packages have a map of Africa logo shaped in the form of a person with the intent of clearly highlighting where the coffee is produced and processed. And to appeal to a wide range of tastes, the company developed a number of coffee varieties, including Espresso roast (a combination of Robusta and Arabica), Rukoki Gold (medium dry roast), Rwenzori Mountains (a medium roast) and freeze-dried instant coffee (Good African, 2013d).

Rugasira's marketing and branding experience, gained while running VR promotions, was instrumental in building the Good African coffee brand. He remarked in an interview with CNN: 'What I brought to Good African was a marketing understanding – understanding of branding, communication and how brands are built' (CNN, 2013). To market its coffee, the company has also skilfully harnessed Internet platforms such as Facebook and Twitter, as well as blogs, that tell the stories of its farmers.

TRADE, NOT AID

An ardent critic of development aid, Rugasira has long been a proponent of trade as a means to economic transformation. Echoing arguments by prominent development economists, including William Easterly (2007) and Dambisa Moyo (2010), he maintains that aid has had very little impact on Africa's development in the last few decades, despite the billions of dollars that have been poured into the continent.

Development aid does not work, he argues, because it damages the responsiveness of governments to their citizens and crowds out more efficient actors of productivity and economic development. In other words, recipient countries become less accountable to their citizens as they prioritise donor demands and become less appealing to efficiency-seeking investors. Moreover, by creating a culture of dependency, aid stifles innovation and entrepreneurship in receiving countries. Because of the many conditions attached to aid by donor countries, it undermines recipient countries' independence and, in so doing, damages the independent management of their economic affairs (Good African, 2013e).

Trade, on the other hand, is a proven mechanism not just for improving the lives of the poor, but also as a powerful driver of economic development, since it is underpinned by a philosophy of self-sustainability. The mantra 'trade not aid' is at the centre of the company's philosophy. Rugasira illustrates this through his experience with coffee: Farmers only earn around $2–$3 per kilogram through the harvesting of green coffee beans, while roasted coffee can fetch up to $15 per kilogram (BBC, 2013). He believes that if African countries are able to process products as well as increase their global trade of value-added commodities such as coffee, this would result in vastly improved lives and economies.

SCALING-UP AND CHALLENGES

Rugasira has ambitious plans for his company. Going forward, he plans to diversify by extending his business model to other commodities, such as tea and chocolate. The company is looking to scale up and expand the brand to the rest of Africa. They are also looking at increasing their presence in both Europe and the USA.

Yet challenges remain. Unlike countries in the West where entrepreneurs have more access to capital, in Africa getting the funds required to start a company or to scale up is still a major obstacle. Rugasira notes in his book, *A Good African Story: How a Small Company Built a Global Coffee Brand*, that accessing affordable capital has been one of his company's biggest challenges. People in sub-Saharan Africa have some of the lowest access to credit. While more than 800 people per 1000 in the developed world can obtain credit, only 28 per 1000 people in sub-Saharan Africa have access (Sulaiman, 2013). If Good African is to seriously compete with other global coffee brands such as Nestlé, it will need to find reliable sources of capital required for it to become the multinational it aims to be.

In addition to lack of capital, poor infrastructure as well as high transportation costs are big challenges to sub-Saharan African companies trying to competitively export their products. Moreover, the heavily subsidised European producers and manufacturers increasingly make it difficult for companies such as Good African to compete globally.

CONCLUSION

Good African Coffee demonstrates that having a social mission as a core part of an organisation does not have to come at the expense of profitability. The company has been successful both in monetary terms and in empowering previously marginalised farmers in western Uganda. Moreover, the company's adoption and commitment to the tenets of Africapitalism, which have played a key role in its success, offers a blueprint especially for other agri-businesses operating in Africa that seek lasting socio-economic transformation in the communities in which they operate. In addition, Good African Coffee's accomplishments show that despite seemingly endless challenges for a small or medium-sized company from sub-Saharan Africa expanding internationally, companies with the right approach, the right strategies and a healthy dose of resilience and agility can not only produce quality products, but can also add value and build brands capable of penetrating markets beyond Africa, which will also benefit the producers and the broader community back home.

REFERENCES

Adams, T. A. 2005. Good Man in Africa. *The Guardian*, 13 November 2005. Available at www.theguardian.com/lifeandstyle/2005/nov/13/foodanddrink .features10. Accessed December 2016.

Amaeshi, K. and Idemudia, U. 2015. Africapitalism: A Management Idea for Business in Africa? *Africa Journal of Management*, 1(2): 210–223.

Bariyo, N. 2014. *Uganda Seeks to Bolster Coffee Exports with 300 Million New Trees*, 19 November 2014. Available at blogs.wsj.com/frontiers/2014/11/19/uga nda-seeks-to-bolster-coffee-exports-with-300-million-new-trees/. Accessed December 2016.

Battilana, J. and Lee, M. 2014. Advancing Research on Hybrid Organizing – Insights from the Study of Social Enterprises. *The Academy of Management Annals*, 8(1): 397–441.

Battilana, J., Sengul, M., Pache, A. C. and Model, J. 2015. Harnessing Productive Tensions in Hybrid Organizations: The Case of Work Integration Social Enterprises. *Academy of Management Journal*, 58(6): 1658–1685.

Bergner, D. 2012. Can Coffee Kick-Start an Economy? *New York Times*, 6 April 2012.

Blas, J. 2014. Uganda Joins African Wave of GDP Rebasing and Gets 13 Per Cent Boost. *Financial Times*, 1 December 2014. Available at blogs.ft.com/beyond-brics/2014/12/01/uganda-joins-african-wave-of-gdp-rebasing-and-gets-13-per -cent-boost/. Accessed December 2016.

British Broadcasting Corporation. 2013. Interview. What's the Best Way to Build New Markets? 20 January 2013. Available at www.bbc.co.uk/programmes/p013 61jj. Accessed October 2016.

Brown, N. 2014. Daily Coffee News, A Brief History of Global Coffee Production as We Know It (1963–2013). *Roast Magazine*, 17 July 2014. Available at dailycoffeenews.com/2014/07/17/a-brief-history-of-global-coffee-production-as -we-know-it-1963–2013/.

Cable News Network. 2013. Interview. Coffee entrepreneur transforms lives. 13 June 2013, https://edition.cnn.com/videos/international/2013/06/17/african-voi ces-andrew-rugasira-a.cnn. Accessed October 2016.

Easterly, W. and Reshef, A. 2010. *African Export Successes: Surprises, Stylized Facts and Explanations.* National Bureau of Economic Research, December 2010. Available at https://williameasterly.files.wordpress.com/2010/12/6_east erly_reshef_africanexportsuccesses.pdf. Accessed October 2016.

Economic Commission for Africa. 2013. *Making the Most of Africa's Commodities: Industrializing for Growth, Jobs and Economic Transformation,* Economic Report on Africa, 2013.

The Economist. 2010. A Good African Tale: An African Entrepreneur Struggles for Recognition in Rich-Country Markets. 11 May 2010. Available at www.econo mist.com/node/16095457. Accessed December 2016.

Food and Agriculture Organisation. 2005 Corporate Document Repository – *Arabica Coffee Manual for Myanmar.* Available at www.fao.org/docrep/008/ae938e/a e938e08.htm. Accessed December 2016.

Frontani, H. 2015. *Success Story from Uganda: Andrew Rugasira's Good African Coffee.* Available at https://africandevelopmentsuccesses.wordpress .com/2015/01/31/success-story-from-uganda-andrew-rugasiras-good-african -coffee/. Accessed December 2016.

Global Data. 2009. *Good African Coffee Plant Project Financing Good African Coffee Plant, Uganda.* Available at www.packaging-gateway.com/projects/good -african-coffee/. Accessed December 2016.

Goldschein, E. 2011. 11 Incredible Facts about the Global Coffee Industry. *Business Insider.* 11 November 2011. Available at www.businessinsider.com/facts-about -the-coffee-industry-2011–11?op=1. Accessed 28 January 2018.

Good African. 2013a. Our Story. Available at http://goodafrican.com/index.php/our -story.html. Accessed December 2013.

Good African. 2013b. Vision Mission and Values. Available at www.goodafrican .com/index.php/our-story/vision-mission-and-values.html. Accessed December 2016.

Good African. 2013c. How the Coffee Is Grown. Available at http://goodafrican.com/ index.php/our-products/how-the-coffee-is-grown.html. Accessed December 2016.

Good African. 2013d. Our Products. Available at http://goodafrican.com/index.php/ our-products.html. Accessed December 2016.

Good African. 2013e. Trade Not Aid. Available at http://goodafrican.com/index.php/ our-story/trade-not-aid.html. Accessed December 2016.

Gosier, J. 2009. Africa's First Coffee Roasting and Packaging Plant Opens in Uganda. *Africa,* 22 July 2009. Available at http://blog.appfrica.com/2009/07/22/

africa%25E2%2580%2599s-first-coffee-roasting-and-packaging-plant-opens-in
-uganda/. Accessed December 2016.

Gouillart, E. 2009. Five Faces of African Innovation and Entrepreneurship. Available at https://web.archive.org/web/20110929022333/http:/jia.sipa.colum bia.edu/files/jia/195–205_Feature.indd_.pdf. Accessed December 2016.

International Coffee Organization. 2014. World Coffee Trade (1963–2013): *A Review of the Markets, Challenges and Opportunities Facing the Sector*, 24 February 2014. Available at www.ico.org/show_news.asp?id=361. Accessed December 2016.

International Coffee Organization. 2017. Available at http://www.ico.org/prices/po -production.pdf. Accessed December 2017.

International Coffee Organization (ICO). 2014. World Coffee Trade (1963–2013): A Review of the Markets, Challenges and Opportunities Facing the Sector, 24 February 2014. Available at www.ico.org/news/icc-111–5-r1e-world-coffee-out look.pdf. Accessed December 2016.

International Monetary Fund. 2016. World Economic Outlook Database, April 2016. Available at https://www.imf.org/external/pubs/ft/weo/2016/01/weo data/index.aspx. Accessed December 2016.

Kalinaki, D. 2011. Selling Ugandan Coffee on US Shelves: A Story of Persistence and Constant Lessons. *Daily Monitor*. 9 November 2011. Available at www.moni tor.co.ug/artsculture/Reviews/-/691232/1270344/-/item/0/-/7x850sz/-/index.html. Accessed December 2016.

Kolb, N. 2016. *The Coffee Tree*. Available at http://justaboutcoffee.com/index.php? file=coffeetree. Accessed December 2016.

MacNamara, W. 2007. Andrew Rugasira: 'Good African' Banks on the Feel-Good Factor. *Financial Times*, 20 November.

Moyo, D. 2010. *Dead Aid: Why Aid Is Not Working and How There Is a Better Way*. New York, NY: Farrar, Straus and Giroux.

Murphy, T. 2012. A View from the Cave. Reporting on International Aid and Development. Available at www.aviewfromthecave.com/2012_03_01_archive .html. Accessed December 2016.

Musiitwa, D. 2013. Trade, Not Aid – Andrew Rugasira Shares His Story as an African Entrepreneur. Africabookclub.com, 1 October 2013. Available at www .africabookclub.com/?p=14516. Accessed 28 January 2018.

Ojambo, F. 2014. Uganda Coffee Exports Climb to Six-Month High as Prices Rise. *Bloomberg Business*, 11 February 2014. Available at www.bloomberg.com/new s/articles/2014–02-11/uganda-coffee-exports-climb-to-six-month-high-as-pri ces-rise.

Padmore R. 2014. Rainy Weather Will Increase Coffee Output in Uganda. *BBC World Service*, 15 September 2014. Available at www.bbc.com/news/business -29210487. Accessed 28 January 2018.

Rugasira, A. 2013. *A Good African Story: How a Small Company Built a Global Coffee Brand*. London: Random House.

Rugasira, A. 2015. The Global African Entrepreneur. *YouTube*. Available at https:// www.youtube.com/watch?v=z6qQHtKkdvA. Accessed December 2016.

Sulaiman, T. 2013. Uganda Coffee Firm: a Pioneer in U.K., U.S. Markets. *The Globe and Mail*. 22 February 2013. Available at www.theglobeandmail.com/re port-on-business/international-business/african-and-mideast-business/uganda -coffee-firm-a-pioneer-in-uk-us-markets/article8976645/. Accessed December 2016.

Sunday Monitor. 2013. Good African Story: How Andrew Rugasira Got into the South African Market. 19 February 2013.

The United Nations Educational, Scientific and Cultural Organization. 1994. Rwenzori Mountains National Park. Available at whc.unesco.org/en/list/684. Accessed December 2015.

Vision Reporter. 2014. Uganda Tops List of Most Ethnically Diverse Countries. *New Vision*. Available at www.newvision.co.ug/new_vision/news/1315155/ug anda-tops-list-ethnically-diverse-countries. Accessed October 2015.

World Bank. 2017a. Uganda. Available at http://data.worldbank.org/country/ugan da. Accessed December 2017.

World Bank. 2017b. Uganda Overview. Available at www.worldbank.org/en/coun try/uganda/overview. Accessed December 2017.

11 Reflections on Africapitalism and Management Education in Africa

Stella M. Nkomo

Africapitalism, in its most basic intent, is an idea for how African businesses can create a new form of capitalism that achieves the dual aim of economic and social wealth for nations on the continent. The purpose of this chapter is to reflect upon the implications of Africapitalism for how the continent educates the next generation of managers. In the first part of the chapter, I reflect upon the relevance of the African context and the basic tenets of Africapitalism. Next, I propose how management education should be approached to support Africapitalism. The eleven propositions offered are broad but applicable for undergraduate, postgraduate and executive management education. My theoretical framing for the chapter draws heavily from postcolonial theories and decolonisation arguments, as well as perspectives from the Global South or what Connell (2007) refers to as 'Southern Theory'. According to Connell (2007: viii–ix):

> Southern theory calls attention to the centre-periphery relations in the realm of knowledge ... The term is not used to name a sharply bounded category of states or societies, but to emphasise relations – authority, exclusion and inclusion, hegemony, partnership, sponsorship, appropriation – between intellectuals and institutions in the metropole and those in the world periphery.

In essence, the theory interrogates the dominance of knowledge from the Global North in the world. Different knowledges and epistemologies (ways of knowing) have generally been silenced. However, marginalised voices from the Global South continue to challenge the hegemony of Western knowledge and its declared universality (Alcadipani, Khan, Gantman and Nkomo, 2012; Mignolo, 2007; Spivak, 1988; Quijano, 2000; Westwood, Jack, Khan and Frenkel, 2014).

AFRICAPITALISM AND THE AFRICAN CONTEXT

In a recent article, Amaeshi and Idemudia (2015: 210) define Africapitalism as 'an economic philosophy that embodies the private sector's commitment to the economic transformation of Africa through investments that generate both economic prosperity and social wealth'. The term itself has been attributed to Tony O. Elumelu CON – a Nigerian banker and economist (Amaeshi and Idemudia, 2015: 210). A reading of further elaborations on Africapitalism suggests it is very much an aspirational ideology rather than a concrete construct. Its current formulation is largely prescriptive – *what should be* – not what already exists. It is an idea rooted in the need for Africa to sustainably resolve its social and economic challenges, weaning itself from its historical dependency position. At its core, Africapitalism stresses a transformed model of capitalism premised upon and responsive to the context of Africa.

The core idea of Africapitalism – that economic and social well-being are not mutually exclusive but can be simultaneously achieved – has surfaced in other initiatives on the continent. For example, the King Principles developed in South Africa provide guidelines that emphasize business responsibility for the triple bottom line: profits, people and planet. King III and its earlier versions have broadened the scope of corporate governance and responsibility in South Africa. The core principles advocated in King III (King Committee on Corporate Governance, 2009) revolve around the intimate relationships between leadership, sustainability and corporate citizenship. Recent treatments of corporate social responsibility found in the management literature reject the long-standing view dating back to the economist Milton Friedman's famous mantra that the only social responsibility of business was to make profits. Instead, they argue that the social responsibility of business cannot be narrowly defined and that business is *in* society, not separate from it (Waddock, Bodwell and Graves, 2002).

However, what makes Africapitalism distinct from corporate social responsibility is its call for an approach to business that is African-centric: that is, an approach embedded within the context of Africa. Although it is dangerous to speak of or write about a homogenous African context, scholars have offered a number of insights about its salient features in juxtaposition to Western, European and Asian contexts (Jackson, 2004; Kuada, 2010; Nkomo, Zoogah and Acquaah, 2015; Zoogah, 2008; Zoogah and Beugré, 2008; Zoogah, Peng and Woldu, 2015). For example, Zoogah (2008) asserts the African context consists of two main features: traditional and modern, reflected in rurality and urbanity. These salient features influence economic activities as well as human behaviour and social practices (i.e. culture). Zoogah's (2008) description recognises the heterogeneity of the continent and its diverse cultures by asserting the relative influence of the two contexts varies among countries.

Other scholars, however, stress the collectivist culture of Africa as an important common contextual factor that must be considered in understanding people and organisations on the continent. Several of the authors in this volume also ascribe collectivism as a key dimension of Africapitalism. The collectivism in Africa is most often represented by the concept of Ubuntu (Kartsen and Illa, 2005; Mangaliso, 2001; Mbigi, 1997; Newenham-Kahindi, 2009). Mangaliso (2001: 24) defined *Ubuntu* as 'humaneness – a pervasive spirit of caring and community, harmony and hospitality, respect and responsiveness – that individuals and groups display for one another. *Ubuntu* is the foundation for the basic values that manifest themselves in the ways African people think and behave towards each other and everyone else they encounter'.

Past empirical studies of national culture that include examples from Africa also found collectivism to be a key cultural dimension (e.g., Hofstede, 1980; House, Hanges, Javidan, Dorfman and Gupta, 2004). Recently, other scholars have failed to find empirical evidence of the practice of Ubuntu by leaders (Littrell, Wu and Nkomo, 2009; Littrell, Wu, Nkomo, Wanasika, Howell and Dorfman, 2013; Thomas and Bendixen, 2000). Littrell et al. (2013) could find little evidence of Ubuntu amongst the businesspeople they sampled. The authors concluded that the Ubuntu movement may be an inspirational goal promulgated by elites to encourage a more humane, community-oriented set of values for sub-Saharan Africans. While it might be tempting to offer the extreme conclusion that Africa in contradistinction to countries in the Global North has a universal collectivist national culture rather than individualistic, Zoogah's (2008) and Zoogah and Beugré's (2013) urban-rural – traditional-modern characterisation of Africa suggests collectivist cultures are more likely to be found in rural regions where traditional customs are still practised.

Postcolonial scholars would remind us of the intimate relationship between capitalism and the colonisation of Africa. So in thinking about what Africapitalism is and how we should align management education to it, we have to be aware of the devastating effect of colonialism on the continent. In other words, understanding Africa's contemporary context requires attention to its colonial history. Colonialism not only disrupted the economic advancement of countries but also denigrated traditional economic, cultural and social practices (Mudimbe, 1988; Young, 2001, Loomba, 2005, Rodney, 1974). Civilising the 'natives' was a central strategy used by colonialists to subjugate Africans, politically, economically, culturally and psychologically. The psychological and cultural assault alienated Africans from themselves (Fanon, 1990).

Although Africapitalism is proposed as a new concept, we must be aware of its precursors: pan-Africanism, African Socialism and African Humanism (Young, 2001). These ideologies were articulated by revolutionary leaders in Africa and the diaspora, gaining full steam during the anti-colonial struggles of the 1950s and 1960s (Fanon, 1970; Senghor, 1964; Césaire, 1972; Cabral, 1969; Nkrumah, 1964, 1970;

Nyerere, 1968; du Bois, 1965). The African critique of and resistance to colonialism comprised an intellectual, economic, political, philosophical and cultural response as well as a vision for an independent, decolonised continent (Young, 2001). These responses were embodied in the linked ideologies of pan-Africanism, African Socialism and African Humanism. While these ideologies had different roots and proponents, over time they often merged. Pan-Africanism first articulated in Africa by Tiyo Soga in the 1860s has been most associated with Kwame Nkrumah, first president of an independent Ghana (Young, 2001: 236). However, Julius Nyerere also developed principles for African Socialism as president of Tanzania (Nyerere, 1968).

Pan-Africanism as well as African Socialism called for a socialist economic policy of industrialisation and cooperative forms of agriculture that would result in an independent Africa (Young, 2001: 236). Its similarity to Africapitalism lies in its focus on economic development suitable for Africa. However, pan-Africanism and African Socialism were based upon socialism; while capitalism is the base for Africapitalism. The goal of the former were to create a socialism for Africa different from Russian socialism (Young, 2001) similar to the aspiration of Africapitalists to create a new form of capitalism distinct from Western forms. Africapitalism and pan-Africanism/African Socialism, however, all share an explicit call for a restitution of traditional African cultural values. The cultural dimensions of pan-Africanism, African Socialism and African Humanism drew from Senghor's (1964) concept of *négritude*. Négritude arose out of a political and cultural movement of the 1930s from anti-colonial intellectuals in Francophone Africa (Young, 2001). While it has been criticised for evoking an essentialist view of 'African' culture, proponents like Senghor (1964) articulated it as a response to the denigration of African culture by colonialists. Négritude called for a re-establishment and affirmation of the rich communal and spiritual values of African culture that is quite similar to Ubuntu (Senghor, 1964; Young, 2001). Communalism and shared values of mutual support were espoused as tools for economic and social transformation (Nyerere, 1968).

Despite the efforts of some leaders of the newly independent nations of the continent to implement these new ideologies, pan-Africanism, African Socialism and African Humanism were never fully realised (Young, 2001). A discussion of the complex reasons for the lack of realisation are beyond the scope of this chapter. However, the fate of these transformative ideologies has a major implication for the actualisation of Africapitalism. This suggests the education of managers and others is a very critical project if we are to move Africapitalism from ideology to practice. Nyerere (1968: 1) also stressed education and *re*-education as the first step for creating the mindset required for African Socialism.

The anti-colonial struggles of Africa brought an end to colonialism. However, the lingering effects of colonialism along with contemporary core-periphery divisions reinforce inequalities between so-called developed and developing nations and regions. For example, Western ideas and concepts still dominate the curriculum and learning materials for management education in Africa (Nkomo, 2011; Littrell et al., 2013). Individualism and the primacy of shareholders have been identified as two core principles underpinning management concepts and theories. The triumph of private interests over public interest is a pillar of capitalism. Shareholders are viewed as the single most important stakeholders, and managers are positioned as agents who must make decisions in their best interests (Ghoshal, 2005; Mintzberg, 2004; Waddock and Lozano, 2013). While there is growing criticism of these core principles, much less attention has been paid to the effects Western management education on countries in the Global South or periphery (for exceptions see Alcadipani and Rosa, 2011; Cooke and Alcadipani, 2015; Darley and Luethge, 2016; Ibarra-Colada, 2006; Nkomo, 2015). These effects have a long history and can be traced to the aftermath of decolonisation and development interventions initiated by the West as African countries gained independence (Dia, 1990). This was the case for other developing nations and regions as well (Alcadipani, Khan, Gantman and Nkomo, 2011; Jack and Westwood, 2009; Ibarra-Colada, 2006; Cooke, 2003).

The discourse on 'third world development' imposed a neoliberal solution to the underdevelopment of Africa and other regions like Latin America (Cooke, 2003). The modernity imposed upon the newly independent African nations was one that valorised Western definitions of progress. Newly independent countries inherited the educational systems of colonial rule. Further, during colonial rule, high-level management education and development was generally not available to Africans. Post-independence, training in Western management theory and practices was ironically imposed as a solution to the economic well-being of the continent (Cooke, 2003; Dia, 1996; Kiggundu, 1991; Safavi, 1991). It is indeed even more accurate to speak specifically about American management education and its global spread through what has been referred to as the Americanisation of management education (e.g., Alcadipani and Caldas, 2012; Westwood and Jack, 2008). Management theories and practices were developed in the United States through the pioneering work of thought leaders like Frederick Taylor and Henri Fayol during industrialisation and the rise of the factory system (Wren, 2005). The dominance of the United States in the development of the management discipline has been difficult to supplant even for other regions of the West. For example, its dominance was recognised in one of the rationales offered for the establishment of the European Foundation for Management Development (EFMD) in 1971: the 'formation of a distinctly European culture and approach in the field of business and management' (Agnelli, 1996: 177).

Solutions for developing post-independence Africa were not determined by countries themselves but often required as conditions for funding from institutions like the World Bank, United Nations and International Monetary Fund (Moyo, 2009). Consequently, in thinking about creating an approach to management education that would serve the realisation of Africapitalism, we must soberly recognise that many Africans in business and management education programmes on the continent continue to be largely taught theories and concepts developed in the United States, particularly those studying at universities striving for global recognition and accreditation (Nkomo, 2015). Thus, creating and institutionalising management education for Africapitalism is in the end a *decolonisation* project (Ndlovu-Gatshensi, 2013a). Decolonisation is a complex concept embodying three interrelated tasks according to Ndlovu-Gatshensi, 2013a: 11–12): (1) it requires an understanding of how the current global geopolitical context or *coloniality of power* is constructed and constituted; (2) it calls for a challenge to Western domination of knowledge including epistemological preferences; and (3) it requires resistance to dominant modes of subjectivity – ways of being – that stress rationality and individualism. The next section offers propositions for how we might begin decolonising management education by offering essential curricular changes to advance Africapitalism.

PROPOSITIONS FOR MANAGEMENT EDUCATION

Africapitalism implies recovering the continent's 'Africanness' or a new form of capitalism that places the values and needs of Africa at its core. Of course, we must avoid homogenising these values and needs, and remain aware of the diversity of Africa. In other words, 'Africanness' can take on many different forms due to local realities. Further, acknowledging that colonialism separated Africa from its precolonial identity, is it really possible to speak of an authentic Africa given Mudimbe's (1988) observation that Africa was an invention of the colonialists? So rather than seeking a return to what was, our task becomes one of imagining the key elements of management education for Africapitalism in the twenty-first century. Pragmatically, we need to take cognisance of the contemporary challenges facing the continent and globalisation.

Proposition 1

Agenda 2063: The Africa We Want, authored by the African Union, should be the starting point for curriculum design (African Union Commission, 2015). It not only describes the key challenges facing the continent but also offers an agenda of how they should be addressed (DeGhetto, Gray and Kiggundu, 2016). Agenda 2063

1. A prosperous Africa based on inclusive growth and sustainable development
2. An integrated continent, politically united and based on the ideals of Pan-Africanism and the vision of Africa's Renaissance
3. An Africa of good governance, democracy, respect for human rights, justice and the rule of law
4. A peaceful and secure Africa
5. An Africa with a strong cultural identity, common heritage, shared values and ethics
6. An Africa whose development is people-driven, relying on the potential of African people, especially its women and youth, and caring for children
7. Africa as a strong, united and influential global player and partner

Source: African Union Commission (2015). Agenda 2063: The Africa we want (p. 43).

FIGURE 11.1: Aspirations of Agenda 2063

embraces a pan-African vision of *an integrated and peaceful Africa, driven by its own citizens and representing a dynamic force in the international arena.* The seven aspirations identified in Agenda 2063 (see Figure 11.1) are important for constructing management education for Africa. Additionally, the vision articulated in Agenda 2063 suggests an approach that reflects the tripartite interrelationships among local, continental and global contexts (see Figure 11.2). The diagram suggests an inside-out perspective where the local context is at the centre of management education but at the same time informed by continental and global realities (Nkomo, 2015). Therefore, in addition to Agenda 2063, country agendas for economic, social and political development are also very important. For example, South Africa's country agenda is detailed in its National Development Plan Vision 2023.

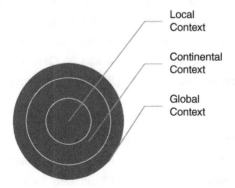

Local
Context

Continental
Context

Global
Context

FIGURE 11.2: Tripartite Context for Management Education in Africa

Proposition 2

The curriculum should be multidisciplinary. The challenges faced by the continent are not just within the traditional scope of management and business education. They are also political, psychological, philosophical, social and historical. While technical skills like accounting and finance are important, they are traditionally taught as being divorced from other influences. Critical management scholars would also point to their deep roots in capitalism and its assumptions. Providing students with a multidisciplinary perspective will hopefully disrupt the dominant portrayal of technical subjects like accounting and finance as objective, neutral and value free. For example, critical accounting scholarship has demonstrated the hegemonic effects of accounting (Cooper and Sherer, 1984); how its prescribed techniques support the appropriation of surplus value between core and peripheral countries (Tinker, 1980; Neu, Cooper and Everett, 2001) and how accounting procedures can be abused for corrupt purposes (Linsley and Shrives, 2009).

Proposition 3

The curriculum should include coverage of the pre-colonial, colonial and post-colonial history of the African continent as well as the different manifestations across countries and regions. This will assist management and business students to develop a well-informed understanding of the complexity of their own local contexts as well as that of the rest of the continent. Despite the general marginalisation of Africa in knowledge production, there are rich and varied sources of its history and postcolonial present (e.g., see the seminal works of Davidson (1959, 2013), Diop (1988), Mazuri (1986), Mbembe (2001) and Mudimbe (1988).

Proposition 4

The curriculum should provide an overview of current local and external political, economic, social and technological influences on business and their implications for management, typically referred to as a PEST assessment. However, this should be done from a broader geopolitical perspective and what decolonisation scholars refer to as the coloniality of power (Ndlovu-Gatshensi, 2013b; Mignolo, 2007; Quijano, 2000). The concept has been largely driven by Latin American scholars with respect to Latin America with some recent application by African scholars like Ndlovu-Gatshensi (2013a; 2013b). Coloniality refers to the imperial/colonial organisation of society with respect to four interrelated domains: control of the economy, control of authority, control of gender and sexuality and control of subjectivity and knowledge (Quijano, 2000; Tlostanova and Mignolo, 2009). Although the concept has been largely driven by Latin American scholars, it provides a lens through which management and business students in Africa can gain a broader understanding of the historical and contemporary manifestations of core and periphery relations.

Proposition 5

The curriculum should include a well-informed discussion of culture and identity in Africa rooted in African philosophy. Unfortunately, current discussions of the culture of Africa tend to be simplistic and romantic. These simplistic treatments tend to homogenise the continent, downplaying its heterogeneity and the ways in which culture has been evoked for less than noble reasons. The negative effects of nationalism as well as the dark side of ethnicity (i.e., ethnocentrism), which has been deeply implicated in conflicts and genocide in Africa should be included. It will also be important to call attention to the hybrid and fluid nature of culture. Culture and identity cannot be discussed without also a focus on gender and other dominant categories of difference in society. Students should be encouraged to develop an intersectional understanding of identity. Intersectionality refers to the inseparability of categories of social difference such as race, gender, class, ethnicity, sexuality and nation, and the systemic power dynamics that arise as multiple dimensions of social difference interact across individual, institutional, cultural and societal spheres of influence (Rodriquez, Holvino, Fletcher and Nkomo, 2016: 201).

Proposition 6

The curriculum must include an opportunity for students to engage reflexively with their identities and potential to practise a different type of leadership – one that is not for individual achievement but motivated by serving a common good. The instruction should allow ample opportunity for the identity work required to develop an approach to leadership that embraces and values people. The values identified as important to Africapitalism as discussed by Amaeshi and Idemudia (2015: 216) are (1) sense of progress and prosperity; (2) sense of parity; (3) sense of peace and harmony; and (4) sense of place and belongingness. Students should have ample time to reflect upon the following: What does it take to lead a human-friendly business that values people and society? The prototype of a 'Good African' business leader (see Chapter 10 by White and Kitimbo in this book) should be quite different from the dominant heroic images in Western leadership scholarship (Nkomo, 2011).

Proposition 7

Social entrepreneurship should be a mandatory module for both undergraduate and postgraduate students. Traditional entrepreneurship theory and practice is premised on individualism in that a passionate and talented individual embarks upon an entrepreneurial venture rather than pursuing paid employment. Social entrepreneurship in contrast as described by Dees in a 1998 paper, 'combines the passion of a social mission with an image of business-like discipline, innovation and determination commonly associated with the high-tech pioneers of Silicon Valley' (Dees, 1998: 1). However, the conceptualisation and practice of social entrepreneurship has taken many forms as noted by Holt and Littlewood in Chapter 8. They present a strong case for the connections between Africapitalism and the new modes of doing business emerging from social entrepreneurship.

Proposition 8

The curriculum should include a mandatory completion of a community intervention that demonstrates a student's (or group of students) ability to develop, plan and execute a project that achieves the dual goals of economic and social improvement. This will require students to learn to work closely with their local communities not in a hierarchical fashion but one that is respectful and responsive.

This intervention should not be one-off but require students to continue with the project post-graduation as a service to their communities.

Proposition 9

Given the current limited Africa-centred management knowledge available, the pedagogical approach should be what has been referred to as a funds of knowledge approach. Such an approach recognises that students' lived experiences can be a valuable source of knowledge. This would mean inviting, for example, practising managers enrolled in MBA programmes or even undergraduate degrees to share their experience from managing organisations to inform the curricula as well as study materials.

Proposition 10

The curriculum should contain alternative theories and examples of different organisational forms and managing and leading people. It is not enough to expose students to critique but to also explore possibilities for doing business and management differently. Africapitalism clearly requires re-visioning and transforming taken-for-granted best ways of governing organisations, structuring organisations and managing the people within them. Students should also be exposed to what is referred to as post-capitalist forms of organisation (e.g., Gibson-Graham, 1996, 2006).

Proposition 11

In redesigning the curriculum, all of the taken-for-granted core functions that are often assumed to be unmarked and neutral (e.g., accounting, finance, management, marketing and strategic management) should be critically interrogated to unmask content counter to the values and principles of Africapitalism.

MANAGEMENT EDUCATION AND RESEARCH

Although this chapter focuses on prescriptions for an approach to management education aligned with Africapitalism, its actualisation requires an acceleration in the generation of context-specific theories and empirical studies of management and organisations in Africa. The current paucity of context-specific management and business knowledge generation could constrain the realisation of an educational approach customised to support the aspirations of Africapitalism (Kan, Apitsa and Adegbite, 2015; George, Corbshley, Khayesi, Haas and Tihanyi, 2016; Nkomo et al., 2015). Knowledge about management and organisations in Africa is at best a field of study in a pre-paradigmatic state without an established epistemology and with continued debates about its very ontology (Kan et al., 2015; Kuhn, 1962).

On the positive side, there seems to be both a surge in published research articles about management in Africa, particularly in the last decade (e.g., Kamoche, 2011; Zoogah, Peng and Woldu, 2015; Zoogah and Nkomo, 2012) as well as recognition from the rest of the world of the need to 'bring' Africa into the scholarly conversation (George et al., 2016). There is also substantial body of knowledge that has done a good job in articulating the problems of Africa's marginalisation in management knowledge and the challenges ahead. On the downside, there needs to be a greater mobilisation of scholarship from scholars on the continent as well as strengthening of doctoral education opportunities in Africa. With respect to the former, there is the danger as noted by Grosfoguel (2007: 211) of the production of studies about management in Africa rather than studies with and from an African perspective. Doctoral education is particularly important as universities on the continent lag behind in the graduation of students. The research performed by new doctoral students has the greatest potential to make significant in-roads into indigenous-based management knowledge in African countries. Currently, five countries in Africa account for the majority of management and economic sciences research from the continent (Nkomo, 2015). The focus now has to be on developing 'African' management theory and empirical research with the aim to build a concrete body of knowledge (Kan et al., 2015). And, it must be actionable knowledge that can assist African managers to improve the effectiveness of organisations and institutions to contribute economically and socially to the development of the continent (Kan et al., 2015).

CONCLUSION

This chapter offers very preliminary propositions for an approach to management education to support the realisation of Africapitalism in Africa. Because Africapitalism is currently an ideology, the proposed curriculum is at best an imagined one or normative in the sense of igniting possibility. That is, the propositions prescribe how management education could be approached to transform the way managers view Africa's challenges, how they feel about them and ultimately act to resolve them in managing organisations and institutions (Nkomo, 2015). Africapitalism is positioned by its proponents as an alternative to Western approaches to modernity and development. There is justified worry about the *capitalism* in Africapitalism as discussed in the chapter by Ferns, Okupe and Amaeshi. How do we do Africapitalism while avoiding the neoliberal trap of superficial or cosmetic changes to capitalist modes of doing business? Critical management theorists remain sceptical about whether capitalism can be reformed as it has the uncanny ability to reinvent itself (Parker, Cheney and Land, 2014).

We should not underestimate the work required to convince educators on the continent of possibilities for an Africa-centred approach to management education. The results of a recent study of leading management educators and stakeholders justify this concern. A small minority of respondents claimed that it was realistic to think in terms of an African model for management education. Slightly less than half of respondents said that it was not realistic to conceive of an African model for management education (Thomas, Lee, Thomas and Wilson, 2016: 60). However, the respondents did concur that management education in Africa was Western dominated. Respondents proposed a hybrid approach with a strong focus on context that resonates with some of the ideas presented in the propositions in this chapter. Ideally, institutions like the Association of African Business Schools and other entities could play a leadership role in transforming management education. The slippery slope of change will not be easily travelled as the remaining question for the decolonisation of Africa is how to create something new, unfettered from what has always been positioned as the universal. As Sium, Desai and Ritskes (2012: ii) have noted, 'Decolonisation is a messy, dynamic, and contradictory process' and so is the project for actualising Africapitalism.

REFERENCES

Alcadipani, R., Khan, F. R., Gantman, E. and Nkomo, S. M. 2012. Southern Voices in Management and Organization Knowledge. *Organization: The Critical Journal of Organization, Theory and Society*, 19(2): 131–144.

Alcadipani, R. and Caldas, M. P. 2012. Americanizing Brazilian Management. *Critical Perspectives on International Business*, 8(1): 37–55.

Alcadipani, R. and Rosa, A. R. 2011. From Grobal Management to Glocal Management: Latin American Perspectives as a Counter-Dominant Management Epistemology. *Canadian Journal of Administrative Sciences/ Revue Canadienne des Sciences de l'Administration*, 28(4): 453–466.

African Union Commission. 2015. *Agenda 2063: The Africa We Want*. Available at www.un.org/en/africa/osaa/pdf/au/agenda2063.pdf. Accessed 29 January 2018.

Agnelli, G. 1996. *Training the Fire Brigade: Preparing for the Unimaginable*. Brussels, Belgium: EFMD Publications.

Amaeshi, K. and Idemudia, U. 2015. Africapitalism: A Management Idea for Business in Africa? *Africa Journal of Management*, 2(1): 210–223.

Cabral, A. 1969. *Revolution in Guinea: An African People's Struggle*. London: Stage 1.

Césaire, A. 1972. *Discourse on Colonialism (1955)*. Trans. Joan Pinkham. New York, NY: Monthly Review Press.

Connell, R. 2007. *Southern Theory: The Global Dynamics of Knowledge in Social Sciences*. Cambridge: Polity.

Cooke, B. 2003. A New Continuity with Colonial Administration: Participation in Development Management. *Third World Quarterly*, 24: 47–61.

Cooke, B. and Alcadipani, R. 2015. Toward a Global History of Management Education: The Case of the Ford Foundation and the São Paulo School of Business Administration, Brazil. *Academy of Management Learning & Education*, 14(4): 482–499.

Cooper, D. J. and Sherer, M. J. 1984. The Value of Corporate Accounting Reports: Arguments for a Political Economy of Accounting. *Accounting, Organizations and Society*, 9(3–4): 207–232.

Darley, W. K. and Luethge, D. J. 2016. The Role of Faculty Research in the Development of a Management Research and Knowledge Culture in African Educational Institutions. *Academy of Management Learning & Education*, 15 (2): 325–344.

Davidson, B. 1959. *Old Africa Rediscovered*. London: Gollancz.

Davidson, B. 2013. *Africa in History*. UK: Hachette.

Dia, M. 1996. *Africa's Management in the 1990s and Beyond*. Washington, DC: World Bank.

Dees, J. G. 1998. The Meaning of Social Entrepreneurship. Available at www .redalmarza.cl/ing/pdf/TheMeaningofsocialEntrepreneurship.pdf. Accessed 15 July 2016.

DeGhetto, K., Gray, J. R. and Kiggundu, M. 2016. The African Union's Agenda 2063: Aspirations, Challenges and Opportunities for Management Research. *Africa Journal of Management*, 2(1): 93–105.

Diop, C. A. 1988. *Precolonial Black Africa*. Chicago, IL: Review Press.

Du Bois, W. E. B. 1965. *The World and Africa: An Inquiry into the Part Which Africa Has Played in World History*. Enlarged edn. New York, NY: International Publishers.

Fanon, F. 1970. First Truths on the Colonial Problem. In *Toward the African Revolution*. Edited by F. Fanon and H. Chevalier, 120–126. Trans. Haakon Chevalier. Harmondsworth: Penguin.

Fanon, F. 1990. *The Wretched of the Earth*. 3rd edn. Trans. Constance Farrington. Harmondsworth: Penguin.

Gerard, G., Corbishley, C., Khayesi, J. N. O., Hass, M. R. and Tihanyi, L. 2016. Bringing Africa In Promising Directions for Management Research. *Academy of Management Journal*, 59(2): 377–393.

Ghoshal, S. 2005. Bad Management Theories Are Destroying Good Management Practices. *Academy of Management Learning & Education*, 4: 75–91.

Gibson-Graham, J. K. 1996. *The End of Capitalism (as We Knew It): A Feminist Critique of Political Economy*. With a New Introduction. Minneapolis, MN: University of Minnesota Press.

Gibson-Graham, J. K. 2006. *A Postcapitalist Politics*. Minneapolis, MN: University of Minnesota Press.

Gonzáles, N. 2005. Beyond Culture: The Hybridity of Funds of Knowledge. Funds of Knowledge: Theorizing Practices in Households, Communities, and Classrooms. Edited by N. Gonzáles, L.C. Moll and C. Amanti, 29–46. Mahwah, NJ: Lawrence Erlbaum Associates.

Grosfoguel, R. 2007. The Epistemic Decolonial Turn. *Cultural Studies*, 21(2–3): 211–223.

Hofstede, G. 1980. *Culture's Consequences: International Differences in Work-Related Values*. Beverly-Hills, CA: Sage Publications.

House, R. J., Hanges, P. J., Javidan, M., Dorfman, P. and Gupta, V. (eds.). 2004. *Leadership, Culture, and Organisations: The Globe Study of 62 Societies*. Thousand Oaks, CA: Sage Publications Inc.

Ibarra-Colado, E. 2006. Organization Studies and Epistemic Coloniality in Latin America: Thinking Otherness from the Margins. *Organization* 13(4): 463–488.

Jack, G. and Westwood, R. 2009. *International and Cross-Cultural Management Studies: A Postcolonial Reading*. Basingstoke: Palgrave Macmillan.

Jackson, T. 2004. *Management and Change in Africa: A Cross-Cultural Perspective*. London: Routledge.

Kamoche, K. 2011. Contemporary Management of Human Resources in Africa. *Journal of World Business*, 46: 1–4.

Kan, K. A., Apitsa, S. M. and Adegbite, E. 2015. African Management: Concept, Content and Usability. *Society and Business Review*, 10(3): 258–279.

Karsten L. and Illa, H. 2005. Ubuntu as a Key African Management Concept: Contextual Background and Practical Insights for Knowledge Application. *Journal of Managerial Psychology*, 20(7): 607–620.

Kiggundu, M. N. 1991. The Challenges of Management Development in Sub-Saharan Africa . *Journal of Management Development*, 10(6): 32–47.

King Committee on Governance. 2009. *Draft Code of Governance Principles for South Africa-2009*. Parklands: Institute of Directors for Southern Africa.

Kuada, J. 2010. Culture and Leadership in Africa: A Conceptual Model and Research Agenda. *African Journal of Economic and Management Studies*, 1(1): 9–24.

Kuhn, T. 1962. *The Structure of Scientific Revolutions*. Chicago, IL: University of Chicago Press.

Linsley, P. M. and Shrives, P. J. 2009. Mary Douglas, Risk and Accounting Failures. *Critical Perspectives on Accounting*, 20(4): 492–508.

Littrell, R. F., Wu, N. H. and Nkomo, S. M. 2009. Preferred Managerial Leadership Behaviour in Sub-Saharan African Business Organisations. In *Proceedings of the 51st Annual Meeting of the Academy of International Business 'Knowledge Development and Exchange in International Business Networks'*. Edited by T. Pederson, and T. Kiyak, 27–30. San Diego, CA, USA, June 2009. East Lansing, MI: Academy of International Business, Michigan State University.

Littrell, R. F., Wu, N. H., Nkomo, S. M., Wanasika, I. and Howell, J. 2013. Pan-Sub-Saharan African Managerial Leadership and the Values of *Ubuntu*. In *Management in Africa: Macro and Micro Perspectives*. Edited by T. Lituchy, B. J. Punnett, and B. Puplampu, 232–248. New York, NY: Routledge Publishers.

Lituchy, T, Punnett, F. J. and Puplampu, B. (eds.). 2013. *Management in Africa: Macro and Micro Perspectives*. New York, NY: Routledge.

Loomba, A. 2005. *Postcolonial Studies and Beyond*. Durham, NC: Duke University Press.

Mangaliso, M. P. 2001. Building Competitive Advantage from Ubuntu: Management Lessons from South Africa. *Academy of Management Executive*, 15(3), 23–32.

Mazrui, A. A. 1986. *The Africans: A Triple Heritage*. London: BBC Publications.

Mbembe, A. 2001. *On the Postcolony*. Berkeley, CA: University of California Press.

Mbigi, L. 1997. *Ubuntu: The African Dream in Management*. Johannesburg, South Africa: Knowledge Resources.

Mignolo, W. D. 2007. Coloniality of Power and De-colonial Thinking. *Cultural Studies*, 21: 155–167.

Mintzberg, H. 2004. *Managers Not MBAs: A Hard Look at the Soft Practice of Managing and Management Development*. San Francisco, CA: Barrett-Koehler.

Moyo, D. 2009. *Dead Aid: Why Aid Is Not Working and How There Is a Better Way for Africa*. London: Macmillan.

Mudimbe, V. Y. 1988. *The Invention of Africa: Gnosis, Philosophy, and the Order of Knowledge*. Bloomington, IN: Indiana University Press.

Ndlovu-Gathensi, S. J. 2013a. Decolonising the University in Africa. *The Thinker*, 51: 46–51.

Ndlovu-Gatshensi, S. J. 2013b. *Empire, Global Coloniality and African Subjectivity*. London: Berghahn Books.

Neu, D., Cooper, D. J. and Everett, J. 2001. Critical Accounting Interventions. *Critical Perspectives on Accounting*, 12(6): 735–762.

Newenham-Kahindi, A. 2009. The Transfer of Ubuntu and Indaba Business Models Abroad: A Case of South African Multinational Banks and Telecommunication Services in Tanzania. *International Journal of Cross Cultural Management*, 9(1): 87–108.

Nkomo, S. M. 2011. A Postcolonial and Anti-colonial Reading of 'African' Leadership and Management in Organization Studies: Tensions, Contradictions and Possibilities. *Organization: The Critical Journal of Organization, Theory and Society*, 18(3): 365–386.

Nkomo, S. M. 2015. Challenges of Management and Business Education in a Developmental State: The Case of South Africa. *Academy of Management Learning and Education Journal*, 14(2): 242–258.

Nkomo, S. M., Zoogah, D. and Acquaah, M. 2015. Why Africa Journal of Management and Why Now? *Africa Journal of Management*, 1(1): 4–26.

Nkrumah, K. 1970. *Consciencism: Philosophy and Ideology for Decolonization* (1964). Rev. edn. New York, NY: Monthly Review Press.

Nyerere, J. K. 1968. *Ujamaa: Essays on Socialism*. Oxford: Oxford University Press.

Parker, M., Cheney, G., Fournier, V. and Land, C. 2014. *The Routledge Companion to Alternative Organization*. Abingdon: Routledge.

Quijano, A. 2000. Coloniality of Power, Eurocentrism and Latin America. *International Sociology*, 15: 215–232.

Rodney, W. 1974. *How Europe Underdeveloped Africa*. London: Bogle-L'Ouverture Publications.

Rodriquez, J., Holvino, E., Fletcher, J. and Nkomo, S. M. 2016. The Theory and Praxis of Intersectionality in Work and Organizations: Where Do We Go from Here? *Gender, Work and Organization*, 23(3): 201–222.

Safavi, F. 1981. A Model of Management Education in Africa. *Academy of Management Review*, 6(2): 319–331.

Senghor, L. S. 1964. *On African Socialism*. Trans. Mercer Cook. London: Pall Mall.

Sium, A., Desai, C. and Ritskes, E. 2012. Towards the 'Tangible Unknown': Decolonization and the Indigenous Future. *Decolonization: Indigeneity, Education & Society*, 1(1): x–xiii.

Spivak, G. C. 1988. 'Can the Subaltern Speak?' In *Marxism and the Interpretation of Culture*. Edited by C. Nelson and L. Grossberg, 271–313. London: Macmillan.

Srinivas, N. 2013. Could a Subaltern Manage? Identity Work and Habitus in a Colonial Workplace. *Organization Studies*, 34: 1655–1674.

Thomas, A. and Bendixen, M. 2000. The Management Implications of Ethnicity in South Africa. *Journal of International Business Studies*, 31(3): 507–519.

Thomas, H., Lee, M., Thomas, M. and Wilson, A. 2016. Does Africa Need an 'African Management Model?' *EFMD Global*, 2(10): 58–63.

Tinker, A. M. 1980. Towards a Political Economy of Accounting: An Empirical Illustration of the Cambridge Controversies. *Accounting, Organizations and Society*, 5(1): 147–160.

Tlostanova, M. V. and Mignolo, W. D. 2009. Global Coloniality and the Decolonial Option. *Kult*, 6(Special Issue): 130–147.

Waddock, S., Bodwell, C. and Graves, S. B. 2002. Responsibility: The New Business Imperative. *The Academy of Management Executive*, 16(2): 132–148.

Waddock, S. and Lozano, J. M. 2013. Developing More Holistic Management Education: Lessons Learned from Two Programs. *Academy of Management Learning and Education*, 12: 265–284.

Westwood, R. and Jack, G. 2008. The US Commercial-Military-Political Complex and the Emergence of International Business and Management Studies. *Critical Perspectives on International Business*, 4(4): 367–388.

Westwood, R., Jack, G., Khan, F. R. and Frenkel, M. 2014. *Core-Periphery Relations and Organisation Studies*. Basingstoke, Hampshire, UK: Palgrave Macmillan,

Wren, D. A. 2005. *The History of Management Thought*. Hoboken, NJ: John Wiley & Sons.

Young, R. C. 2001. *Postcolonialism: An Historical Introduction*. London: Blackwell.

Zoogah, D. B. 2008. African Business Research: A Review of Studies Published in the Journal of African Business and a Framework for Enhancing Future Studies. *Journal of African Business*, 9(1): 219–255.

Zoogah, D. B. and Beugré, C. D. 2013. *Managing Organizational Behaviour in the African Context*. New York, NY: Routledge.

Zoogah, D., Peng, M. W. and Woldu, H. 2015. Institutions, Resources, and Organizational Effectiveness in Africa. *Academy of Management Perspectives*, 29(1): 7.

Index